Antique Fairs and Auctions

The paper in this book meets archival paper standards for libraries in ANSI Standard Z39.48-1984

Manston's
Flea Markets
Antique Fairs and Auctions
of Britain

Including where to find
markets, how to ship items,
clear customs, and much more.

Peter B. Manston

A Travel Key Guide
Published by Travel Keys
Sacramento, California U.S.A.

Published by Travel Keys
in association with Prima Publishing
and distributed by St. Martin's Press,
except in Canada distributed by Raincoast Book
Distribution, Ltd.

Travel Keys
P. O. Box 160691
Sacramento, California 95816 U.S.A.
Telephone (916) 452-5200

Prima Publishing
P. O. Box 1260
Rocklin, California 95677
Telephone (916) 624-5718

St. Martin's Press
175 Fifth Avenue
New York, N. Y. 10010
Telephone (212) 674-5151

Designed by Peter B. Manston
Edited and cover photo by Robert C. Bynum
Drawings and maps by Claudia R. Graham
Type Galleys by The Electric Page
Printed and bound by The Haddon Craftsmen
Manufactured in the United States of America
First Printing September 1987

Library of Congress Cataloging-in-Publication Data

Manston, Peter B., 1951-
Manston's Flea Markets, Antique Fairs, and Auctions of Britain.
"A Travel Key Guide." Includes Index.
   1. Flea Markets—Great Britain. 2. Antique Dealers—Great Britain. 3. Auctions—Great Britain. I. Title. II. Title: Flea Markets, Antique Fairs, and Auctions of Britain.
   HF 5482.M3125   1987   381'.1   87-16221
   ISBN 0-931367-10-7 (pbk.)

Contents

Acknowledgements

Many people helped provide information and support during the time while this book was written. Most of them provided help, but it isn't possible to thank them all. A few I'd like to specially thank include: Robert C. Bynum, who provided thoughtful editorial comments and strong moral support, Paula R. Mazuski for excellent help in clarifying the objective of this book, Will Renner, Joyce Williams, and Agnes A. Manston (my mother). In addition, thanks to many members of the British antiques trade.

Disclaimer of Responsibility

Markets move as the result of urban renewal, sometimes close during bad weather, or are rescheduled around holidays. Dates can change because the hall, square, or other location has already been reserved for another conflicting use, or because there are not enough sellers reserving a place. Bus lines are sometimes renumbered, parking lots turn into buildings, parking garages raise their rates, and occasionally new subways are built.

This book is as complete and accurate as possible. Facts have been exhaustively checked and rechecked. Therefore, though the information is deemed to be accurate as of press date, it may not exactly mirror your experience. Neither the author nor the publisher can be responsible if you are inconvenienced by information contained in this book.

The persons, companies, institutions, and organizations named in the book are believed to be reputable and engaged in the work they purport to be in. Any questions should be directed to them rather than the author or publisher. Inclusion or exclusion of a firm or organization is no reflection on the suitability of its service or product.

When you find differences, will you let us know? Fill out the "Will You Help?" form at the end of the book (or in a letter). What you find and suggest can make the next edition even more complete and more useful to those who follow your path.

Portobello Road ~ London

Introduction

Britain is a treasure-trove of antiques, collectables, and bric-a-brac. Even better, the British antiques trade is well organized, so that markets and fairs are frequent and large.

Britain has a centuries-old tradition of markets, and cities and other locations have vied to have the best. As early as 1100 A.D., royal charters authorized markets either once a year or more frequently. The market cross in many a town became the focal point of the town, and gave legal status to buying and selling in the market precinct.

While few of the antiques fairs and markets date back to the Middle Ages, a large number have been in existence for many years. At some, the right to sell is granted to all willing to pay a few pounds for a small spot on the ground; at others, one must wait for years until a permanent place is available; and at the most prestigious, one must be invited to display, and all merchandise is carefully checked for authenticity.

You can find almost anything: British specialties such as porcelain, pottery, silver, linen, furniture, glass, old industrial tools, and all types of other items too numerous to mention. There are also relics and artifacts brought from around the world.

5

As the result of empire and trade, some of the finest antiques and other items from parts of the world that weren't directly under British rule: therefore, Britain is one of the best places in the world to find antique Persian carpets, French furniture, and Oriental wares of all types.

Today, hundreds of markets offer all types of items, from carefully checked items that could grace a museum, elegant country estate, or castle, as well as your home, to just plain junk.

There are also hundreds of auctions a year. Some auctions in London may offer only paintings, others may restrict themselves to silver, wine, books, or militaria. Many in the country sell whatever people bring in. Often, country auctions are where true finds may be made. Many occur on a regular schedule: weekly, or once or twice a month. Occasionally, an entire estate is auctioned, but finding these is a matter of luck and timing, since they are most often announced only in local newspapers and posters glued to walls.

This book will give information vital for the antique dealer and collector; most isn't conveniently available elsewhere. It includes:

- when and where to find flea markets, antique fairs, and boot sales
- types of markets and what you can expect to find at each
- names, addresses, and specialties of auction houses, as well as the regular schedule of auctions
- how to determine if a special permit is needed for export, and how deal with the Export Licensing Branch if it is
- and much, much more.

This pocket-sized book provides all this information. At the back, you'll find a complete index, and detailed maps to help you find what you need fast.

This book is dedicated to you, the ever-hopeful collector of exciting experiences and warm memories, as well as the collector of antiques, junk, and hidden treasures.

Can You
Still Make Finds?

All of us have heard about long-lost masterpieces found in a junk shop or bought for a few dollars at a flea market. We would all like to make a "great find"—a long lost painting, an old Wedgwood service, or a piece of original Chippendale or Adam furniture, or a teapot by famed silversmiths Paul de Lamerie, Paul Storr, or Hester Bateman.

These items do exist, and can occasionally be found, usually accompanied by great publicity and newspaper headlines. Finds of this type are rare.

But minor finds can more readily be made—the antique 18th-century spoon for only a few pounds; or a massive Queen Anne sterling chocolate pot for a few hundred to several thousand; finely detailed Victorian clothing; or a minor artist's 17th- or 18th-century painting.

The more you know about a given period or class of objects, the likelier you are to recognize and make a true find. This merely reinforces the fact that specialized knowledge has potentially great value.

Remember, you're searching for the proverbial needle in a haystack; there are thousands of British dealers and collectors in competition for the same things you are. You, however, can have the advantage of broader exposure, and you know about a radically different antique market unknown to most Europeans: the United States and Canadian markets, where the selection is smaller and the prices are higher.

Many British dealers only know about specialties of their own locality or country, while you can take the broader view, surveying the products of the entire world. Often, your best finds will be products or artworks far from their home, and, therefore, whose true value is unappreciated or unknown locally.

Charnock Richard

Why Search for Antiques in Britain?

Britain is probably the best antique warehouse in the world. There are more antiques available than any other single country, with the possible exception of France.

Britain has many attributes that makes it an excellent source of antiques: large quantities of goods, the willingness to export antiques and art, and past wealth coupled with economically difficult times.

Britain has huge quantities of goods at attractive prices. British craftsmanship has been renowned since the Middle Ages, particularly in silver and gold, porcelain, and furniture.

British sterling is particularly well noted for its craftsmanship, sense of good design, and its generally good state of preservation. Every antiques market and flea market will have lots of sterling, ranging from racks of sugar tongs and spoons to 18th-century teapots, coffee and chocolate pots, and serving pieces.

Britain has long been noted for furniture, from Welsh cabinets and pine work to carefully made furniture of exotic woods. The British taste in furniture tends to be for simplicity of line and exquisite taste. The Victorian age produced an unparalleled amount of furniture, possibly not quite so beautifully designed and made as in earlier times, but far more available and reasonable in cost. (Unfortunately, much modern British furniture has lost this quality.)

Britain has long been known for pottery or porcelain—who hasn't heard of Wedgwood, Royal Doulton, and a number of other famous porcelain works? Their products often span the centuries. Pottery works have been producing everything from common brown-glazed teapots to Toby mugs, and everything in between.

Now, the products of the early 20th century are becoming widely available in British markets. British Art Deco is distinctive and noteworthy, slightly understated when compared to the designs of the same period in Germany, France, and the United States.

In addition to British-made goods, many foreign items have trickled into Britain over the centuries, making Britain a prime source of Persian carpets, Oriental art, religious art from Eastern Europe, and enough other specialties that it would take an entire page to list them all.

British vendors are willing and able to sell most antiques, and the government doesn't interfere the export of most of them. Several factors contribute to this:

- Trade and commerce have traditionally been the main source of British wealth.
- The late 20th century has been a difficult time for Britain's economy, with the result that many treasures of the past are surfacing for sale at attractive prices. This phenomenon is particularly marked in the economically devastated areas mainly in Britain's north, such as Lancashire and parts of Scotland. This factor is helped by the relative fall in the value of the British pound sterling during this century when compared with both American and Canadian dollars. (At the turn of the century, the British pound was worth about $5; today it is worth about $1.60/1.80 U.S. and about $2.00/2.30 Canadian.)
- The British sense of fair dealing has made the legal export of most antiques and collectables possible and the rules governing export of antiques and works of art clear and understandable.

The British antiques trade is large and well organized. Thousands of dealers have immense stocks of antiques. Many take their choicest items to markets, shows, and fairs. It would take a number of people to canvass all of the markets, fairs, sales, and auctions where antiques and collectables are sold.

Export arrangements are also easier to make in Britain than almost everywhere else. Many collection and packing companies provide nationwide or regional pickup, and can pack at any given standard of packing, from just jamming huge containers full of miscellaneous lots of furniture, to careful item-by-item museum-quality coddling.

Britain, for a number of reasons, is probably the best country for hunting antiques in the world today.

Bermondsey Street~London

Learning to See What You're Looking At

Without preparation, you can find antiques, collectables, and assorted items by the thousands. You're limited only by your money, your patience, and your transportation. But discoveries of real artistic quality items will be made only from good luck, maybe aided by intuition. But for the real finds, you must know what you're looking at.

You'll be will repaid later by the effort spent now, when you are knowledgeable enough to tell a good piece from a poor or fake one later at a boisterous flea market, auction, or antique show. You'll be faced with hundreds and thousands of items, but only a few are of interest to you, and even fewer are very good value for the serious collector.

At well-known dealers and some dealers' marts, you will often be able to obtain certificates of authenticity and provenance papers, more or less guaranteeing that you're really buying a genuine antique. Naturally such guarantees and paperwork have their (high) price.

At flea markets and junk shops, however, the motto is "let the buyer beware." The market in fakes sold to the unwary is large, and buyers' cupidity and ignorance are prime sales tools for these sellers. In Britain this is somewhat less of a problem than countries such as Spain, Portugal, and Italy.

The time to start learning about antiques and collectables is right now. Read everything you can—style guides, price guides, antique-trade and fine arts magazines, museum catalogues, and applied arts and fine arts history. Catalogues from Christie's, Phillips, and Sotheby's auctions are treasure-troves of knowledge, with illustrations of sale items, descriptions of the creator, the item, and characteristics of the style, and estimated sales prices. These catalogues are sometimes available at libraries or museums, and, of course, are sold through the respective auction houses.

Study the text and illustrations carefully—what you remember will make it much easier to sort through the thousands of worthless pieces for the few excellent items at the market, show, or fair.

Your local library is an excellent place to begin your search. Search through "Books In Print" to supplement your search of library shelves. Small and medium-sized libraries can often obtain books through the "interlibrary loan" system. For details and to make a request, see the reference librarian.

Many college and university libraries have more extensive and specialized collections, particularly in the area of art and antiques. Usually the public is admitted to "open-stack" libraries and can use the books in the library at no charge. Often you can become a "friend of the library" at modest cost to obtain borrowing privileges.

Museums are another place to learn. In major museums you will be able to see actual examples of authentic works. Study the lines, the artistic qualities, and materials carefully. When you have a bit of knowledge but want more, seek out the curators in the museum.

Sometimes museums also have excellent art libraries, but rarely can their library materials be checked out.

Antique dealers in your area represent a valuable source of knowledge. How do you find a dealer knowledgeable in a particular field? Many dealers have specialties: the most knowledgeable, specialized and expensive dealers are often clustered in cities such as New York, Boston, Chicago, San Francisco, Los Angeles, and Toronto. In short, dealers congregate where there are large numbers of people with a taste for European antiques and art, and who have money to indulge their taste. For obvious reasons, dealers won't usually share their sources of supply.

When buying, you're likely to find more interesting and beautiful items if you know what you're buying.

Let your sense of beauty and value for money guide you: learn to trust your instincts, based on a firm foundation of knowledge.

London, 1800

British Sterling Silver

The work in silver is one of the greatest of all British art forms. For centuries, British royalty and gentry have carefully nurtured, encouraged, patronized, and carefully regulated silversmiths and goldsmiths. Several periods are unequalled in artistry and quality, but perhaps the greatest age of British silver was from the Restoration (1660) to the Regency (1820). The design and execution of silver was particularly distinguished from about 1690 to 1730.

Origin of Hallmarks

All solid British silver (but not silverplate) has been hallmarked since early in the Middle Ages. The first hallmark was introduced in 1180, and assay of precious metals was required under Henry III in 1238. The reason for hallmarking was to guarantee the purity of precious metals, both silver and gold. By requiring every piece to be assayed (tested for purity), the mark of the maker and the guild furnished proof that the metal was up to standard. As time went on, additional marks were added to record such diverse facts as the city, year of manufacture, payment of tax, and other items.

Regulation of the trade was under the protection of the government, delegated to the Worshipful Company of Goldsmiths and Silversmiths.

14

Standards for Silver

There are two legal standards for British silver: Sterling (925/1000 fine) and Britannia (958/1000 fine). Sterling is shown by a lion, and Britannia by a seated figure. Foreign silver must be marked as an import with an inverted "U" in a circle before it can be sold.

Hallmarks

Silver hallmarks have changed over time, so that it is relatively simple to date British silver. The first mark was a leopard's head, introduced in 1180 by the guild of goldsmiths.

Beginning in 1336, the crowned leopard's head was joined by the maker's mark (always two letters), and the date letter.

Beginning in 1393, a city mark was introduced: each assay office had (and still has) its own mark. These are shown below.

Beginning in 1545, the sterling standard was shown by a lion in a shield. Beginning in 1697, a higher silver standard (Britannia) was introduced to prevent the melting of coins for silver work.

Since 1719, British silversmiths have been able

 Sterling   *Britannia*

to use either the sterling or Britannia standard.

Marks on British Silver

Modern British silver will have four marks. Each of the following must be included: the initials of the maker, the town of manufacture, the date-letter, and the lion guarantee of sterling or seated Britannia figure for Britannia standard silver. If it also has a monarch's head (1758—1890) you can be sure that the tax on silver items was paid before its initial sale.

Date letters are particularly helpful when dating silver, since they change every year. At the end of a series of letters, the style of the letters and surrounding shields are changed. Therefore, every nineteen years the letter has changed (most date-letter alphabets do not include J, W, X, Y, or Z).

Beginning in 1975, all year marks and the lettering style were standardized. In that year, date-letters began with "A"; the cycle is expected to repeat every 25 years (the letter J is not used.)

Sample Marks

Here are some samples of the marks used on British sterling:

 Chester   *Sheffield*

 Exeter   *York*

 Newcastle   *London*

 Birmingham

 Scotland   *Glasgow*   *Edinburgh*

The lion is found on all sterling (.925) work, the Britannia on all Britannia (.958) work.

The city stamp will be one of those shown.

Note: British silver marks have changed to some degree as the result of the Hallmarking Act 1973. There are now only four assay offices: London (using the leopard's head), Birmingham (using the anchor), Sheffield (now using a rose instead of the traditional crown), and Edinburgh (using the castle). Date letters are now to be standard between assay offices, and each year's letter must coincide with the calendar year (January 1 through December 31).

A full explanation of British hallmarks can be found in a small book often sold at British markets for about £1.50.

Why is It Called Sterling, and What Was a Pound Sterling?

Coins in the Middle Ages were given value by their precious metal content. A sterling was a medieval silver coin, which for many centuries was distinguished by a star (stoer in Middle English). The silver was of a consistent standard of purity: 10 troy ounces 11 pennyweights of pure

London, 1687

metal in the troy pound (12 ounces). One pound by weight in sterlings equalled a "pound sterling."

From the early 1800s until 1966, one pound's (£1) worth of copper pennies (240 pence) weighed exactly 16 ounces. Copper coins were measured at banks by weight rather then value.

The name for the main unit of British money remains today, though no coin or combination of coins worth £1 weighs anything close to a pound.

Silver Plate

Silverplate can be distinguished from solid silver, because it has very different marks. Some may be merely for decoration, but in Britain, non-silver must be marked as plated ware. This can be shown by the initials EPNS (Electro-Plated Nickel Silver), the words "Silverplate" or "Silver Plated," or if on a base of copper, "Sheffield Plate".

Gold

Pure gold is 24 karats. In Britain, to be legally sold as gold, it must contain least 9 karats (375/1000 fine). Usually, modern cheap gold chains and earrings are 9 or 10 karat. However, good quality gold in Britain is often 18 carat (750/1000 fine).

All gold must state its gold content in carats, and be assayed and hallmarked.

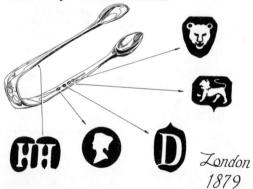

London
1879

Ardingly

When to Go for the Best Finds

The British antiques trade is a year-round activity, except for the week between Christmas and New Year's Day. While there are seasonal highs and lows to various components of the trade, some events take place all through the year. The weekly antiques markets are always going. Auctions take place on a regular basis. And antiques fairs at hotels and conference halls are also continual.

In winter, there are few tourists and the business is more for the locals. The quantity of merchandise is almost as large, but it is almost all under cover and indoors. The weekly antiques markets—many outside—are open in unpleasant weather: the dealers don't let a bit of dampness, cold, and rain interfere with the pursuit of profit and finds. However, only a few of the major, one-day sales held before March.

In spring, outdoor sales become more frequent: the first of the large, one- or two-day sales are held. These large fairs often have 1000 vendors, some under cover in exhibition halls and some offering their wares from trucks and vans outside. Some of the major auctions of the season take place. And the weekly antiques markets continue.

Summer is the high point of the outdoor market season, with seemingly the whole country involved in the buying and selling of collectables, antiques, and just plain junk. Every town and apparently every village has its market. There are also plenty of auctions in most parts of the country. Every weekend, at hundreds of "boot sales," private parties unload all types of treasures and trash from the trunks (boots) of their cars.

Autumn is probably the most active season in the antiques trade, with the major fairs and exhibitions taking place between September and Christmas. Many of the most publicized auctions of famous paintings also take place during this season, as well as the last of the one- or two-day antiques fairs. And the open-air antiques markets continue.

Any time of year will opportunities to pursue and acquire antiques and collectables. And at any time of the year, there are more events than you could ever thoroughly cover.

Time of Day

Most open-air markets begin early in the morning, some as early as 3 or 4 a.m. The best finds are made as the vendors unpack. When an interesting load arrives, potential buyers cluster around to inspect. Many sales are made before the goods are all unloaded. Markets usually run until noon or early afternoon.

Most antiques fairs start later in the morning, most often 9:30 or 10 a.m., and end at 5 p.m.

Night Sales: A Special Caution

You can lose the right to any purchase made during the night at an open market, if it can be proven that the goods were stolen. In 1973, and Appeal Court ruled that all purchases made at open markets during the night could be challenged. If goods could be proven to be stolen, they can be returned to the rightful owner without recourse. Purchases made during daylight hours are yours without this restriction, as long as you don't know that goods were stolen.

This ruling doesn't seem to affect the early morning markets, probably because few stolen goods are offered at the markets.

Market Cross - Stratford

Origins of the British Markets

Britain has had recognized markets since the Roman occupation, from 100 to about 400 A.D. In Roman Britain, London was the trading center and largest town. There were at least two markets, one of which has left its name in "Cheapside" and other streets and squares with the word Cheap in them. (*Ceap,* spoken "cheap," was the old Saxon word for market.)

The lords of the land (who could be the Crown, a monastery, or a local lord of the manor) often were granted the right to hold specific types of markets at various times and places. Generally, competing markets within a certain distance (often a league, or six and two-thirds miles) were forbidden, as was buying and selling the prescribed items outside of the market precincts. The lords were also given the right to levy various fees and taxes in order to pay for services, and, more frequently, provide the market lords with revenue.

Some of the great London markets, such as the Sunday Petticoat Lane market (hardly the place for finding antiques!), the Billingsgate fish market, the old Covent Garden vegetable market, and the Smithfield meat and cattle market developed as the result of grant of market rights.

Most antiques markets have developed much more recently, especially since the Second World

21

War. Many of the larger and more elite markets and fairs have grown in stature along with the British realization that there is quite a lot of money to be made in antiques.

Some fairs have charitable origins: many parish churches and beneficial organizations sponsor sales to raise money. Other fairs are run strictly to provide a location for efficient buying and selling of antiques and collectables. Naturally many of these fairs are run strictly for the profit of the participants and especially the organizers. Britain has many markets surviving centuries that are not antiques or collectables fairs. Many street markets can trace their origins back for centuries, and the original royal charter granting the right to hold a fair may be on file in some dusty records office. Some street markets in the provinces are still property of the lord of the market.

With the passage of time, however, cities and other local authorities have leased or bought the rights to hold fairs and markets from private owners.

Market Crosses

Many traditional markets were marked by a market cross, erected under the authority of the owner of the fair, and blessed by the church. This allowed the owners to bring all sales under the obligations of fair dealing and (especially before the 19th century) regulated prices.

Some of the largest and best preserved market crosses (such as Malmesbury, Wiltshire) are large enough to shelter small offices and other amenities under them, even if they no longer have a large market to serve.

Some market crosses are relatively recent, such as the one in Stratford-on-Avon, which dates from the late Victorian era, and still marks the site of a boisterous street market (no antiques) once a week.

All market crosses are out in the open; only in modern times have some gained walls to turn the interior into buildings.

Boot Sale
Ascot~

Types of Markets

Britain is almost overwhelmed with fairs, markets, and auctions at which antiques are sold. In addition, there are hundreds of special-interest fairs. Most of them take place in England, with only a thin scattering in Wales, Scotland, and Northern Ireland.

Many weekly markets are organized by city or regional governmental entities, such as local councils or city governments.

In addition, a number of regular markets are organized by market companies and promoted in the antiques trade press. While most of the important markets (and some of the less important ones) are listed here, you may want to check the "Antique Dealer and Collector's Guide" monthly magazine, or the weekly "Antiques Trade Gazette."

Antiques Fairs

Regularly occurring shows are often called "antiques fairs," or "antique fairs." Often, they are held indoors at a hotel or convention hall. They consist of anywhere from twenty to two or three hundred dealers who bring all kind of things to try to sell. While most of these dealers have regular shops, some strictly travel the fair circuit.

The merchandise is carefully studied by experts hired by the organizer before being offered for sale. Generally, true finds will be rare at this type of show. Some of them require sellers to be members of either of the two largest British antique dealers' associations, the British Antique Dealers Association (BADA), and the London and Provincial Antique Dealers Association (LAPADA).

Antiques Shows

Antiques shows are similar to antiques fairs, but it is often even harder for dealers to obtain the right to sell there. There is no restriction on who may come to look and to buy. Generally, admissions are more costly than at other events, (as much as £5), but the price of admission often includes a wonderful, fully illustrated glossy catalogue. At the best of these shows, most of the items are of museum quality; all will carry a guarantee, and sometimes complete papers of provenance (the history of the item). Items for sale must be in perfect condition. Some shows limit those offering goods to members of the two British antiques associations, BADA, and LAPADA.

Dealers are invited to display at these shows; some dealers wait decades before they're invited to display. These shows form the high point of the British antiques circuit, and generally take place in the spring and, especially, during the fall months.

Collectors Fairs

Specialized fairs catering to limited types of items are often called collectors fairs. They are often smaller than antiques fairs; some may be limited to Toby mugs or antique swords, or Belgian postage stamps, or almost any other type of collectable. Often, they are announced in the hard-to-find specialist newsletters and magazines rather than (or in addition to) the general antiques trade newspapers.

Britain is certainly a nation of collectors! These specialists are knowledgeable, and often are fountains of information for the interested amateur.

These fairs are held as much for enlightenment of the collectors as well as the purchase and sale of items. As a result, they are generally more relaxed and informal than the larger antiques events.

Boot Sales

Boot sales are more or less like an American or Canadian flea market or swap meet. They're called "boot sales" because sellers can sell whatever they can fit into the car's "boot" (trunk). Many are small, local affairs; others are still local but may have hundreds of sellers and thousands of potential buyers. While a few of the larger, most regular ones are listed here, often many can be found only by small, tacked-up signs along the road with an arrow pointing in the right direction.

Most sellers are private parties rather than regular dealers. Most prohibit dealers from selling, though these are some of the most fertile grounds for bargain hunters. Many dealers regularly canvass the boot sales, since this is one place where the sellers may not know what they have.

Boot sales are usually a summer, fair-weather event: they're extremely scarce from November through April. Some are held rain or shine, but others are only held if it isn't raining. Saturday and Sunday are the usual days for boot sales.

Admission charges are usually low—anywhere from 10p to 50p, and parking will often be available either for free or a modest fee.

Jumble Sales

Jumble sales are no more or less than what in the United States and Canada is called a "rummage sale." Often these sales are sponsored by churches or civic or charitable groups. The quality of items is usually low—old clothes, broken small appliances, and other leftovers of the industrial age. But also, many discoveries and finds can be made here for bargain prices. Jumble sales take place on an irregular basis; they are often advertised in local newspapers, and local tourist offices may list them on the calendar of the week's events.

Exhibitions

Exhibitions are usually displays of antiques, where the items are not for sale (though the dealers or exhibitors sometimes will talk discreetly about selling). Many are specialist meetings, held to show what is currently of interest in the antiques trade.

Sometimes, an antique show or fair is called an exhibition to imply exclusivity and large size. In this case, sales are openly promoted.

Antiques Markets

Indoor antiques markets are regular collections of full-time dealers, usually open during regular business hours. While some are located in the vicinity of markets (such as the Bermondsey Antiques Market in London, adjacent to the Bermondsey Market), others are free-standing.

Often from twenty to one hundred dealers share quarters in these buildings. They are efficient ways for travelers to see large quantities of antiques and collectables quickly. Sometimes, finds may be made. However, only a few of these full-time collections of dealers are listed, when either they are very large, or when there just isn't much else in the neighborhood.

Crafts Fairs

Crafts fairs are usually the fruit of one of the most endearing of British characteristics: the love of the amateur endeavor. Many of the fairs are for new work only, and only the people who created the work can offer the goods for sale. As a result, few antiques will be found at a crafts fair. There are lots of interesting people, as well as products ranging from the best of British crafts to some items that, because of low quality and poor conception, make you wonder whether anyone would buy them.

Flea Markets

British flea markets differ from the North American version, in that they are mainly for the sale of lower-quality, new and cheap goods: pots and pans, clothes, motor oil and car parts, hardware, tools, and plumbing fixtures. For example, the St. Martin's Market in Birmingham (Tuesday, Thursday, and Saturday) is a huge hall and adjacent outdoor lot, with hundreds of vendors of cheap, often poorly made clothes, new pots and pans, a few fruit and vegetable vendors, and a man selling toothpaste, aspirins, and similar items with the help of an amazing, home-built computer system hooked to an old television. (However, every six weeks, usually on a Wednesday, this site is the location of one of the best antiques and collectors markets in Britain.)

Street Markets

Street markets come in all types, but most are general collections of fruit and vegetable vendors, fish mongers, sellers of new and used clothes, demonstrations and sales of kitchen gadgets guaranteed to cut corkscrews of potatoes and mile-long curls from carrots, and shred mountains of cabbage for cole slaw.

   Though they are interesting and great events in themselves, few of them offer antiques or collectables of any type.

Terms That Define a Market

Every trade has a shorthand that quickly communicates to potential visitors the type and special conditions that the fair offers. Here are several you're likely to find:

"Dateline"

Usually you'll see this term in conjunction with a year, frequently 1880 or 1930. It signifies that nothing newer can be offered for sale at this event. Generally, only the higher quality and carefully monitored events have formal datelines.

"No New or Reproduction"

This term means that only items of a certain age (dependent on the organizer) can be sold. Reproductions are widespread in Britain and are not always very clearly marked. New items in the style of old are also easy to find. Fair organizers often state the minimum age in their contracts with sellers, and advertise it in announcements of forthcoming fairs and markets. However, this doesn't mean that experts have screened every item.

"Vetted"

When this term appears, it means that experts have inspected every item offered to ensure that it meets stated requirements for items to be sold at the fair, and that the goods are authentic and of good quality. Generally this term (and procedure) is only used at the very top quality fairs.

"BADA"

BADA, the British Antique Dealers Association, is the most prestigious organization of antiques dealers. It is elitist in character, with membership limited to the upper crust of dealers. Dealers must be nominated, and if admitted, must subscribe to a strict code of ethics. Member dealers usually have the portrait logo prominently affixed in their shops or displays, and sometimes put it on their cards and letterheads as well.

This organization can be contacted at its headquarters:

British Antique Dealers Association
20 Rutland Gate
London SW7
Telephone 01-589 4128

"LAPADA"

LAPADA, the London and Provincial Antique Dealers Association, is the other major organization of antique dealers. It is newer, and was frankly formed as an alternative to BADA. While membership requires several years in business and adherence to a strict code of ethics, its character is not as elite as BADA. Member dealers often display the organization's logo, a Chippendale chandelier.

This organization can be contacted at its headquarters:

London and Provincial Antique
Dealers Association
3 Cheval Place
London SW7
Telephone 01-584 7911

(Note: some dealers are members of both organizations)

"PBFA"

PBFA, the Provincial Booksellers Faris Association, an organization of antiquarian book sellers, have formed an association to promote their interests and organize book fairs. This organization sponsors a regular London fair every month, and issues a free calendar of other antiquarian book fairs all over Britain. Members of this organization can be identified by the logo of a cat sitting on a book. For a calendar schedule and list of members, contact:

Provincial Booksellers Fairs Association
P.O. Box 66
Cambridge, Cambridgeshire CB1 3PD
Telephone (0223) 240921

Sugar tongs - Bath

Special Favors for the "Antiques Trade"

The antiques trade is highly organized. As in so many other fields, special favors and terms are given to those individuals who are in the same line of work. These favors can range from preferential pricing to early and/or free admission to fairs and markets.

How to Identify Favors to the "Trade"

Many times, notices of fairs and markets will include one or two code words to let you know that special courtesies are extended to others in the antiques trade. In advertisements, look for words such as "Trade Free," "Trade _____ Only," "Open 11.0; 9.30 by Invitation or (Trade) Card Only," or similar half-hidden wording, often placed in fine print in a corner.

Special Favors to Dealers

Many but not all antiques fairs, boot sales, and other events discriminate in favor of members of the antiques trades. Several different types of discrimination are practiced, though with forethought and planning, they can be minimized.

Early Admission

Most antique fairs and shows held one to four times a year allow (and encourage) dealers and others clearly in the antiques trades to have an advance look at the goods to be sold, and to "skim the cream" from the goods offered before the public is allowed to enter.

Individual organizers set the rules as they choose. Early admission for some fairs is only an hour or two before the public is admitted. At others, it may be a whole day.

During the "trade" periods, you're expected to know what you're looking at, or at least not betray your ignorance.

On the other hand, prices are more favorable, even if you admit that the items you're interested in are for export. (Your clothes and accent will announce this even if you don't state it out loud.)

A few organizers (such as Penman Fairs) utterly refuse to allow dealers to have first pick during the trade preview.

A few other organizers let members of the antiques trade in early, but charge a higher admission to the early birds.

Free Admission

Many fairs (but not many boot sales) allow members of the antiques trade in for free, while the general public has to pay admission fees, running anywhere from 10p to £4. At some of the very famous and exclusive sales, usually those with beautifully printed color catalogues, members of the antiques trade pay just as much as anyone else.

How to Prove You're in the "Trade"

The best proof that you're in the antiques trade is printed. A business card (in Britain often called a "trade card") announcing the name of an antiques shop with address, telephone number, and your name, fills the bill.

If your card shows that you have a shop in North America, you won't ever be asked for a tax number.

Additional proof can be in the form of the copy of a business license or state or provincial resale tax certificate.

Membership in an antiques trade organization (as shown by a membership card) also is usually considered proof.

A number of knowledgeable collectors have secured "trade" privileges by merely having business cards printed before they leave home.

British dealers may have to provide their VAT number and, rarely, show a (pocket-sized) VAT Special Scheme Stockbook.

Discounts to Members of the "Trade"

Almost without exception, you can obtain a discount if you can demonstrate you're in the "trade." Often, merely asking, "What is the best price to the trade?" will obtain a reduction of 10 to 15%. Occasionally, you may have to produce some proof; as above, your card or business certificate will be the best proof. Don't be bashful about asking for the "trade price," since it offers a way of saving money.

Naturally, the more you know about the subject, and the more you can talk knowledgeably about the items and the trade, the more credible your request for trade treatment becomes. (Often, discussing the antiques trade where you live will be of great interest to your listener, and then they may reveal more about how they perceive that the British antiques trade operates.)

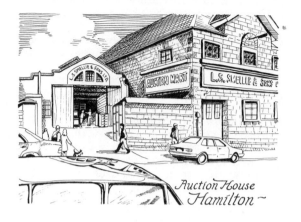

Auction House
Hamilton ~

Auctions

Probably a larger proportion of antiques and collectables passes through the auction houses in Britain than most other countries. And at auction, occasionally great finds can be made and prices can be quite reasonable. The vast majority of items offered for auction are sold for less than £200.

Auctions vary greatly in formality and how they are conducted. Some country auctions are rowdy, informal gatherings mainly consisting of local dealers and used-goods merchants where it seems that everyone knows each other, with auctioneers joking with the bidders. At these auctions, to bid you need only raise or wildly wave your hand, shout out, or almost anything else to have your bid noted.

Other auctions, primarily those dealing with very expensive fine arts often held in London, are formal, tension-laden affairs, with bidders risking huge sums to buy well-known, unique items. Suits and ties and dresses are expected. The atmosphere is formal. Buyers must pre-register to obtain admittance or to bid.

And there are all types of auctions in between.

If You Wiggle Your Ears Will You Spend All Your Money?

One of the fears that many people have at auction is that they'll spend an outrageous amount of money for something that they don't want by wiggling their ear, looking at their watch, or scratching their nose. However, these discreet signs are usually used only by prior arrangement at auctions where the privacy of the buyer is important.

When this hasn't been arranged, this type of bid has been known to occur. They are extremely rare and, if you shake your head, are not binding. (When a bid has not been truly made, the auctioneer will restart the bidding on the spot at a lower price.)

In addition to the auctioneer watching for bids, there are usually one or more assistants also watching.

They are skilled at gaining bidders' eyes, and rarely misinterpret.

Often, auctioneers will determine early in the sale who is likely to bid on certain types of items, and direct most of their attention to those potential bidders.

Auction Schedules

Auctions basically are held when the auctioneer knows (or hopes) that there will be enough goods to draw lively bidding.

In London and other large cities, a number of auction houses hold regular auctions, with greater or lesser specialization.

Other auction houses hold auctions only infrequently on a schedule or irregularly when there are enough goods to sell. Finding the dates and times can be difficult; while local newspapers and antiques trade newspapers will invariably carry auction notices, the best source of information is the auction house itself. Most will be glad to answer when you write or telephone and request information.

Most auction houses will, upon request, provide a calendar of all auctions for three months to a year at a time.

Inspection (Viewing) Before the Sale

Every auction (except the extremely rare mail-order auction) provides inspection periods before the auction. While the exact times may vary, generally inspections can be made on the day before the sale, sometimes two days before the sale, and on sale day before the auction begins.

If a catalog has been issued, and you don't want to buy one, several will be available for reference during the inspection period. If you don't see them around, ask at the information desk for a catalogue.

Catalogues

Most auction houses issue a catalogue, often several weeks before the sale. The catalogue can range from crude, mimeographed sheets with conditions of sale on one side and one- or two-line descriptions of each lot to lavish, full-color catalogues with knowledgeable commentary. If the lot is very important or unique, it will usually have a longer description, and often a photograph as well.

For the auctions of Old Masters and similarly rare items, catalogues may be issued a month or two before the sale date.

For regular sales, catalogues will usually be available about one month before the sale date.

If the auction is a regular weekly sale, the catalogue may not be available until a week before the sale.

At country auctions offering miscellaneous items, there may not be a catalogue.

Most catalogues aren't free: for the exquisite catalogues of the finest antiques and artwork, you may have to pay as much as £1 to £4. In addition, you may have to pay extra if you want it mailed to you.

Major auction houses have catalogue subscription services. If you want all catalogues for sale of a particular class of item, you can arrange to have catalogues sent to you (even by airmail or air express). Contact the auction house's "general office" for further information.

How to Read a Catalogue

Most catalogues are easy to read. Somewhere on the first few pages, you'll find the Standard Conditions of Sale. This may be from one to five pages of legalese; however, read the conditions carefully to avoid surprises when the time comes to pay the bill.

General Conditions of Sale

Every catalogue includes the auction house's general conditions of sale. Variations are minor. They generally state that the highest bidder will purchase, that the auctioneer has the sole discretion to accept or reject bids for any reason or for no reason, and special provisions for items on with a minimum reserve.

The general conditions will also cover payment policy, whether a buyer's premium is charged, and policy for removing purchased goods.

Estimated Sale Price

Many auction catalogues, particularly when the sale is relatively specialized, will provide estimated sales prices for every lot. Invariably, these figures do not include any buyer's premium or Value Added Tax. Somewhere, most catalogues will have a disclaimer about estimated sale prices such as this notice in Phillips catalogues, "The estimated figures are our opinion of the prices we expect lots to realise."

Lots and Items

Auction houses decide how they want to sell various items: either as a single item or as a lot. Frequently items which were brought in together by one seller and have a relationship (for example, a tea set) will be sold as one lot. Sometimes, however, a set can be divided into two or more lots. For example, if the tea set has a matching coffee pot as well, the coffee pot may be sold as a separate lot.

The auction house has total discretion in the matter, and how and whether related items are divided depend on how the auctioneer believes they will bring a higher price.

Bidder Registration

Bidders in most auctions are requested (or required) to register before they make their first bid. The bidder's registration form asks for you name, address, sometimes verified by some identification such as a passport or identity card. At this type of auction, as you bid, a record of your purchases is kept, and you can pay for all of your purchases at the cashier.

At other auctions, most likely country auctions, you need not register; you just go in and bid. When the item is sold to you, you're handed the item, and you hand over the money to the roving auctioneer's assistant.

The Hammer and Hammer Price

The hammer is auctioneer's symbol of office. The hammer, a small eight- or ten-inch long mallet, is actually used at every auction, and no item is considered sold until it is "knocked down" by three taps of the hammer.

The "hammer price" is the price you bid. However, at many auctions, this is not the total price you'll pay. Some auctions add a charge called a "buyer's premium," and Value Added Tax as well.

Buyer's Premium

When you buy and item for perhaps £100, that doesn't mean that is the price you must pay. Many auctions, particularly those run by the largest three auction companies (Christie's, Phillips, and Sotheby's) also charge a buyer's premium. This charge, actually a commission, which is added to your bill. Some buyer's premiums are as high as 10%. Since this charge is determined by the auction house, different auctions often have a different percentage as a buyer's premium.

Even when there is a buyer's premium, the auction house still also collects a seller's premium (see "seller's premium" below).

Value Added Tax

Value added tax (VAT), a general tax on most sales and other transactions, is added to the buyer's premium, and therefore, to your bill. This tax is 15% of the buyer's premium (if it is charged), and is added to the auctioneer's commission or premium.

In addition, on some types of items, generally newer items, you may have to pay VAT on the price of the item as well. However, antiques, art, and most types of used goods are exempt from VAT.

Seller's Premium

Every auction house makes its money on commissions, also called premiums. These commissions are charged on a percentage basis, although the percentage may be on a sliding scale at some auction houses. It may range from about a maximum of 15% down to about 5%. The seller's premium or commission is included in the price that you pay for the goods.

If the lot is not sold because it doesn't meet the reserve price (see next section), the commission is still charged to the would-be seller.

Reserve Prices

Many items are consigned to auction houses with a firm reserve price: that is, the minimum price for which the item or lot must bring. If the item doesn't bring the minimum it is not sold, but a commission is still charged to the person consigning the item.

The amount of the reserve (if any) is a secret between the auctioneer and the person consigning the item. It will not be revealed, even if you ask. You won't even be able to find out which items (if any) have a minimum reserve price. Some auction houses have general rules for minimum reserve amounts. This will be stated in the General Conditions of Sale. Often, if an item isn't sold at the reserve on the first try, it will reappear at the next sale with a lower reserve, or no reserve at all. Surprisingly, often it will bring not only the lower reserve price, but the final hammer price may exceed the higher reserve at the earlier auction.

Bought-In Items

Sometimes the auction house will itself purchase an item (or acquire it in other ways, such as non-payment of storage fees), and sell it on its own behalf. In this case, the auction house treats it exactly as it would a consigned item, and may set a reserve and collect the premiums from the buyer in the normal way.

Bidding When You're Not There

Most auction houses welcome bids from bidders who aren't in attendance during the sale. These bids are called "Commissions." There is no charge for this service. If you wish to use this process, you must make arrangements before the auction begins. When you contact the auction house, ask for the "Commissions" office or department.

Bids can be made by telephone, mail, or by a bid left with the auction house after you have inspected the items to be sold.

Left Bids and Mail Bids

A left bid is a bid that you leave in person after inspecting the goods for sale. For mail bids, you must first obtain a catalogue or inspect the merchandise personally at the sale site. If you wish to make a bid, fill out a form (usually provided by the auction house) in which you state the maximum hammer price you're willing to pay for each separate item.

You must also provide your name, signature and date, address, and telephone number where you can be reached during the sale.

List the items you wish to bid on: lot number, description, and maximum price. The auction's commission bidder will bid for you, only to the maximum price (usually called the "limit") you have stated.

Note that the "limit" is the price before any buyers premium and VAT: if you want your price to include these figures, lower the amount of your limit. Do not put the total price and state "including premium and VAT."

Telephone Bids

For telephone bids, the procedure is a bit more complicated. You must register as a bidder, and inform the auction house about how you intend to pay, and the items you wish to bid on.

Contact the Commissions office well in advance of the sale to arrange for telephone bidding.

Bidding by the House

When you're at the auction and you see employees of the auction house making bids, don't worry. In reality, they are making bids not for themselves or for the house, but rather for people who have left written bids or are relaying bids from telephone bidders.

Shills

Shills are prohibited at British auctions. Owners of items at auction are also generally prohibited from bidding on the items they're trying to sell. Failure to follow these rules will exclude the seller from future auctions.

Storage and Shipping After the Auction

Generally, most antiques auctions require that all purchases be removed in a short period. Some require removal by dark, while others will let you take as long as one week. The free period depends on the auction house's policy.

After this period expires, all items are put in storage at your expense; you'll have to pay the storage and sometimes transportation charges before you can claim the purchases.

In any case, you won't be permitted to take the goods until you have a bill of sale in your possession.

If you have a shipping company making collections, you may make arrangements with the auction house to hold the items until the collection truck arrives. Make sure that you work out arrangements before you leave the sale! Make sure that the collections truck driver has the original or copy of the bill of sale and your authorization to take the items.

Paying for Purchased Items

You must pay for the items you bought before you can take them. Since most auctions do not accept credit cards, payment must usually be made in pounds, either by British check drawn on a British bank, by sterling travelers' check, or by cash.

Usually, large antiques auction houses allow up to several days to make payment before action will be taken. Small country auctions may wish to collect payment on the same day as the auction. It is entirely up to the auction house to set its own policy.

Usually, payment in foreign currency is not accepted. If you need to make special arrangements such as having money cabled, discuss this with the management before you begin bidding.

Receipts and Other Documents

When you pay for your purchases, you'll be given a receipt with the lot number, probably a short description of what the lot contains, and the price, plus an additional amount for any buyer's premium and VAT.

You have the right to a receipt for every purchase.

Regulation of Auctioneers and Auctions

Legally, auctions are not considered retail sales. Unlike antique dealers, auctioneers are not bound by the "Trade Description Act," which requires accurate descriptions of items sold, and are specifically excluded from coverage under the "Unfair Contract Terms Act," which in general prohibits general disclaimers of responsibility. As a result, while auctioneers try to accurately assess the goods they offer, they are not legally liable for misdescription of merchandise and often offer no guarantee.

However, remember that many of the true experts in identification of antiques are found at the auction houses. The larger firms often have specialists in particular types of items.

Usually, if you can prove that the item was misrepresented or a fake, you can take your evidence and information to the auction house, which will often have the sale annulled, and you may be able to get your money back.

Fine Art Auctioneers Trade Association

Most auctioneers of antiques belong to the trade association. You can contact this organization if you wish:

Society of Fine Arts Auctioneers
7 Blenheim Street
London, W1Y 0AS
Telephone 01-620 2933

Birmingham

Who Are the Sellers?

You always hope to find friendly, helpful vendors who don't know the value of what they're selling, and therefore sell it to you for a song. While such sellers do exist, they are only slightly more common than hens' teeth. Do not expect to find them very often.

Sellers may vary widely in knowledge of their chosen field. Most use reference books and price guides to help them keep their pricing current with the British market. The day of the untutored and ignorant seller of antiques has passed almost completely.

Most sellers at antiques fairs, shows, and regular antiques markets are full-time dealers, who may close their shops or leave an assistant to mind the main store. Depending on the nature of the market, they either take their best or worst—whatever they think will sell.

Some dealers have no fixed place of business, except their vans and trucks, and maybe a dusty barn at their home in the country or part of an old warehouse. They are "pickers"—that is, picking up the best around the country, and serving as the city dealers' source of supply. If you can find them, they can also be a cheaper source of supply for you as well. These traveling dealers have the time and patience to seek out house sales, country auctions, and fund-raising sales of charity groups. They often cultivate a grapevine to lead to tips and sources of supply. Because they have no fixed place of business, they often thrive on large turnover and take low markups. Some vendors are junk dealers pure and simple. They clean out basements and attics, old barns, warehouses, and garages. Some even go on early morning safaris looking for salvageable items in the trash! Even so, they may ask the same amount that the price guides suggest and consider their time as their investment.

Part-time vendors are usually found in strength only at weekend flea markets where permanent stands aren't available. During the week, they are members of other trades and professions. While many do not have the choicest items, they may be more willing to negotiate and they are often more happy to share experiences. Many of their items may only be of garage-sale or rummage-sale quality.

Bermondsey Street—London

Bargaining

While prices at antique fairs and shows are often marked, they are rarely fixed—you can usually obtain reductions of 10 to 30 per cent of the first asking price if you try. These reductions are often possible in the most elegant of fairs and exhibitions. Knowing the economics of the market helps.

As a rule of thumb, most dealers try to double the prices of everything they sell. They feel entitled to this for their time, trouble, skill, and luck.

British bargaining is unlike the "let's make a deal" attitude so common in Italy. It's much more likely to be a softly spoken, "Is that your best price?" answered by "I think I could do a little better."

The first price almost always include a "fudge factor," since most sellers (and most buyers) expect to haggle and reduce the initial price. In fact, if you fail to bargain, some vendors may be puzzled and deprived of the conversational ritual to set the final price. The conversations as well as the money constitute much of the income many part time vendors expect and enjoy.

Here are a number of tactics to try to bring the price down:

1. The seller will always make a profit: his or her initial cost is also the base price. Some sellers

keep markups low to increase turnover; this will make initial prices seem more reasonable, but there maybe less price flexibility.

If the dealer just obtained the item, the price may be reduced to provide a quick profit to raise cash. The dealer may know of another more desirable object he or she may need some added money to buy. On the other hand, if the item has been a longtime dust collector, and you're the first person even casually interested, the price may be less.

2. Have enough cash to buy what you want. At flea markets, all payments are expected to be cash—in British pounds. You'll be amazed at some of the sums of cash discreetly changing hands. No checks, no credit cards, no foreign money such as dollars.

3. The price is usually on an "as is—where is" basis. If there's an imperfection, use it as a way to try to reduce the price.

4. Bargain even if you know an item is an incredibly good buy. You can still always pay the initial asking price later. Failure to bargain may make the vendor believe that either you're foolish or that the item is very valuable (and the seller may decide to keep it).

5. Treat sellers as *people* first—this will solve many of your price problems. Politeness, courtesy, and consideration will almost always make a difference.

6. When you first see an item you want, set a price on it in your mind even before you pick it up to examine it. Don't pay more if you can help it. The "get it now" mentality used by auctioneers and high-pressure salespeople can lead you to spend far more than you planned. Conversely, there are sometimes a few items you must have, or you'll regret it forever.

7. If you find an item you know is unique, don't wait and plan to come back later. You probably won't, or it will be sold when you do return. You may never see a similar item again, and be

reminded of it every time you see the empty space on your mantel at home.

8. Don't make a beeline for the only item you want. Showing too much interest right away may lead to a higher final price. Better to pick up five or six items of lesser interest and look at them as well as the items you want.

One maneuver that sometimes works well is to ask the price of a group of unrelated items, then ask the price of smaller groups, single items, and eventually ask the price of the item you really want.

Often, using this approach, the price of the item you want is less than its proportional share of the whole group—and a bargain besides.

9. Ask for the "best price to the trade." If you use this tactic, it helps if you know or can act knowledgeably about the field, and if you can "prove" you're a dealer by possession of a business card of an antique dealer with your name as owner or manager.

Not a Tactic

Some dealers are contrary and won't reduce the price at all. Don't insult them by being loud and rude. The fixed price may be only for a particular item, only for foreigners, or people with certain color eyes. The firmly fixed price is uncommon in antique markets, even in the very expensive ones in London and Bath.

Bristol

Transportation in Britain

Britain has a very good public transportation system. The Intercity trains are fast, on time, and frequent. Most cities, compact by American and Canadian standards, are well served by public transportation. London's Underground (tube) is one of the easiest systems to use in the world. It's also often the fastest way to get around.

Where information about access via convenient public transit is available, it's included in the description of each market, fair, or auction.

Public transit as the basis for a tour of markets, fairs, and auctions has serious drawbacks, however. Not all markets are conveniently reached using public transit. Many are in suburbs, obscure country villages, or even motorway rest areas beyond the reach of subway, train, or bus service.

Most markets start early; they're at their best early Saturday and Sunday morning (and Friday for Bermondsey in London) soon after dawn. Busses and the Underground will probably be running on a night or weekend schedule—which means long waits or even no service. As the market opens, dealers and regulars pick over and buy the best of this week's harvest of antiques, while you still stand in the station waiting for a train or bus to come along. Or, you can easily spend two or three hours getting to a suburban market only 10 miles away; when you finally arrive, you may find the market has been cancelled, or is packing up.

When using public transit, you have to carry your purchases with you, send them along, or arrange for a collection service to gather them together. There's a limit to how much luggage you can carry, and porters or baggage carts are often scarce. Sending your treasures to a central point in London or other major port for a single shipment or shipping small parcels home every day or two can be an exercise in frustration, and cost a fortune in postal and express shipping charges.

In London, there are often half a dozen markets to cover on a single day. Each market has its own character and unique offerings. The markets are an hour or more from each other by public transit—but 20 minutes by car or van.

Public transit is often the fastest way to get around large cities on weekdays. During the week, a car or van in a city can be a hindrance. During the week, city driving is an exercise in fighting through the thick molasses of traffic. Cars are often best left in a parking place.

Car or Van—The Advantages

A vehicle is almost a necessity for serious collector or dealer.

Take a hint from the sellers: they don't usually arrive on public transit. They drive.

Drive Everywhere

Small towns and villages in the countryside or city suburbs often hold antique markets, antique fairs, and auctions. Public transport is either unavailable or very inconvenient.

If you limit yourself to major cities, you eliminate a large proportion of items for sale. You also deprive yourself of some of the most picturesque market settings, and friendly (and often lower priced) provincial sellers. You may also miss country style furniture, folk art, and new but traditional artifacts.

Your Vehicle as Depository

Carrying purchases around a flea market can be exhausting—especially if you have bought heavy crystal, small bronze statues, or delicate porcelain. If you have a car, you can slip back to it to unload your purchases, reducing fatigue and worry.

If several of you travel together, you can search the market independently and find the car a convenient meeting place. Each separate marketer should have a car key. (Keys are made at a locksmith, and may cost as much as £4.)

Probably Save Money

Unless your entire expedition is limited to London and its suburbs, renting a small car or a basic van (not a fully equipped camper!) can save you a substantial amount of money, even after you consider the 15% Value Added Tax and the high price of gasoline.

The price of renting or leasing a very small car in Britain is little more than the price of a BritRailpass or other discounted rail and bus ticket for the same period of time. It is rarely more than one and a half times the price of a BritRailpass. Therefore, with two or more people, it is cheaper to rent a car than to take the train.

City center hotels cost more than those in the outskirts and in the countryside. With a car, you'll have a wider selection of hotels to choose from. You'll also be able to stay in country inns and Britain's famous Bed and Breakfast establishments, which are unserved by any public transportation at all.

Parking: A Potential Problem

One drawback of driving is parking. British cities (except for the New Towns and the old cities totally reconstructed after being flattened during the

Second World War) were not designed for motor vehicles, or for parking. If you arrive at the market early, you'll probably get a parking place within a few blocks of the market's center—impossible later in the day. Street parking places may be free, especially on Sunday. Watch, however, for no-parking signs. Sometimes the police will tow illegally parked cars away. Towaway zones are usually signed: there will be two yellow lines embedded or painted on the side of the road, and a small yellow sign with black writing will be near by. To redeem a towed car may cost as much as £100.

You may find signs directing you to pay car parks, where for 10p to £2 you'll have a legal parking place.

British pay parking garages almost operate several payment systems. Some require you to take a ticket as you enter, and you pay a cashier as you leave. Others operate on a self-serve system: you find a parking place, find the coin-operated ticket machine, buy a ticket, and place it on the windshield of your car (Pay and Display). At still others, you just pay as you enter.

Parking meters are also unfortunately widespread in Britain. Some in London take £1 coins, while giving as little as twenty minutes of freedom from the meter maid (formally known in Britain as traffic wardens).

Antiques Market-Windsor

Carrying Your Finds at Market

Sellers' Packing Materials

Few sellers have adequate, secure, convenient packing materials. Most will hand you the item, possibly wrapped in an old newspaper or a flimsy shopping bag. These bags, though better than nothing or a newspaper, are lightweight, and stretch and tear if filled with heavy or sharp-pointed objects. Bring your own bag.

One exception to the general rule of "carry and ship it yourself" is when you buy a large quantity of merchandise from one seller. Often the seller can crate it and arrange for its shipment. In that case, you can generally rely on the seller's packing materials and procedures. Try to watch the crating or container-packing operations. It will be interesting, and you'll also ensure that the correct items are packed. Buy adequate insurance for the shipment.

Selecting a Market Bag

There is a large variety of carry bags available. Take a day pack or gym bag. Nylon bags are best: they are strong, light, fold into small places, and shield the contents from the prying eyes of potential thieves. Shoulder straps leave your hands free to inspect items. In general, bags of this type are cheaper and more strongly constructed when bought in the United States and Canada.

Carefully check a bag before you buy it. Look for durability and convenience, not style. A good bag has these qualities:

1. The material is strong. Rip-stop nylon is the most durable lightweight fabric. Canvas is heavier (in weight, not strength) and can rot if left in the damp for extended periods.

2. The stitching is strong and seams are secure.

3. The zippers are strong and substantial, and open and close easily.

4. All metal parts are thick and strong: solid brass is best.

If you plan on extensive purchases of small items, take an extra bag with you.

Luggage Carriers

Tourists at very large markets sometimes bring wheeled luggage carriers. They have a number of limitations that make them less useful there than at airports and train stations. Many markets have a lot of barriers to the small wheels of these devices. Markets are often held on dirt, gravel, or uneven cobblestone surfaces. Curbs may interfere with smooth rolling. Many indoor markets have stairs, which further reduce the utility of these carriers.

Flea markets and antique fairs by their very nature are very crowded, full of jostling people intent on their business. They don't expect to find luggage carriers in their way and may trip over them.

If you do use a luggage carrier or dolly, be sure it is strong and will take a lot of punishing use without breaking. And be sure that boxes or suitcases can be securely fastened to the carrier.

London

Amenities at the Flea Market

Food at the Fair

Most markets and fairs have food and drink for
sale at concession stands. Such convenience food,
not noted for offering quality or good value, can
range from vendors of soda pop, sandwiches, and
meat pies, to fish-and-chips, small pizzas, and, at
the elegant hotel shows, the entire dining room of
the hotel.

Snack food sold at markets is usually as safe as
any food elsewhere in Britain. Use the same
precautions you would use anywhere.

If the market is also a general market with
vegetable vendors as well as a antiques and junk,
you may find lower prices, better variety and
more quality for your money.

Toilets

There are toilets at most markets or close by.
Some can be most portable, primitive, smelly, and
ill-maintained. There may not be any toilet
paper—or the paper may have the texture and
consistency of waxed paper. Some of the worst
ones have an attendant to collect money, usually
5p, 10p, or 20p per use.

Often facilities for women are unequal to the demand—plan to wait.

In a number of markets held in open spaces or fields, toilets may be placed in portable trailers. Look for the trailers looming up above the stands. They are often but not always marked.

If there are toilets in the area, look for these signs: Toilets, W.C., Public Conveniences.

Scotland~

Export Laws and Regulations

As in most of the rest of Europe, Great Britain
regulates and restricts the export of antiques and
other items deemed part of the national heritage.
Unlike some other countries, particularly Greece,
Turkey, and all of the Eastern European
countries, the laws in Britain are relatively
reasonable, and are impartially and fairly enforced.

The first laws regarding the export of art
works, antiques, books, and armor came into
force in 1952. Prior to this date, there were no
restrictions.

Current Laws

The current law governing the export of antiques
and artwork is the Act of 1985 #849, Export of
Goods (Control) Order. It provides that under a
general license, most types of goods may be exported. Restrictions are described below.

Special laws apply to the export of manorial
and tithe records: the Law of Property
(Amendment) Act of 1924 relates to manorial
records and the Tithe Act of 1936 relates to tithe
records.

What Can Be Exported?

In general, export permits are needed for export of most antiques and items of cultural value. There are, however, broad exceptions to this rule. Export licenses are not required for:

- All items (or sets of items) less than 50 years old regardless of value.

- All items regardless of age or content which were imported into Great Britain less than 50 years before the date of exportation if proof of importation is provided.

- All items over 50 years old which are valued at less than £16,000, with exceptions described in the next section.

- All items from 50 to 100 years old valued under £16,000, unless otherwise restricted. (However, a declaration on ELB Form A must be made.)

- Coins.

- A shipment of antiques or other collectables with a total value of over £16,000 if every individual item or related set is worth less than £16,000.

Specially Restricted Items

The following items require a an export license:

- Documents, manuscripts, architectural renderings and archives produced by hand which are older than 50 years, regardless of value. (However, there are no restrictions on printed books, pamphlets, and other printed matter.)

- Any item found in the soil and sea bed other than coins, and those items buried more than 50 years before they are exported.

- Representation of British historical personages in any medium with a value of over £4,000, or which has a value between £4,000 and £16,000, and the exporter produces a certificate from the Director of the National Portrait Gallery or the Keeper of the Scottish National Portrait Gallery that the item is not a work of national importance. (Coins may be exported regardless of age or portrait.)

- Photographs or albums of photographs when the work as a whole has a value of over £400.

- Motor vehicles more than 50 years old.

- Official papers of any value.

- Documents and manuscripts when each article or collection has a value of over £250.

- Manorial and tithe records. For special requirements for these particular records, contact:
Secretary
Royal Commission on Historical Manuscripts
Quality House, Quality Court
Chancery Lane
London WC2 1HP
Telephone 01-242 1198

These requirements may be changed at any time: if you have any questions, ask for information at the Export Licensing Branch (see next section). (This office is more responsive by telephone than in person.)

How to Apply for an Export License

Applications can only be made by permanent British residents; travelers resident outside of Britain cannot make an application on their own behalf. However, usually auction houses and antique dealers or shippers will be willing to make the declarations for you.

Applications must be made on ELB Form C to:

Export Licensing Branch
Department of Trade and Industry
Millbank Tower
Millbank
London SW1P 4QU
Telephone 01-322 3115
Telex 8811075

A photograph of every item for which an export license is requested must accompany the application.

When an application for export is made, it is referred to an official Expert Adviser, who will review the application and may either recommend that the export license be granted, or that it be refused because the item is of national importance.

If the Expert Adviser recommends refusal, the application is referred to the Reviewing Committee on the Export of Works of Art. The applicant will always be informed of this referral. Both the applicant and the Expert Adviser are asked to make a formal written statement of why they believe that the work should or should not be exported.

The committee will review both the applicant's information and the information from the Expert Adviser and will make its decision based on both submissions.

This committee can be contacted at:

The Reviewing Committee on the Export
  of Works of Art
Office of Arts and Libraries
Great George Street
London SW1P 3AL
Telephone 01-233 4797

If the committee decides to deny a license, the applicant has several choices: the art can remain in Britain, or the applicant may request that it be purchased at his or her cost by a public museum or trust. If the item is not purchased within the time permitted in the law (six months or one year), an export license must be granted.

Warehouse along the Clyde

Getting Your Purchases Home

Once you have your antiques and other items, you need to be able to get them home. How you do this depends on many factors: how much material there is, its weight and volume, and how soon you need or want it. You have several options: you can take your purchases with you as baggage, ship them by mail, package express, air freight, or for large items, in a shipping crate. If of great volume, it can be shipped in a 20-foot, 40-foot, or 45-foot (jumbo) shipping container.

Bringing Purchases Home with You

Packing Your Bags

When ready to return home laden with your purchases, you can carry them on the plane as hand luggage or check them as baggage. Remember that your baggage is not insured against loss or damage to precious metals, glass and crystal, money, and jewelry. Therefore, you may wish to consider carrying those items onto the plane.

If you decide to check your valuables as baggage, surround breakables with clothes, and, if available, plastic bubble-pack or Styrofoam packing peanuts and shells. These materials are available from shipping supply merchants and moving companies (check "Packers," "Packing Case Manufacturers," and "Removals and Storage" in the Yellow Pages). Sometimes you can find these materials in the early morning along sidewalks in retail shopping areas or wholesale markets.

Sturdy cardboard boxes provide excellent protection. Cartons made for shipping household goods (available from moving companies) and those made in China for shipping food (available in early morning before trash pickup in front of Chinese restaurants and grocery stores) provide the most protection. Almost as durable are cardboard fruit shipping boxes made in France and Italy (available at open air markets and food stores). Those used for apples are very good in size and durability.

Avoid boxes made of a soft grade of cardboard. If you try to fold a corner of a box flap and it bends easily, cracks, or tears, don't use that box.

Reinforce every cardboard box, especially at seams and corners, with filament tape. Since this tape is not widely available in Britain, you may want to take a roll with you. Have a sharp knife to cut it—the tape is extremely strong. A flimsy shipping tape is available in some stationery stores as well as shipping supply companies.

Baggage Allowances Between Britain and North America

Checked baggage on air flights between Britain and North America is counted on the piece system, rather than strictly by weight. If you return from Europe by air, you are entitled to check two pieces of luggage free and take a carry-on with you onto the plane. Each checked package must have a combined length, width, and height less than 62 inches (1.60 meters) and weigh no more than 70 pounds (32 kilograms). Some airlines limit the second piece of checked luggage to 55 inches (1.50 meters) and 70 pounds (32 kilograms). The limits are enforced sporadically, depending on the airline and the airline counter agent.

Carry-on luggage can weigh up to 70 pounds (32 kilograms), but sometimes some airlines will, on some airplanes, limit the luggage to 22 pounds (10 kilograms). In addition to your carryon, you can often take your camera, purse, day pack and duty-free shopping bag.

Generally, if your purchases are small items and you travel light, the transatlantic baggage allowance will prove sufficient. However, if you have excess baggage, charges can vary wildly between airlines. If you believe (before you make your reservation) that you'll have excess baggage, find out the charges. If they seem excessive, consider changing to an airline with lower excess baggage charges.

If you are not flying directly from Britain to North America, you can expect to have baggage treated on the European weight-based system (see next section).

Baggage Allowances Within Europe

Airlines in Europe (and, most of the rest of the world) accept baggage strictly on weight. Each first-class passenger is entitled to 66 pounds (30 kilograms) of checked luggage and one carry-on. Each business and coach passenger is entitled to 44 pounds (20 kilograms) of checked luggage and one carry-on.

The strictness with which the rules are applied will vary between different airlines at the same airport, the same airline at different airports, and even between one airline counter agent and the next.

Excess baggage charges are often steep! The rule of thumb is to charge one per cent of the first-class fare to every kilogram (or fraction), even if you're not in a first-class seat.

Shipment by Mail (Parcel Post)

There is usually a per-package limit of 50 pounds (22-1/2 kilograms) to the United States and 22 pounds (10 kilograms) to Canada, and costs are relatively high.

You pack the items yourself, either with your own box or an approved carton sold at the post office. Packing requirements are found in the brochure, "Wrap Up Well," available at most British post offices. Detailed requirements are found in the "Post Office Guide," available for reference at every post office.

At the post office, go to the window marked "Parcels." You'll have to complete a customs declaration. Use form C1 (small, green, both in French as well as English) for shipments worth under £50, and form C2 or CP3 if valued over £50. These are available at the counter. On the declaration, you have to state the contents and the value. In addition, you'll have to pay postage, which varies with the type of contents. (Books and papers have a special reduced rate.)

Expect packages to take one to two months to arrive at their destination.

Parcels for delivery in the United States are inspected by the United States Customs Service at the port of entry and then forwarded to you. If any duty is payable, the post office will bill you the amount of duty, a $5 Customs fee, and a collection surcharge. If the shipment is entirely duty free, there is no charge.

If the package contains a gift, it can be admitted duty free if you write "Unsolicited Gift—Value Under $50." You cannot mail gifts to yourself, and only one will be admitted duty free if addressed to the same party and passes Customs the same day.

Canadian Customs and Excise inspects parcels at the port of entry, and assesses duty. You pay any duty when the parcel is delivered.

Gifts can be sent duty free if they are marked "Unsolicited Gift—Price Under $40."

Package (Railway) Express

If the package weighs over 44 pounds (20 kilograms) to the United States or 11 pounds (5 kilograms) to Canada, you may ship it by rail to a port, by sea passage, and, in North America, accept delivery from the post office or freight express office.

Take the package to the baggage and left luggage office at any main railway station. You will have to fill out a customs declaration, as described above. Often, smaller stations don't have these forms: get one from a post office.

Delivery takes approximately four to eight weeks. United States or Canadian Customs inspection is the same as detailed above in the "Shipment by Mail" section.

Air Freight

When you need quick delivery, you can send packages by air freight. When shipping by air freight, your parcel is best packed in a wooden shipping carton.

You can take the parcel to the city check-in terminal in major cities such as London, Birmingham, or Edinburgh, or directly to the air-freight (cargo) terminal at the airport. You can also call air-freight shippers, who include pickup and delivery. (See "Airlines" and look for "Cargo" in the Yellow Pages listings.)

Costs are higher than surface transport, but delivery is between three days and one week, including Customs clearances.

While air freight is charged by weight, in general the larger and heavier the item, the less the charge per pound will be. The exact cost will vary, often with the category of merchandise the package contains.

If you ship through an air express company (many familiar names also operate out of Britain) the company will handle United States or Canadian Customs clearance. If you ship with an airline, you can either clear the package yourself or hire a customs broker to perform these formalities. Find the air express companies under "Courier Services" in the Yellow Pages.

A number of offices consolidate air freight and send it to your destination for much less than overweight charges. Some advertise in the handouts given to tourists. Compare costs between these operations and regular air freight companies carefully

Shipping Through Packers/Shippers

If your purchases are too bulky to take with you or ship by parcel post or express, or because of their age or importance to the British national heritage require permits for export, you'll probably become involved with a packing and shipping company. If you choose to work through a packer/shipper, most of the small but important details will be taken care of.

For large shipments, the packer's and shippers's costs are more than justified by the time and energy saved. There are several types of shipment, but the packer's and shipper's involvement and most of the paperwork will be the same.

Many shippers' services include:
- picking up of merchandise within a metropolitan area (such as London or Birmingham), or anywhere in the country
- packing the merchandise in a shipping crate or container
- preparing care of all export documentation (such as customs forms and a bill of lading)
- carrying freight to the port or airport, or to any North American port of entry you designate, or even to the final delivery location.

While to some extent the costs will vary with the shipper, you can expect to pay in the neighborhood of £2,200 to £6,000 for a 20-foot container and £3,200 to £10,000 for a 40-foot container for pick up in a single metropolitan region, packing, export documentation, and delivery to the port. The differences in costs are often reflected in the pickup radius, and care taken to cushion the items and to tightly fit them in for minimum shifting during the shipment.

Note: If you have the shipper perform the pickup, you'll need to provide the shipper with the name and address of every vendor, as well as the invoice for every item. This will ensure that all of the pickups can be scheduled and all items can be accounted for. Pickup usually can be accomplished within a week to ten days.

Choosing a Shipper

Shippers can be found in several ways: by discussion with antique dealers and auction houses, through shippers' and packers' advertisements in the antiques trade press, and at shipping offices at major antique shows and fairs, and the Yellow Pages (look under "Packers—Export," "Packers—Fine Art," and "Removals and Storage"). Many shippers have specialties or limitations. Ask carefully and listen to the answers, and obtain competitive bids for the exact same services.

Most reputable shippers will be pleased to quote a price and specify exactly what the price includes.

You should ask to see the premises where from which the packer operates: some resemble laboratories and specialize in the shipment of fine arts and rare paintings, while others are in run-down warehouses and fit huge loads of miscellaneous furniture and bric-a-brac into large shipping containers at a lower price.

Ask for references from the shipper before entering a contract: any reputable shipper will have a number of references.

Crate or Container?

Generally, smaller loads are packed into wood shipping crates. Some are standard size, while others are custom made for particular items. Larger loads are packed into metal shipping containers eight feet high, eight feet wide, with lengths of 20-feet, 40-feet, or 45-feet (jumbo). Since the price between a crate and a container may be small, it may be worth buying cheap items just to fill up a container. Containers are strong and are sealed at the packer's and are generally opened only by customs officials. Crates are more easily damaged and a bit easier to pilfer.

Delivery times are approximately the same for containers of any size. Sometimes crates take longer than containers.

Air Freight

Smaller, lightweight items of great value are usually sent by air freight. Some shippers, often those specializing in shipping paintings for museum exhibitions, are specialists in this type of shipment.

Air freight, though not cheap, takes only a few days. In addition, air freight insurance is much less that marine insurance. Generally it costs between one and two per cent of the value declared on the invoice, air bill, and customs declaration.

Shipping By Sea

All international sea shipping companies quote prices in U. S. dollars. Rates fluctuate, sometimes wildly, both between companies, and over time.

When considering sea shipment, be sure to consider several factors.

Shipping companies are divided into "Conference" lines and "non-Conference" lines. The "Conference" is a price-fixing group of shipping lines. In general, Conference lines charge several hundred dollars more per container, and consist of many of the largest shipping lines with the most frequent schedules.

Non-Conference lines are independents, often working with agents to line up complete cargoes for shipment. Non-Conference lines are more numerous, and service appears to be as reliable as with the Conference lines. The costs are approximately 10 to 20 per cent cheaper than the Conference lines.

Shipping rates (known as "tariffs" vary by the type of goods you ship—often widely. The approximate cost to ship used furniture and bric-a-brac to an East Coast port (such as Montréal, Boston, New York, or Baltimore) is: 20-foot container—Conference $2000, non-Conference $1900; 40-foot container—Conference $2400, non-Conference $2200.

The approximate cost to ship to a Gulf port (such as Miami, New Orleans, or Houston) is: 20-foot container—Conference $2100, non-Conference $1900; 40-foot container—Conference $2400, non-Conference $2250. The approximate cost to ship to a West Coast port (such as Los Angeles, San Francisco/Oakland, Seattle, or Vancouver, B.C.) is: 20-foot container—Conference $1925, non-Conference $1800; 40-foot container—Conference $3190, non-Conference $3050.

If shipping to the West Coast, be sure to specify shipment through the Panama Canal; some shipments have been routed on a "land bridge" via Houston and truck or rail from there, with delays and damage en route.

When deciding whether to make your own sea shipment arrangements leave or it to your packer, remember that most packers and some shipping companies add a premium (often around 11 per cent) of the estimated shipping charge to ensure that they don't lose money on currency fluctuations. (This is because the pound-to-dollar rate is calculated at the time it passes midpoint in the ocean rather than at delivery on board the ship.) If you deal directly with the shipping company and pay in U.S. dollars, you can sometimes avoid this premium.

Marine Insurance

You can purchase two basic types of marine insurance: all-risk or total-loss. Many importers of less valuable antiques and used items purchase only total-loss insurance, since proving when or how breakage occurred can be difficult if not impossible. However, when shipments of great value are made, the additional cost of all-risk insurance is worth paying. Generally, total-loss insurance costs from one to three per cent of value declared on the bill of lading and customs declaration. All-risk insurance (which covers water damage and damage during port operations, but not damage due to strikes, acts of violence, nuclear disaster, or certain other exclusions) costs about twice as much as total loss insurance.

If you choose all-risk insurance, be sure to document the condition of goods shipped before they are packed. Invoices and photographs of all items are the best proof of condition and value.

Delivery to the Port of Your Choice

Be sure to specify which port you wish to have as the port of entry in the United States or Canada. Avoid entering the shipment through a distant port; although customs brokers at any port of entry can solve many problems, the farther away the port of entry is from the ultimate destination, the more you'll have to pay for truck or rail shipment inside the United States and Canada. Even though it may be landed far from the port of entry, it can be shipped "in bond" to the port of entry you choose.

Clearing United States Customs

Customs inspection! The very words can strike terror or great amounts of irritation into many travelers: visions of weary inspectors pawing through your luggage in search of contraband are not pleasant, particularly when you have a tight connection to your final destination.

Constitutional protections, such as freedom from arbitrary search or the right to be warned if you're suspected of a crime, don't apply when dealing with any Customs officer at the border. The Customs Service is virtually unique in American government in this regard. The laws relating to the search of vehicles and persons are found in the United States Code at 19 U.S.C. Section 482. Case law interpreting this section gives the Customs Service the "broadest possible authority for search." Border searches may be conducted with or without cause.

However, bringing in antiques and collectables can require anything from a simple oral statement of what you bought to what seems to be an almost endless round of paper shuffling and frustration.

If you completely and fully declare every item at the correct price, and make it available for inspection, you shouldn't have to worry.

What Customs Can Inspect

Every item brought into the United States from any other country must be presented to United States Customs for inspection. The customs inspector, at his or her discretion, can decide to accept your word and inspect nothing, whether a simple suitcase or an entire shipping container. The inspector can decide for any reason, or no reason, to pull every item out of every package and inspect every item.

The reasons for customs inspection include not only the collection of customs duty but also to ensure that all imports are safe, don't violate copyright or trademark laws, meet varying federal regulations, and are not prohibited (such as narcotics or items made from endangered species).

In general, the procedures fall into two categories: "informal entry" for all shipments whose purchase price or value is less than $1,000, or "formal entry" for all shipments valued over $1,000.

Informal Entries

Informal entry is the easiest and least time-consuming way to ensure that your purchases quickly pass through customs.

In general, all shipments (whether commercial or for your own use) whose purchase price (including packing but not transportation) is less than $1,000 qualify for informal entry whether with your baggage or sent by mail.

When your purchases accompany you, you can usually use an informal entry. When they are over $400, fill out the simplified declaration form handed out on most planes, ships, and busses. If you're in a car (for example from Canada or Mexico), you can make an oral declaration.

In addition, if the importation is for your own use and is with you as baggage, you can also usually use the informal entry procedure, even when the value of your purchases is over $1,000. An oral declaration to the inspector is often sufficient.

In all cases, you should have every bill of sale and receipt readily available to show the customs inspector upon request.

If you have packed goods in boxes, you should have shipping tape, twine, or other materials to reseal the containers when the inspector has finished. While some officers have some tape or other materials available, you can't count on it.

Remember that true antiques are duty free, but the inspector may demand proof. Paintings (but not frames) and many products from under-developed nations are also duty free.

Duty-Free Allowance

If your purchases cost under $400 and you have been outside of the United States for at least 72 hours, you can bring in your purchases duty free as part of your baggage once every 30 days. Duty is assessed at 10% on the next $1,000 of goods. After that, the agent will assess duty as prescribed by regulations: the amount will vary depending on the exact classification of the merchandise. (This exemption is valid only when the items are part of your baggage and you present them in person for inspection.)

Unsolicited Gifts

You're permitted to send unsolicited gifts duty-free if no more than one package to one individual clears Customs on the same day. The gifts must be worth less than $50. The outside must be clearly marked "Unsolicited Gift—Value under $50." You're not permitted to send these packages to yourself or residents of your house.

Informal Mail Entries

If you mail antiques home, obtain a customs declaration form from the British post office, complete it, and glue it to the package when you mail it.

Enclose a copy of the invoice inside the package. Customs will inspect the parcel at the port of entry. If duty is payable, the post office will collect the duty and a $5 inspection fee from you when the parcel is delivered to you. (There is no fee for completely duty-free items.)

Formal Entries

For all commercial shipments entering the United States with a purchase price or value over $1,000, you have to make a formal entry.

Inspectors in some airports may sometimes treat amounts over $1,000 as informal entries when the purchases are part of your baggage. When you're not actually there with the shipment, the formal entry procedure is invariably followed by the Customs Service.

Here are the steps that must take place when your purchases arrive at the port of entry:

1. Provide Customs with an acceptable commercial invoice (as defined in the section on steps to clear Customs), or "pro forma invoice" (an invoice you make up reflecting the actual conditions of the sale; later you will have to provide a commercial invoice).

2. File an Entry Manifest (Customs Form 7533) or other equivalent form (usually taken care of by the shipping company).

3. Complete the Entry Summary (Customs Form 7501).

4. Provide a bond or deposit with the Entry Summary to ensure the payment of duty.

5. Make the goods available for inspection.

6. Pay any estimated payment of duty.

7. Arrange for local delivery of the goods.

If you live near the port of entry and want to oversee each step of the process, you can do it yourself. However, you can also hire a customs broker to handle this process for you.

Why Hire a Customs Broker?

Customs brokers are licensed and bonded and can handle all of the details of clearing customs if you can't or don't wish to. Naturally they charge a fee for service.

When using a broker, you must still play a part by providing a complete commercial or pro forma invoice and ensure that a complete bill of lading (or air bill) accompanies the shipment. The bill of lading should (if possible) specify the broker who will be clearing the shipment.

Customs brokers cluster around all major ports of entry; they're listed in the Yellow Pages. The local Customs office often has lists of brokers in the area. However, the Customs staff will not recommend brokers.

How to Select a Broker

Since there may be at least several dozen brokers near most major ports of entry, you need to carefully select the one that will work best for you. Sometimes antique dealers specializing in imported items will tell you which brokers they use, if any (some dealers take care of this themselves).

Ask these questions of any broker you're considering:

1. What experience do you have with antiques and collectables (or type of merchandise you're importing)? How many shipments of such items have you recently cleared?

2. Can you refer me to several recent customers for whom you have cleared this type of merchandise?

3. How much do you charge? Get a breakdown and ask:
• is this fee all inclusive?
• if not, what extra charges can be added?

Some brokers provide all services for a set price, plus the exact amount of any customs duty payable. Others may have a reasonable base price, plus a charge for every single entry they type on forms and every phone call they make or every paper they handle. There is often no relationship between charges and quality of service.

Brokers will commonly charge between $75 and $300 to clear a single shipment, and the value of the shipment often does not have a bearing on the fee.

A knowledgeable broker should be able to clear your shipment in just a few days.

Steps in Clearing Customs (If You Do It Yourself)

1. Provide Customs with an acceptable commercial or pro forma invoice.

Every formal entry must be accompanied by a commercial invoice. While most of the things that must appear on the invoice are commonplace, the requirements for a complete invoice are spelled out in Federal regulations (1 CFR Title 19, Sections 141.83 (c) and 141.86 through 141.89).

In general, the invoice must state the exact type and quantity of each item, what each type of item is made of, and the price paid (including and specifying whether containers and packing were included). It must also include the name and address of both buyer and seller, and specify the U.S. port of entry. The invoice should be signed or sealed by the exporter. If you have a number of invoices from different sellers, you can combine the items in one shipment. In this case, you can make out a combined invoice, but all of the original invoices should be attached to the combined invoice.

Pro forma invoices can be used to clear Customs but a true invoice must be provided within six months of entry. Otherwise a penalty will usually be assessed out of the customs bond (see below in Section 4).

A special U. S. Customs invoice can be used in place of a regular commercial invoice; contact Customs for more detailed information.

2. File an Entry Manifest, Customs Form 7533 or other equivalent.

(This is usually taken care of by the shipping company.)

3. Complete the Entry Summary (Customs Form 7501).

The Entry Summary form provides, together with the invoice, the basis upon which duty will be determined and assessed.

When filed, it must be accompanied by the invoice, the bill of lading, and bond (or acceptable alternative).

You or your customs broker must complete the form and present it with the rest of the entry documents at the Customs office within five days the shipment's unloading. (While Customs officers may provide information, you or your agent must complete the form, and propose the correct classification for entry.) For exact information to complete the Entry Number, Entry Type Code, Port Code, and similar codes, you will have to contact the regional Customs office.

You must also complete the Description of Merchandise (Items 29-32). This includes not only the description (quantity, value, duty rate, amount of duty payable), but also the tariff classification, which is found in the Tariff Schedule of the United States of America (T. S. U. S. A., usually pronounced "Tsoosuh").

The Entry Summary form must then be signed (press hard—this is a five-part form) and submit these with your Customs bond or equivalent and the invoice.

Using T. S. U. S. A.

This document, usually in the form of a large binder, contains tens of thousands of tariff classifications and rates. What you must do yourself is to determine both the correct classification for the merchandise and the correct rate of duty.

Customs officers will not usually tell you what the exact classifications your items fit.

The tariffs are broken down into seven major categories, and then further subdivided. T. S. U. S. A. is available for reference at all Customs offices, major "depository libraries" (usually public or university libraries), or found in bound form in the United States Code Annotated (19 U.S.C. Section 1202 and following sections). Related provisions are found in 19 CFR Chapter 1. Both of these are available in large law libraries, or you can buy a copy from the:

United States Government Printing Office
Washington, D. C. 20402
Telephone (202) 783-3238

4. Provide a bond or deposit with the Entry Summary to ensure the payment of duty.

This must be submitted even if you believe the goods are duty free. The purpose of the bond is to ensure the correct payment of duty.

Customs bonds must be issued by an approved customs bonding company. The local customs office will have a list of local bonding companies. (Most customs brokers include the bonding with their other services.)

The amount of a single entry bond varies, but is generally the value of the shipment and the estimated amount of duty.

A customs bond can be issued either on a permanent basis for importers on a regular basis, or as a single entry bond for a single shipment.

Alternatives to a Customs Bond

There are several alternatives to a customs bond, but they are less convenient. They include:
- A cash deposit equal to the value of shipment (no interest is paid and the cash is held for two years).
- Personal surety (requiring two signatories with real assets in the state in which the port of entry is located).
- Treasury bills, notes or bonds (but not U. S. Savings Bonds) which will also be held for two years, but you eventually receive the interest.

The bond or its alternative must be presented to Customs when you present the invoice and Entry Summary (Customs Form 7501).

5. *Make the goods available for inspection.*

Usually shipments are held in a customs warehouse at the port of entry for up to 10 days. During this time, the inspection should take place. Under certain circumstances, the shipment can also be shipped in bond to a more convenient place (usually a bonded warehouse), or opened in the presence of a Customs officer.

6. *Pay the estimated payment of duty.*

You already have estimated the amount of duty (at the rate found in T.S.U.S.A.) and included it on the Summary Entry form. Make payment of any amount needed; the goods won't be released until the estimated duty is paid.

Rates of Duty

From the thousands of rates found in T. S. U. S. A., most of the ones needed by antique dealers and collectors are here:

All antiques (defined as certifiably at least 100 years old) enter the United States duty free.

All paintings made entirely by hand are duty free, regardless of age (but you may have to pay duty on the frame and packing).

All sculptures made and signed by a "recognized" artist in an edition of 10 or fewer (usually a photocopy of an entry in a bibliography of art and artists will suffice).

Items that are old but do not qualify as antiques are assessed duty as found in T. S. U. S. A.; duties on most items are much lower than you might expect, in the neighborhood of free to about 8 per cent. Naturally exceptions exist, and depend not only on the item but also where it was made or acquired. Duty is imposed based on the classification of the merchandise and its country of origin. In general, imports from Great Britain receive the "most favored nation" rate.

7. *Arrange for local delivery of the goods.*

When you have paid the estimated duty, you are able to pick up or have your goods shipped to their final destination.

While for most purposes, the procedure is finished when you pay the duty, Customs has 90 days to review the paperwork and finalize the transaction. The entry (shipment of merchandise) is completed in 90 days; at that time the entry is "liquidated" (the paperwork is considered final by Customs).

Clearing
Canadian Customs

Customs inspection! These words make many
people a bit nervous, and can strike terror in
some people. However, when entering Canada, a
full and truthful declaration of merchandise will
speed re-entry of both you and your purchases. If
your purchases are shipped, you'll have to clear
them through Customs and Excise yourself or
hire a customs broker. Depending on where the
merchandise enters Canada and how much there
is, clearing customs can require anything from a
simple declaration to the customs officer to a formal entry, with all of the paperwork that may en-
tail.

What Customs Can Inspect

Every item brought into Canada from any other
country must be presented to Customs and Excise
for inspection. The customs officer can, at his discretion, accept your declaration or open and inspect any and all portions of the shipment. In
general, procedures fall into two categories: informal clearance of items included in personal baggage that you have with you, or formal clearance
for shipments of high value, whether with you or
sent separately.

Customs inspections are carried out for the purposes of collection of duty, federal sales tax, excise taxes, and to ensure that imports are safe, don't violate copyright, trademark, or drug laws, and that no items made from endangered species are imported.

Informal Entries

Once a year, travelers returning to Canada after an absence of at least seven days may import items for personal use without paying duty or federal sales tax to the value of $300. After the first trip abroad, Canadian residents can bring up to $100 duty free with them once every calendar quarter after an absence of at least seven days.

All goods exceeding that amount or for resale are subject to duty and federal sales tax (12 per cent), though some items are exempt from sales tax. Excise tax (usually 10 per cent) is added to some categories of imports as well.

Mail Entries

If you send a package by mail or package express, it will be inspected by Customs and Excise at the port of entry. The assessment will, in large part, be based on the customs declaration you attached in Britain. Any duty, federal sales tax, and excise tax payable will be collected upon delivery.

Formal and Commercial Entries

If your goods are for resale, you must follow the procedures for commercial entries. In general, all shipments must follow this procedure. The process is much more complex than a simple traveler's declaration to a customs officer at the border or airport. In general, you must complete customs forms, including the "Canada Customs Import Entry Coding Form (B3)." This includes determining the correct tariff classification, correct duty, excise, and federal sales tax. This form, along with copies of your purchase invoice(s) and various other documents must be presented to

Customs and Excise. Payment must also be made if duty and taxes are due.

You can take care of this procedure yourself, or hire a customs broker (see below).

Commercial Entries Under $900

Until December 31, 1987, commercial entries valued at less than $900 can use the simplified form, called the "Commercial Short Import Entry Coding Form (B8)." In general, it requires less data. Information about this simplified procedure is available at every Customs office. After January 1, 1988, all commercial entries must use the regular B3 form.

New Commercial Entry System

Canada is now extensively revising Customs procedures. Changes began in 1987 and should be complete early in 1988. The changes include revised forms and procedures, and the introduction of new tariff categories. Be sure to contact the customs office before entering each shipment, at least through mid 1988. The new procedures are being introduced region by region during the second half of 1987. The objective is to make the customs procedure smoother and to automate the process. Eventually, the possibility of on-line computer transmission of import data to Customs and Excise will greatly reduce the paperwork involved—although the required information must still be provided. However, the paper procedure will also be an alternative on a permanent basis.

Additional changes will occur in 1988. The main change will be the total reclassification for tariff purposes of all imports. The new classification is called the "Harmonized Commodity and Coding System," or more frequently, "Harmonized System," because the system is in accord with international agreements and a treaty. The final new tariff classifications will be published during the last half of 1987, and go into effect on January 1, 1988. While the objective of the reclassification is to leave the tariff the same on all merchandise, because of the differences between the old and new systems, certain items will have higher or lower duty. In general, duty- and tax-free classifications keep this tariff treatment.

Other changes require a transaction number to be assigned to every entry. Contact Customs for the details.

Importer Number

If you aren't using a customs broker to clear your goods, you must either use your Federal Employer Number or obtain your own Importer Number from Customs and Excise. Contact the nearest Customs and Excise office to obtain the number. It is required for almost all commercial entries.

Financial Security Guarantee

If you plan regular shipments, you should contact Customs and Excise to arrange a "security account," in the form of a deposit or bond. Criteria for importer security are found in Memorandum D17-1-5-D, available at any Customs and Excise office.

If you maintain acceptable security, you can qualify for the "Release on Minimum Documentation," also called "RMD." This allows clearance and release of goods on minimum documents, or even by computerized data submission, as long as full documentation is presented to Customs and Excise within five working days.

When the Shipment Arrives

Before or when the shipment arrives at the port of entry, you will receive a copy of the bill of lading, waybill, manifest, and a cargo control document from the shipper. You need to check to be sure that it contains the cargo control number, shipment routing, and quantity of cartons or other containers.

Before your purchases can clear be released by Customs, you (or your customs broker) must complete entry an form (see next section). Three copies of your commercial invoice or a Canada Customs invoice must be submitted along with the Customs forms.

The minimum information on the commercial or Customs invoice includes seller, buyer, quantity, type of goods, price, country of origin, and similar information. Exact details of required information can be obtained in Customs Memorandum D1-4-1, available at every Customs office.

Complete the "Canada Customs Import Entry Coding Form (B3)"

Note: Requirements will change during the next two years, as Canada automates and revises Customs clearance procedures. You will encounter changes in 1988, including procedures and new tariff classifications as Canada moves into the "Harmonized System."

The B3 forms are available from any Customs and Excise office at any port of entry (seaports, land crossings, or international airports) and the headquarters in Ottawa. *Note: a new version of this form (B3 9/86) is required as of January 1, 1988—don't use prior versions after that date!*

In general, you must code any version of the form to account for a variety of information:
- Importer's name and address
- Importer number (Federal Employer Number or Customs-assigned CAEC number)
- Vendor's name
- Customs office (a three-digit number available from Customs)
- Country of origin (Great Britain is 101 until January 1 1988, then becomes GB, and includes Northern Ireland. The Irish Republic is 117 until January 1, 1988, then becomes IE.) Note: if at least 50% of the value of an item, it is considered to be completely from that country.
- Country of export (Great Britain is 101 until January 1, 1988, then becomes GB, and in-

cludes Northern Ireland. The Irish Republic is
117.)
- Tariff treatment (Britain is Most Favoured
  Nation, code 2)
- Currency (The British pound (£) is GBP)
- Quantity of each item
- Value of each item
- Value in foreign currency
- Value in Canadian dollars
- Classification number (tariff category, a 10-
  digit code in the new system)
- Amount of duty, federal sales tax, excise tax,
  and total payable to Customs and Excise
- Declaration and signature
- Cargo control number (a number attached to
  each shipment by a form called the "Cargo
  Control Document"

Special Notes for Properly Completing the B3.

Country of Origin

Note that with antiques, this isn't as critical,
since true antiques (over 100 years old) are duty
free. If the merchandise originally is from more
than one country, refer to Customs Memorandum
D17-1-10.

Time Limit

Generally, leave this blank, unless you are completing special types of entry, such as a 60 or 120
day entry. Contact Customs if you have questions.

Tariff Treatment

Use this space to enter the tariff category of the
shipment. All goods of British origin are generally entered under Most Favoured Nation Tariff
category, which is "2." (The rest of Western
Europe is also entered in this category.)
    (See "Tariff Schedules" below for information
about classifying merchandise for tariff
purposes.)

Rate of Duty

This is the rate at which the duty is calculated. You need to obtain this from the Tariff Schedule. The rate can be a percentage of value (10%); if duty is an amount plus percentage of value, quantity, enter 10 and 0.15 per piece. (Do not use % and $ signs.)

When duty free, as in the case of antiques, enter "0.00."

Sales and Excise Tax Status

If paying excise and sales tax, when entered, or no taxes are payable, enter zeroes in this field. If not paying, consult with Customs for the correct entry, or refer to Customs Memorandum D-17-1-10.

Sales Tax Rate

If paying federal sales tax, enter the percentage without the % sign. (Example: enter 12% as "12.")

Excise Tax Rate

If paying excise tax, enter the rate. Do not include symbols such as %, $, or ¢. If there is no excise tax payable, enter zeroes.

Value for Duty (Canadian Dollars)

Enter the pre-duty and pre-tax value of the item(s) in Canadian dollars. Do not use a dollar sign ($).

Regular Duty, Sales Tax, Special Assessments

Enter the amount of duty, sales tax, or special assessments payable for the goods in these fields. (Enter zeroes for none.) If you have a sales tax license, enter zeroes in that blank. If no excise tax is payable (as in antiques) or you have an excise tax license, enter zeroes. Special assessments are generally anti-dumping duties that do not usually apply to antiques and collectables.

Total

If there is no duty or tax payable, enter "0.00" in that box.

Signature and Date

You (or your agent or broker) must sign and date the form at the bottom left on the lines shown.

The Tariff Schedules

The Tariff Schedules consist of a large book containing thousands of different Tariff Items. The Tariff Schedules can be reviewed at any Customs and Excise office. You can also buy a copy from:

Supply and Services Canada
Canadian Government Publishing Centre
Ottawa, Ontario K1A 0S9
Telephone (613) 997-2560

You must decide the exact classification under which each item falls (there are thousands). You must determine which the correct tariff classification.

If you're not sure of the correct classification of an item or group of items, you should discuss the matter with a Customs officer rather than make a guess.

Note: Classification numbers are being changed when the Harmonized System of classification is introduced January 1, 1988. An entire new Tariff Schedule will be introduced and must be used beginning January 1, 1988.

(While tariff classifications will change, and some duty rates will also change, antiques will keep the same duty and tax treatment found below.)

For further information, and the new tariff item numbers and descriptions, please contact the nearest Customs office.

Some common classifications in the Canadian International Tariff Classification (C.I.T.C.) and Harmonized System (H.S.) for antiques and collectables include:

- C.I.T.C. 69315-1, H.S. 9706 series: Articles (other than spirits or wines) produced more than 50 years prior to the date of importation. Antiques are admitted duty free but those less than 100 years old must pay 12 per cent federal sales tax. Antiques over 100 years old are exempt from both duty and federal sales tax. Proof of age is usually required.

- C.I.T.C. 51900 series, H.S. 9400 series: Furniture. There are about seven relevant categories, with duty from 10 per cent to 45 per cent, depending on the exact classification and original country of origin. In addition to the tariff, a 12 per cent federal sales tax must be paid.

- C.I.T.C. 32600 series: Glass. There are several dozen separate tariff categories, with duty rates ranging from free (glass eyes) to 32.5 per cent (carboys and demijohn jugs), plus 12 per cent federal sales tax.

- C.I.T.C. 36200-1, Sterling or other silverware (except silver plate) and gold, with duty ranging from 7 per cent to 45 percent plus 12 per cent federal sales tax plus 10 per cent excise tax on some items.

- C.I.T.C. 28700-1, H.S. 6911.10: All tableware of china, porcelain, semi-porcelain (such as faience), or white granite, but not including earthenware, with duty rates ranging from free to 35 per cent, plus 12 per cent federal sales tax.

- C.I.T.C. 28600-1, H.S. 6912 series: Earthenware and stoneware, with duty rates ranging from 11.3 per cent to 35 per cent, plus 12 per cent federal sales tax.

• H.S. 9701 through 9706: Artwork, mostly duty free.

Determining Duty Rates Within a Tariff Classification

If duty is payable, the rate depends to a great extent on the country of origin. The Tariff Schedules include three categories: Most Favoured Nation Tariff, General Tariff, and General Preferential Tariff. Goods from Britain are entered at the Most Favoured Nation Tariff category.

The U.K. and Ireland Tariff

Until January 1, 1987, all goods with at least 50% British or Irish content entered under a special tariff, "The U.K. and Ireland Tariff." This special tariff has been abolished.

Release of Goods

Goods will not be released from Customs until all duty, federal sales tax and excise taxes have been paid, or a deposit is made sufficient to cover all expected taxes, or you open a security account with Customs and Excise. If you do these, you can obtain approval for "Release on Minimum Documentation (RMD)." Contact Customs for more information.

Customs Brokers

Customs brokers are licensed and bonded and can handle all of the details of customs clearance if you can't or don't wish to. They charge fees for all services they perform.

Customs brokers are found in all major ports of entry, particularly seaports. They are listed in the Yellow Pages under "Customs Brokers."

How to Select a Broker

Since most ports have at least several brokers, and charges for customs entries are not uniform between one and another, consider several factors before choosing a broker.

Ask these questions of any broker you're considering:

1. What experience do you have with antiques and collectables (or the type of merchandise you're importing)? How many shipments of similar items have you recently cleared?

2. Can you provide references of recent customers for whom you have cleared this type of merchandise?

3. How much do you charge? Request a breakdown of fees and ask:
- is this fee all-inclusive?
- if not, what extra services will be incur a charge? And how much are the extra charges likely to be?

Carefully compare brokers' charges and services: some specialize in certain types of imports, and some have fee schedules better suited to certain types of shipments.

Information Sources

The Customs and Excise information office has a number of general brochures and technical publications.

In addition to the Tariff Schedule, Customs and Excise puts out a great number of detailed instructions in the form of "Customs Memoranda." These are on file at every Customs port of entry and regional office. For additional, detailed information, contact either the nearest Customs and Excise office, or:

Customs and Excise
Information Services
Revenue Canada
360 Coventry Road

Ottawa, Ontario K1K 2C6
Telephone (613) 993-0534
Hotline (613) 954-6300

This office has also published a series of brochures and books called "Customs Commercial System," which describe in detail the changes occurring in the customs clearance area.

However, Customs and Excise doesn't publish a detailed step-by-step how-to manual. For every detail and procedure, you can obtain the annual "McGoldrick's Handbook of the Canadian Customs Tariff and Excise Duties." It also includes the complete customs tariff classification. Most customs brokers have this for reference. It is expensive; the exact 1988 price was not determined as of the writing of this book, but will probably be $120—$150. The book is published by:

The McMullin Publishers Ltd.
417 St. Pierre
Montreal, P.Q. H2Y 2M4
Telephone (514) 849-1424

The Barras ~ Glasgow

Writing and Calling

Many fair and market organizers do not give out their addresses; they can easily be reached only by telephone. In most cases, we've been able to obtain addresses as well as telephone numbers, and have included them in the listings.

British addresses can be long and have many variations: particularly in the countryside, an address may have only the name of the house, the village, town, and the post code. In towns, there is usually a number, but the building's name can be used in place of or in addition to the number.

You can omit the county if you have the complete and correct postcode. Otherwise, include the county, since there can be many towns with the same name.

Telephone numbers have the city code (called STD code) in front of the local number. Telephone numbers can vary from three to seven, STD codes vary from 01 (London) to five numbers. Sometimes in the same town, there can be two separate STD codes with different numbers of digits in each STD code area.

London phone numbers are written 01-XXX XXXX; in other regions, numbers are written (02734) XXXXXX or 02734 XXXXXX, or sometimes Slough XXXXXX (in which case you need to find out the STD if calling long distance). Dial 100 for information.

Complete descriptions of how to use the British telephone system are in "Manston's Travel Key Europe" and "Manston's Travel Key Britain."

Birmingham

Volvo Station Wagons—
Sign of a Good Market

You *know* you're at a good market to find antiques and collectables when you see lots of Volvo
station wagons parked close to the market. Many
British antique dealers and pickers use these
vehicles, because Volvos are boxy and hold a
larger volume of merchandise than streamlined
wagons. Many are fitted with roof racks, to hold
the excess.

Sometimes, Volvos seem to outnumber all other
cars!

While the illustration above was seen at the
Birmingham antiques market held every six
weeks, the scene could have been seen at many,
many markets.

Markets A to Y

Abbotsbury, Dorset

(Please also see Weymouth.)

"Antique Fair at Strangways Hall" every other Saturday from late May through early October from 10 a.m. to 5 p.m. at Stangways Hall. This small regional fair has all types of collectables and some antiques as well. Admission is 20p. Access by car is on B3157 between Weymouth and Bridport. Free parking is available at the Car Park, 200 yards from the fair. Public transportation is not convenient. For exact schedule and further information, contact Mrs. S.J. Lunn, Lunn Antiques, Flat 2, Stanton Court, 11 Greenhill, Weymouth, Dorset DT4 7SW, telephone (0305) 789193.

Alcester, Warwickshire

"The Ragley Hall Antiques Fair" twice a year (near the start of March and October), Friday from 1 to 9 p.m., Saturday from 11 a.m. to 6 p.m., and Sunday from 11 a.m. to 5 p.m., at Ragley Hall, about one mile southwest of Alcester on A441. This fair, held in a historic home, offers all types of very good quality antiques, including clocks, Persian rugs, glass, porcelain, jewelry, silver, and other objets d'art. All items are vetted by outside experts. The dateline is 1885 to 1920 depending of the particular type of item (for example, furniture 1885, paintings 1920). Admission is £2.50. Free parking is available. This fair is not easily accessible by public transit. For exact dates and further information, contact Robert Bailey Antiques Fairs, 1 Roll Gardens, Gants Hill, Ilford, Essex IG2 6TN, telephone 01-550 5435.

Aldershot, Hampshire
(Please also see Farnham, Godalming, Guildford, and Hook.
Antiques and collectors fair every eight to 10 Sundays at The Princes Hall. This is a local antiques fair; most items are small items rather than furniture. For exact sale dates and further information, contact Kingston Promotions, 157 Plymouth Drive, Hill Head, Fareham, Hampshire PO14 3SN, telephone (0329) 661780.

Alnwick, Northumberland

"The Border Antiques and Interior Design Fair" held the second weekend of June, on Friday from 11 a.m. to 9 p.m., Saturday and Sunday from 10 a.m. to 6 p.m. at Alnwick Castle, an 18th- and 19th-century restoration of a 12th-century castle. This event mixes antiques with a few modern items for interior design purposes. All types of antiques are sold, including furniture, silver, clocks, paintings and prints, and other items. All items are vetted. The general dateline is 1880. Admission is £2, accompanied children free. This is a good regional fair by an established organizer. Access by car to Alnwick Castle, just east of the town. Free parking is available at the grounds. Access by public transit is by bus from Newcastle-upon-Tyne, or by rail to Bilton and then by bus or taxi to Alnwick. For exact dates and further information, contact Mr. Robert Soper, Castle Fairs, Bowcliffe Road, Bramham, Wetherby, Yorkshire, telephone (0937) 845829.

Ampleforth, North Yorkshire

"The Dales Antiques and Interior Design Fair" the last weekend of March, on Friday from 11 a.m. to 9 p.m., Saturday and Sunday from 10 a.m. to 6 p.m. in the village of Ampleforth. This event mixes antiques with a few modern items for interior design purposes. All types of antiques are sold, including furniture, silver, porcelains, clocks, and other specialized items All items are vetted. The general dateline is 1880. Admission is £2, accompanied children free. This is a good

regional fair by an established organizer. Access
by car from York, north on B1363 to Ampleforth
College. The event is signposted. Free parking is
available at the grounds. There is no easily used
public transit to this fair. For exact dates and further information, contact Robert Soper, Castle
Fairs, Bowcliffe Road, Bramham, Wetherby,
Yorkshire, telephone (0937) 845829.

Ascot, Berkshire

(Please also see Windsor.)

"Ascot Boot Sale" every Saturday from March
through October from 8 a.m. to about 2 p.m. This
is one of the largest regularly held boot sales in
England and offers hundreds of vendors selling
all types of used goods, including some collectables and antiques. Admission is 20p, which is
donated to charity. Parking is available on the
roads (free) and in adjoining fields. The sales are
not held in the racecourse, but are across the
street under the oak trees. Access by car from
Windsor on A332 and A329. This market is not
easily accessible by public transport.

Ardingly, Sussex

(Please also see Haywards Heath and Horsham.)

"Antiques Trade and Collectors' Fair" five times a
year on Wednesday, on varying dates (end of
January, late April, mid-July, late September,
beginning of November) from 7:30 a.m. to 4 p.m.,
except July 2 to 8 p.m. (1988 dates: 27 January,
20 April, 20 July, 21 September, 9 November).
These fairs are held at the South of England
Showgrounds five miles north of Haywards
Heath on B2028. The September fair is the oldest
and largest one-day fair in the southern part of
England, with more than 900 covered stands.
Every sale has at least 300 stands. Antiques and
collectables of all types, sizes, ages, and authenticity are in profusion. The management does not
inspect or vet the items offered. Food, toilets, and
currency exchange booth are available. Admis-

sion is £2 until 9 a.m., £1 after 9 a.m. Access on B2028 north of Haywards Heath. Plenty of free parking is available. Access by British Rail to Northgate or Haywards Heath station, then take courtesy busses to the show. Also, charter busses from and returning London are available for about £10, leaving Marble Arch about 6 a.m. (for information call 01-249 4050). The antiques trade is not admitted before the public or for free. Organized by Geoffrey Whitaker Antique Fairs, 25B Portland Street, P.O. Box 100, Newark, Nottinghamshire NG24 1LP, England, (0636) 702326.

Arundel, West Sussex

(Please also see Fontwell.)

"Treasure House Antiques Market" every Saturday year round from 9 a.m. to 5 p.m. at 31 High Street. Most of it is indoors but in summer the courtyard is also used. It is accessible from High Street through a passage next to the Red Lion. All types of antiques and collectables are sold at this relatively small market, including silver, Victoriana, china, copper, brass, and miscellaneous odds and ends. There is no entry fee. Parking is free in Winter and 50p—£1 in summer at the Crown Yard Car Park. Access by public transit on the Southdown Bus to High Street, or British Rail to Arundel and walk to High Street. For further information, contact Treasure House Antiques Market, 31 High Street, Arundel, West Sussex BN18 9AG, telephone (0903) 883101.

Ashburton, Devon

(Please also see Newton Abbot).

"Antiques & Collectors Fair and Book Fair" last Saturday of February, May, August, and October from 10 a.m. to 4 p.m. at The Town Hall. Admission is free. This is a small local fair. Organized by West Country Antiques & Collectors Fairs, The Dartmoor Antiques Centre, Off West Street, Ashburton, Devon TQ13 7DV, telephone (0364) 52182.

"The Dartmoor Antiques Center" open every Wednesday from 9 a.m. to 4 p.m. is an indoor gallery off West Street of regular dealers offering all types of antiques and collectables. Organized by West Country Antiques & Collectors Fairs, The Dartmoor Antiques Centre, Off West Street, Ashburton, Devon TQ13 7DV, telephone (0364) 52182.

Ashbourne, Derbyshire

Antiques fair every three months, usually around the March 1, June 15, end of August, and first weekend of December at the Town Hall. This is a regional fair, with all types of collectable items and antiques. Admission is 25p, but is free to members of the antiques trade. Parking is available near the hall. For exact dates and further information, contact Peak Fairs, Hill Cross, Ashford, Bakewell, Derbyshire DE4 1QL, telephone (062981) 2008.

Ashford, Kent

Cobb, Burrows, & Day Auctions
One auction per month is held on a Tuesday (often third or fourth but varies) at Victoria Crescent, Ashford. Each auction consists of several hundred lots, mainly of Victorian and more recent furniture, plus any odds and ends of bric-a-brac and other good that are offered. Previews are offered the say before the sale, and the morning of the sale. Exact sale dates and further information is available from Cobb, Burrows, & Day Auctions, 39-41 Bank Street, Ashford, Kent, telephone (0233) 24321.

Hobbs Parker Auctions
This general auctioneer holds one Thursday of every month except May and November, offering various but unspecialized antiques and collectables. Auctions of household furniture are often held on the second Wednesday of the month. (This auction house also offers sales of cars, livestock, farm machinery and other items on other days.) A free annual calendar of sales is available

upon request. Auctions are held at and further information is available from Hobbs Parker, Romney House, Ashford Market, Elwick Road, Ashford, Kent, telephone (0233) 22222.

Bakewell, Derbyshire

(Please also see Buxton and Matlock.)

Antiques fair held every Monday from 10 a.m. to 5 p.m. at the Town Hall. In addition to the Monday fair, the same organizers hold fairs every second weekend (Friday, Saturday, and Sunday) from mid-April to the end of July and almost every weekend in August. The fairs are small regional and local ones, but offer various interesting small items. The region offers tourists famous stately homes, including Haddon Hall and Chatsworth. Access by car to Bakewell, which is a small town. Free parking is available near the hall. Access by bus is possible from Derby, Manchester, and Sheffield, but can be infrequent. For further information, contact Peak Fairs, Ashford, Bakewell, Derbyshire DE4 1QL, telephone (062981) 2008.

Barnstaple, Devon

"North Devon Antique Dealers' Fair" last Thursday and Friday of May and of December at Queens Hall in Barnstaple. On the first day, hours are 2 to 8 p.m.; the second day from 10 a.m to 5 p.m. This is a regional fair. Only dealers may sell here. Organized by West Country Antiques & Crafts Fairs, The Dartmoor Antiques Centre, Off West Street, Ashburton, Devon TQ13 7DV, telephone (0364) 52182.

Bath, Avon

Antiques market every Wednesday year round from 7 a.m. to 3 p.m. in the old school building on Guinea Lane and Walcott Street. About 60 to 100 dealers cram the nooks and crannies of this old building with collectables and junk as well as medium-quality antiques. There is no admission charge. For information contact (0225) 22510.

"Bath Saturday Antiques Market" every Saturday year round from 7 a.m. to 5 p.m. on Walcot Street along the wide part near Guinea Lane. This market offers all types of antiques and collectables. There is no admission charge. For further information contact (0225) 60909.

"West of England Antiques Fair" second Tuesday through Saturday of the month at the Assembly Rooms, Bennett Street at Alfred Street. This is a long-established fair, regional in scope. Organized by Anne Campbell-Macinnes, 9 George Street, Bath, Avon BA1 2EH, telephone (0225) 63727.

Antiques and collector's fair second Sunday morning of every month at the Pavilion next to The Leisure Centre on North Parade Road, off A36 along the river Avon. This is a fair with all types of items, including furniture, glass, jewelry, postcards, and bric-a-brac. A car park is right next to the Pavilion. Organized by Parade Fairs, Bath, telephone (0225) 66497.

A number of indoor, year-round collections of permanent stalls (such as the Bartlett Street Antiques Centre, Great Western Antiques Centre, and Paragon Antiques) are open Monday through Saturday all along Bartlett Street. Better quality antiques and collectables abound, including large quantities of glass and furniture. Worth a browse, but few bargains are found in these markets.

Several auction houses are also found in Bath. Contact them for exact sale schedule and further information:
Aldridges of Bath
130-132 Walcot Street,
Bath, Avon
Telephone (0225) 52839

Stanley, Alder & Price
The City Auction Rooms
4 Princes Buildings, George Street
Bath, Avon

Phillips & Jollys
(an affiliate of Phillips of London)
1 Old King Street
Bath, Avon BA1 1DD
Telephone (0225) 31 0609.

Battle, East Sussex

Antiques market every Saturday morning from
early morning until about noon. The market
takes place in open fields along the main road
near Battle Abbey. A varying number of dealers
and collectors offer all types of junk, collectables,
and antiques.

Burstow & Hewett, Auctioneers
Auctions are held two or three times per month at
the different two salesrooms in Battle. The Abbey
Auction Galleries (Lower Lake, Battle) offers antiques, clocks, watches, porcelain, silver, and
collector's items. These auctions start Wednesdays at 11 a.m. Viewing for these sales is on the
Tuesday before the sale from 9 a.m. to 8 p.m. This
saleroom also has one Wednesday evening auction of paintings and other pictures at 6:30 p.m.;
viewing is held from 9 a.m. to 1 p.m. and 2 to 6 p
m. on the day of the sale. The Granary Salerooms
(Station Road, Battle) is the site of monthly sales
on a Wednesday at 10:30 a.m. Items offered include antique and modern items, with an emphasis on household furnishings. Viewing is held
the Tuesday before the sale from 9 a.m. to 1 p.m.
and 2 to 9 p.m. A free listing of all sales during an
entire year is available upon request. Catalogues
are issued for all sales, and cost between 20p and
£1, depending on the sale. Bids may be left or
made by mail or telephone. There is no buyer's
premium. For sale dates and further information,
contact Burstow & Hewett, Abbey Auction Galleries, Lower Lake, Battle, East Sussex TN33
0A7, telephone (04246) 2374 or (04246) 2302.

Beaconsfield, Buckinghamshire

Beaconsfield Antique Market second Thursday of
each month from 9:30 a.m. to 4 p.m. at Burnham

Hall. Information from the organizer in Beaconsfield, telephone (04946) 5338.

Antiques fair Spring Bank Holiday (last Sunday and Monday of May) from 11 a.m. to 6 p.m. at The Bell House Hotel about two miles west of the town center on A40. This is a midsized regional fair. Free parking available. Organized by Midas Fairs, Beaconsfield, telephone (04946) 4170.

Beaminster, Dorset

"Antique and Bygone Fairs" held the third Saturday of every month (occasionally second or fourth Saturday) from 10 a.m. to 4 p.m. at the Beaminster Public Hall. This is a small local fair. Free parking is available. For further information, contact the organizers at (09389) 395.

Beckenham, Greater London (suburb of London)

(Please also see London and Streatham.).

Antiques fair every Wednesday from 9:30 a.m. to 2 p.m. at The Old Council Hall on Bromley Road. Access by British Rail to Beckenham, or by Green Line bus. Organized by Ray Ratcliff, London, telephone 01-764 3602.

Bedford, Bedfordshire

Antiques and collectors' fair seven Sundays per year (third of January, February, first of April, third of July, second of September, and first of November and December) from 11 a.m. to 5 p.m. at the Corn Exchange (telephone (0234) 59691). These are good regional fairs, but most items are small. There is not much large furniture. The dateline is 1930. Admission is 50p, but members of the antiques trade are admitted free. The fairs are signposted, and parking is available. Organized by Herridge's Antiques and Collectors' Fairs, Tickencote Mill, Tickencote near Stamford, Lincolnshire PE9 4AE, telephone (0780) 57163.

Bexleyheath, Kent

(Please also see Crayford, Greenwich, and London.)

Antique and collectors' fair on May and August Bank Holiday (last Monday of May and August) from 10 a.m. to 5 p.m. at the Crook Log Sports Centre on Brampton Road. These are large fairs, with over 300 stands. All types of antiques and collectables are shown, but reproductions and modern items are prohibited. Access by car on A2. Free parking is available at the site. Access by train to Bexley Station. Organized by Bartholomew Fayres, Executive House, The Maltings, Station Road, Sawbridgeworth, Hertfordshire CM21 9JX, telephone (0279) 725809.

Billingshurst, West Sussex

(Please also see Horsham.)

Sotheby's
Sotheby's new country vaults and sales rooms were recently built as a center for the auctioneer. Sales are held every two weeks on Tuesdays, and consist of all types of items, including furniture, paintings, books, silver, carpets, porcelains and other ceramics, glass, and all other types of items. Catalogues are issued in advance of the sale and can be obtained in at Sotheby's London. The buyer's premium is 10%. Access by public transit on BritRail to Billingshurst, but the last distance may call for a taxi or long walk. Parking is available for cars on the site. Information and sales site is Sotheby's, Summer Place, London Road, Billingshurst, West Sussex, telephone (040381) 3933.

Blechingley near Godstone, Surrey

Lawrence's Fine Art Auctioneers
Auctions are held every six weeks from Tuesday through Thursday, during which more than 2000 lots are sold. The sales include antiques, specializing in furniture, silver, and porcelain,

plus all types of collectables, bric-a-brac, and some rather uninteresting modern items. Previews are held the Friday and Saturday before the sale. There is a 10% buyer's premium. There is no readily available public transit. Access by car on M25 to Exit 6, south to Godstone, and on A 25 to Blechingly. The sales take place and information can be obtained from Lawrence's Fine Art Auctioneers, Norfolk House, 80 High Street, Blechingley, telephone (0883) 843323.

Birmingham, West Midlands

(Please also see Bridgnorth, Kinver, Knowle, and Wombourne.)

"St. Martin's Rag Market," a general market place and large covered market hall in the middle of Birmingham, is the location for a number of markets. It is easily accessible by public transit: take British Rail to New Street Station, and walk south through the Bull Ring Shopping to the market, or from the Birmingham Bus Station across the street, through the Bull Ring Shopping Centre, and across Edgbaston Street. Street parking is impossible, since on most streets, parking is forbidden and cars will be promptly ticketed and towed. Off-street parking is available in the Moat Lane Car Park (pay and display), and other structures on Queensway and Digbeth Street.

The "Flea Market" offers many different types of items, mostly new and cheap, such as clothes, pots and pans, tools, etc., and is of small or no interest to the antique collector. These markets take place every Tuesday, Thursday, and Saturday from 11 a.m. to 5:30 p.m. No admission charge. For further information, contact the City of Birmingham Markets Department, Manor House, 40 Moat Lane, Birmingham, West Midlands B5 5BD, telephone (021) 622 3452.

The "Monday Antique Market" takes place at the same site as the St. Martin's Market every Monday from 7 a.m. until 2 p.m. Between 150 and 200 dealers from all over central England offer collectables and antiques. For information, contact Alan Kipping, Wonder Whistle

Enterprises, 1 Ritson Road, London E8, England, telephone 01-249 4050. There is no admission charge. For further information, contact the City of Birmingham Markets Department, Manor House, 40 Moat Lane, Birmingham, West Midlands B5 5BD, telephone (021) 622 3452.

"The Big Brum" antique market, a true antique dealer's and collector's paradise, is held every six weeks on Wednesday, from 10 a.m. to 6 p.m. inside the hall. Between 600 and 800 dealers and thousands of buyers cram the hall. All types of items are displayed, but the emphasis is on small items such as silver, porcelain, coins, and all types of collectables rather than furniture. However, the real buying and selling begin on the surrounding streets at dawn. Almost no selling takes place on the grounds to the north of the building, since the market police are vigilant. However, on the south and east, as the dealers wait to get in (there is no admission by either dealers or buyers until 10 a.m) all types of transactions are common. The greatest crush takes place within the first 15 minutes after the doors are opened. Most of the good buys are gone by noon, and by 1 p.m. some of the dealers are packing up. Information about exact dates and charter busses from London to this fair (leaving Marble Arch about 6:50 a.m.) are available from Alan Kipping, Wonder Whistle Enterprises, 1 Ritson Road, London E8, England, telephone 01-249 4050. Organized by Antique Forum, Flat 2, 98 Maida Vale, London W9, telephone 01-624 3214 (after 6 p.m. only). The Birmingham Markets Department also can inform you about dates of these fairs, telephone (021) 622 3452.

"British International Antiques Fair" the entire first week of April at the National Exhibition Centre. This is a large fair, held indoors. All types of items are shown, including furniture, jewelry, silver, and all types of miscellaneous items. Admission is charged.

"Miniatura," a twice yearly specialists fair of dollhouse crafts, last Sunday of March and September from 10:30 a.m. to 5 p.m. at the Pavilion Suite, County Cricket Ground, Edgbaston Banqueting Centre, Edgbaston, southwest of the city center on Bristol Road. This is one of the largest specialist shows for dolls, dollhouses, and miniature pottery, furniture, miscellaneous items. About 100 exhibitors show. Most but not all items are 1/12 scale. Nothing larger than 1/10 size may be shown. Merchandise is inspected by the management, but there is no date line. Admission is £1.75, children 50p, no discounts or free admission to the antiques trade. Parking on the grounds is free. Access by public transit is on bus lines 45 and 47 from New Street British Rail Station. Organized by Bob Hopwood, Miniatura, 41 Eastbourne Avenue, Hodge Hill, Birmingham, G34 6AR, telephone (021) 783 2070.

"Warwickshire Antiques Fair" last Thursday, Friday, and Saturday of September at the Warwickshire County Cricket Ground at Edgbaston, southwest of the city center. This fair has approximately 50 stands. Only antiques may be sold—no reproductions or new items. There is enough parking on the site; admission is £1. Organized by Bob Harris & Sons, Birmingham, telephone (021) 743-2259.

"The Birmingham Antiques Centre" is an indoor market at open every Thursday from 9 a.m. to midafternoon 141 Bromsgrove Street. Thirty dealers offer all types of antiques and collectables. It is It is located at 141 Bromsgrove Street, telephone (021) 622 2145. (Weller & Dufty, auctioneers, are at this location. Please see next entry.)

Weller & Dufty Ltd.
Auctions of arms, armor, and militaria are held every five weeks on Wednesday and Thursday, beginning at 10 a.m. at 141 Bromsgrove Street. Hundreds of lots of rifles, shotguns, ammunition, and other related items as well as armor are offered by this specialist auction house. Catalogues are issued for all sales at least two weeks in advance, price £2 plus postage (one catalogue for each day). Catalogues can also be obtained by annual airmail subscription; in the U.S. and Canada for £50 per year. Viewing is held the day before the sale from 9 a.m. to 5 p.m. and each morning before the sale begins. Bids may be left,

or made by mail or telephone. Telephone bids must be confirmed in writing by letter, telegram, or telex before the sale begins. The buyer's premium is 10%. All items must be paid for and removed within one day, except that special arrangements can be made for postal, telephone, and left bids. If known to the auction house, purchasers have 28 days to pay for and remove their purchases. All firearms purchasers must be non-residents or, if British residents, must hold firearms certificates of the correct category for that item. Access by car is to central Birmingham. Street parking is difficult, but any of the Pay and Display Car Parks near the Bull Ring Market and New Street Station are within walking distance. Access by train to New Street Station and walk. For further information and exact sale dates, contact Weller & Dufty Ltd., 141 Bromsgrove Street, Birmingham, West Midlands B5 6RO, telephone (021) 692 1414 and 692 1415.

Boston Spa, West Yorkshire

Antiques fairs five Sundays per year (end of May, beginning of July, September, mid-October, and end of November) at The Village Hall. This is a small regional fair, always held indoors. Admission 50p. Dateline 1930. Organized by Borough Fairs, 83 Huntstanton Road, Old Huntstanton, Norfolk, telephone (0485) 33732.

Botley, Hampshire

(Please also see Southampton.)

Antiques and collectors fair every sixth Sunday (approximately) from 11 am. to 5 p.m. at The Botley Centre. This is a local fair. Small antiques and collectables are available, but not much furniture. Admission is 25p, accompanied children free. For exact dates and further information, contact Kingston Promotions, 157 Plymouth Drive, Fareham, Hampshire PO14 3SN, telephone (0329) 661780.

Bournemouth, Dorset

Antiques and collectors fair the second Saturday
of every month from 10:30 a.m. to 4 p.m. from
March through December at The Sacred Heart
Institute Hall on Richmond Hill. This is a local
fair with about 20 to 25 stands. Admission is 20p.
Street parking can be difficult, but there is a
parking garage at Richmond Hill and Wessex
Way. Organized by Linda Forster, Forest Fairs,
28 Glenwood Road, West Moors, Dorset,
telephone (0202) 875167.

"The Marsham Court Hotel Antiques Fairs," held
on a mid-February weekend, Friday from 1 to 9
p.m., Saturday from 11 a.m. to 6 p.m., and Sunday from 11 a.m. to 5 p.m., at the Marsham Court
Hotel (telephone (0202) 22111) in East Cliff near
the beach and pier. This fair offers all types of
very good quality antiques, including clocks, Persian rugs, glass, porcelain, jewelry, silver, and
other objets d'art. All items are vetted by outside
experts. The dateline is 1885 to 1920 depending
of the particular type of item (for example, furniture 1885, paintings 1920). Admission is £2.50.
Parking is available. Access by public transit to
Bournemouth Central Station, then walk or take
a taxi. For exact dates and further information,
contact Robert Bailey Antiques Fairs, 1 Roll Gardens, Gants Hill, Ilford, Essex IG2 6TN,
telephone 01-550 5435.

Antiques and collectors fair the first Saturday of
June from 10 a.m. (9 a.m. for members of the antiques trade) to 5 p.m. at the Bournemouth International Centre. Reproductions and new work
are prohibited. This is a large regional fair, with
more than 250 dealers, who each take up one or
more tables, selling all types of antiques and collectables. Admission is 25p. Access by car to the
Bournemouth International Centre along the
shore; the route is AA signposted. Parking is
available at the site, for which a charge is made.
Organized by P S Enterprises, P.O. Box 268,
Poole, Dorset BH14 8DE, telephone (0258)
840224.

Bradford-on-Avon, Wiltshire

Antiques and collectors' weekly market every
Thursday from 9 a.m. to 4 p.m. at St. Margaret's
Hall. This is a newly-established fair, and is small
and local in scope. Organized by Westfairs Ltd.,
P.O. Box 43, Weston-super-Mare, Avon BS23 2DS
telephone (0934) 33596.

Brecon (Aberhonddu), Powys, Wales

"Welsh Antiques Fair" third week of September
(usually Thursday through Saturday) at the
Castle Hotel (telephone (0874) 4611). This is a
good, long-established regional fair; most items
offered are older than 1890. Only dealers may
sell. Organized by Antiques in Britain Fairs, Hopton Castle, Craven Arms, Shropshire SY7 0QJ,
England, telephone (05474) 356.

Bridgnorth, Shropshire

Antique fair the fourth Sunday of every other
month from January to November from 10 a.m. to
5 p.m. at Bridgnorth Leisure Centre, on the outskirts of town. This is a small regional sale of approximately 40 vendors of small antiques and collectables. Organized by Waverly Fairs, Boreley
Cottage, Boreley Near Ombersley, Worcestershire, telephone (0205) 620697.

Brighton, East Sussex

*(Please also see Lancing, Fontwell, Haywards
Heath, and Worthing.)*

"Brighton Saturday Morning Market" held every
Saturday from 7 a.m. to 1 p.m. on Upper Gardner
Street, near the Brighton Rail Station. This
market offers about 80 stands of antiques and collectables, including coins, silver, porcelain, some
furniture, glassware, and other items, as well as
additional stands of fruit, vegetables, and
flowers. Access by car is simple: the market is between Gloucester Road and North Road, between

Grand Parade and Queens Road. Parking, however, can be difficult, though there are some car parks, for which a charge is made. Access by train to Brighton Station (Main Line from Victoria Station in London) then walk 200 feet along Queens Road, then left at Gloucester Road. Access by many busses to Brighton Station or Queens Road. Organized by the Patrick Smith, Upper Gardner Street Traders Association, 47 Hove Park Way, Hove BN3 6PW, telephone (0273) 505560.

"Brighton Sunday Market and Boot Sale" held every Sunday from about 10 a.m. to 2 p.m. at Brighton Station. This boot sale offers a bit of everything: collectables, antiques, clothes, and food. It is a general market as well as offering odds and ends. Street parking can be difficult, but there are car parks in the area. Organized by Bray Enterprises, telephone (0883) 42671.

"Brighton Racecourse Antiques Market" every several weeks from April through December from 8 a.m. to 2 p.m. at the Brighton Racecourse, about one mile northeast of the city center on Elm Grove Road. About 400 dealers inside and up to 50 outside stalls, with a 1930 dateline, free admission. Yellow AA signs lead to free parking on sale days, also accessible by city bus. Organized by Mostyn Fairs, 64 Brighton Road, Lancing, Sussex, telephone (0903) 752961.

"Hove Town Hall Antiques Fair" second or third Tuesday of every other month from May through November at the Town Hall at Church Road and Norton Road in Hove. About 65 indoor stalls, 1930 dateline. Admission 30p, parking in structure across the street. Nearest train station: Brighton, about a mile east of the hall, also access by city bus. Organized by Mostyn Fairs, 64 Brighton Road, Lancing, Sussex, telephone (0903) 752961.

Antiques and collectors fairs every month (days vary) from 10 a.m. to 5 p.m. at the Brighton Centre on the sea at King's Road and West St. Between 100 and 200 vendors (mostly but not entirely dealers) offer all types of antiques and collectables, dateline approximately 1930. Admission is 60p; free to the antiques trade. All of this is indoors. Parking is difficult, but available at the Council Car Park at the adjacent Church Street Shopping Centre. For exact dates and further information, contact Brenda Lay, Dyke Farm, West Chiltington Road, Pulborough, West Sussex, telephone (07982) 2447.

"The Brighton Antiques Fair" held the second Wednesday through following Saturday from 11 a.m. to 6 p.m. (Friday 11 a.m. to 9 p.m.) at the Corn Exchange on the grounds of the Royal Pavilion. This is one of the best regional fairs, with about 70 stands. All types of items are offered, including furniture, glass, porcelain, some silver, and collectables. The dateline is 1870, except for 1900 for jewelry and collectables, and 1920 for paintings. All items are vetted; new items and reproductions are prohibited. Admission is £1.50 in 1987, and £2 in future years, which includes a brochure. Readmission is free. Access by car to the Royal Pavilion; there is parking on the street or the Church Street Car Park. Access by train to Brighton, and then a 15-minute walk to the Royal Pavilion. Organized by Penman Fairs, P.O. Box 114, Haywards Heath, West Sussex RH16 2YU, telephone (04447) 2514.

Raymond Philip Inman Auctions
Auctions of antiques, used goods, and some reproductions are held every five weeks on Monday. Viewing is the previous Friday and Saturday from 9:30 a.m. to 4 p.m. and just before the sale. Sales are held at Raymond Philip Inman Auctions, 35-40 Temple Street, Brighton, East Sussex, telephone (0273) 774777.

Graves, Son, & Pilcher Fine Arts
Auctions of antiques of all types are held every month, usually on a Thursday and following Friday at Palmeira Fine Art Auction Rooms, 38 Holland Road, Hove. Catalogues are issued at least one week before the sale. Viewing is held on Tuesday and Wednesday before the sale. Bids may be left or made by mail or telephone. The buyer's premium is 8%. Parking can be difficult, and is not available on the premises. Access by

public transit by train to Brighton or Hove stations, then by bus. For exact sale dates and further information, contact Graves, Son & Pilcher Fine Arts, 71 Church Road, Hove, East Sussex BN3 2GL, telephone (0273) 735266.

"The Lanes," the quaint and well-touristed old area between the Royal Pavilion and the Brighton Centre, offers lots of antiques in small, often elegant shops, but does not have an antiques market at regular intervals.

Bridport, Dorset

Antiques stalls as part of the general Wednesday and Saturday market from early morning until about noon in the town center. A few dealers of antiques, bric-a-brac, and junk are next to vendors of fruit, vegetables, and other new items.

Bristol, Avon

(Please also see Portishead, Weston-super- Mare, and Yatton.)

Antique and collectable section of the regular weekday market at the Exchange Hall on Corn Street. Antiques are mixed in with all other types of merchandise, including glass, baking, art, and crafts. Over 180 stands are full most days, and many vendors are regulars.

Antique market every other Saturday, early morning to early afternoon, held at the Hope Centre. This is a regional market worth visiting if you're in the area.

Antique and collector's fair third Saturday (or very occasionally third Sunday) of every month from 10 a.m. to 4:30 p.m. at The Watershed Gallery 2, next to the Exhibition Centre. This fair has all types of collector's items and antiques, dateline approximately 1930. Admission is 50p, not charged to members of the antiques trade. Pay parking is available on the site. Access by public transit to Temple Meads rail station, then busses. Organized by Evergreen Promotions, 118 Main Road, Cleeve, Bristol, Avon BS19 4PN, telephone (0934) 833629.

Antiques and collectables market second Sunday of every month from 10 a.m. to 5 p.m. at The Brunel Great Train Shed at Temple Meads Station. All types of antiques and collectables are offered. Admission is 50p, not charged to members of the antiques trade. A charge is made for parking. Access by train or bus to Temple Meads Station (the main Bristol station). Organized by Evergreen Promotions, 118 Main Road, Cleeve, Bristol, Avon BS19 4PN, telephone (0934) 833629.

Antique and collectables market every Monday from 8 a.m. until midafternoon at St. John's Hall, Whiteladies Road (A4018), northwest of the city center. This indoor market is of moderate size, with an unexceptional collection of antiques and collectables.

"Antique and Collectors Fair and Book Fair" on New Year's Day, last Sunday of March, August Bank Holiday Monday (last Monday of August), and third Sunday of October at the Bristol Exhibition Centre from 10 a.m. to 5 p.m. These are large regional fairs worth attending if you're in the area. Organized by West Country Antiques & Crafts Fairs, The Dartmoor Antiques Centre, off West Street, Ashburton, Devon TQ13 7DV, telephone (0364) 521 82.

Antique and collectors fair the first or second Sunday of January, April, August, and October at Ashton Court Mansion, at Long Ashton, across the Suspension Bridge from Bristol. These are regional fairs of some interest. Admission is 40p, but free for children and retired persons. For further information, contact the organizers at Yatton (0639) 833629.

"Antique and Collectors Fair" several Sundays a year (usually the beginning of March, June, October, and December) from 10 a.m. (members of the antiques trade 9 a.m.) at Transport House on Victoria Street. About 100 dealers set up stalls and tables to sell all types of and collectables. For further information and exact dates, contact Hallmark Antiques Fairs, Keynsham (02756) 3975.

Lalonde Fine Art Auctioneers
Auctions of fine arts and antiques every two weeks on Wednesday at 11 a.m. at the Bristol Sales Rooms at the auctioneers offices. The items offered are general antiques and collectables, but every two months there are specialized sales of antiques, models, books, and silver, also on Wednesday. Catalogues are issued and sold (usually £1) two to three weeks before sales. Viewing is the day before the sale from 9:30 a.m. to 6 p.m. and morning of the sale. Bids may be left or made by mail or telephone. The buyer's premium is 10%. Parking is not available at the salesrooms, and street parking can be difficult. Sales are held at and more information is available from Lalonde Fine Art Auctioneers, 71 Oakfield Road, Bristol, Avon B58 2BE, telephone (0272) 734052.

Brockenhurst, Hampshire

(Please also see Bournemouth, Christchurch, and Ringwood.)

Antiques and collectors fair second Sunday of most months (occasionally first Sunday) from 11 a.m. to 5 p.m. at the Balmer Lawn Hotel on Lyndhurst Road (hotel telephone (0590) 23116). These are local fairs; small items are sold. Admission is 25p, accompanied children are free. Organized by and further information is available from Kingston Promotions, 157 Plymouth Drive, Hill Head, Fareham, Hampshire PO14 3SN, telephone (0329) 661780.

Buckingham, Buckinghamshire

"The Stowe School Antiques Fair" on a mid-April weekend (Friday from 1 to 9 p.m., Saturday from 11 a.m. to 6 p.m., and Sunday from 11 a.m. to 5 p.m.) at Stowe School, an 18th-century estate a mile northwest of the town on A421 and then local lanes. This is a major regional fair, offering all types of good quality antiques, including Persian rugs, glass, porcelain, jewelry, silver, and other objets d'art. All items are vetted by outside experts. The dateline is 1885 to 1920 depending of the particular type of item (for example, furniture 1885, paintings 1920). Admission is £2.50. Free parking is available. Access by public transit to Burton-upon Trent, then or take a taxi. For exact dates and further information, contact Robert Bailey Antiques Fairs, 1 Roll Gardens, Gants Hill, Ilford, Essex IG2 6TN, telephone 01-550 5435.

Budleigh Salterton, Devon

"The Budleigh Salterton Spring Antiques Fair" second Friday and Saturday of May at the Rosemullion Hotel along the ocean. Hours vary day by day; usually on Friday the fair isn't open until 2 p.m., but on Saturday is open at 10 a.m. Organized by West Country Antiques & Crafts Fairs, The Dartmoor Antiques Centre, off West Street, Ashburton, Devon TQ13 7DV, telephone (0364) 52182.

Burnley, Lancashire

Antique and flea market every Wednesday from early morning until noon at the market hall. The rest of the week, this is a general market. The five days following the first Saturday in July is a large pot fair. Access by road to the market hall. Access by rail to Burnley, then walk. For further information, call (0204) 691511.

Burton Agnes, Humberside

"The Burton Agnes Antiques Fair" the last
weekend of October at Burton Agnes Hall, just
northeast of Burton Agnes village. This is a good
regional antiques fair. All items are vetted. The
dateline is 1920 for painting and sculpture, and
as early as 1860 for all other items. Admission is
£2.50. Access by car on A166 from Bridlington or
Great Driffield. Free parking is available at the
fair. There is no convenient public transport. For
exact dates and further information, contact
Robert Bailey Antiques Fairs, 1 Roll Gardens,
Gants Hill, Ilford, Essex IG2 6TN, telephone 01-
550 5435.

Burton-upon-Trent, Staffordshire

"The Hoar Cross Hall Antiques Fair" fourth
Friday through following Sunday of May (Friday
from 1 to 9 p.m., Saturday from 11 a.m. to 6 p.m.,
and Sunday from 11 a.m. to 5 p.m.) at Hoar Cross
Hall, several miles west of Burton-upon-Trent on
B5017, A515, then on local lanes. This is a major
regional fair, offering all types of very good
quality antiques, including clocks, Persian rugs,
glass, porcelain, jewelry, silver, and other objets
d'art. All items are vetted by outside experts. The
dateline is 1885 to 1920 depending of the particular type of item (for example, furniture 1885,
paintings 1920). Admission is £2.50. Free parking
is available. Access by public transit to Burton-
upon-Trent, then walk or take a taxi. For exact
dates and further information, contact Robert
Bailey Antiques Fairs, 1 Roll Gardens, Gants
Hill, Ilford, Essex IG2 6TN, telephone 01-550
5435.

Bury St. Edmunds, Suffolk

Antiques fair last Friday and Saturday of Aril at
the Athenaeum. This is a middle-sized regional
fair with about 40 sellers. In the area, follow the
yellow AA signs to the fair. Parking is available
on the grounds. Organized by Crown Antiques
Fairs,   55   Barton   Road,   Cambridge,

Cambridgeshire CB3 9LG, telephone (0223) 353016.

"East Anglia Antiques Fair" first weekend of March and September (sometimes starts Thursday and ends Saturday) from 10:30 a.m. to 8 p.m. at the Athenaeum (telephone (0284) 4785). This is a regular and long-established regional fair with about 60 vendors. Most items are older than 1890, and a money-back guarantee is offered on all items. Organized by Antiques in Britain Fairs, Hopton Castle, Craven Arms, Shropshire SY7 0QJ, telephone (05474) 356.

Antiques and Collectors' Fair six Saturdays per year (first of February, Easter Saturday, August Bank Holiday Saturday, third of October, and second of September) from 10 a.m. to 5 p.m. at the Corn Exchange (telephone (0284) 3937). These are regional fairs with all types of small and medium sized antiques and collectables. Admission is 50p, free to members of the antiques trade. The fair is signposted, and parking is available. Organized by Herridge's Antiques and Collectors Fairs, Tickencote Mill, Tickencote near Stamford, Lincolnshire PE9 4AE, telephone (0780) 57163.

Buxton, Derbyshire

(Please also see Bakewell.)

"The Buxton Antiques Fair" second through third weekend of May at the Pavilion Gardens. This is a long- established, good-size regional fair. Antiques include furniture, paintings, prints, clocks, books, silver, and metalware. All antiques are vetted, and must be older than 1851. Admission is charged to all; price includes an illustrated catalogue. Organized by Roger Heath-Bullock, Cultural Exhibitions Ltd., 8 Meadrow, Godalming, Surrey GU7 3HN, telephone (04868) 22562.

This site is frequently used during the year by other organizers for antiques show: some organizers using this site include: Unicorn Fairs (five weekends per year) P.O. Box 30, Hereford, Herford & Worcester, England, telephone (098) 987339. Information on forthcoming events is available from the Pavilion Gardens office, telephone (0298) 3114.

Caerleon near Newport, Gwent (Wales)

"Antique and Collectors Fair" last Sunday of every month from 11 a.m. to 5 p.m. at the Priory Hotel in High Street, Caerleon, about three miles northwest of the Newport rail station. Several dozen dealers display indoors; reproductions must be clearly marked. Welsh specialties including furniture, brass, copper, and china are offered. Admission is 30p to the public, free to the trade. Access by car on M4 to Junction 25, then northeast to Caerleon; access by public transit on the hourly Sunday bus from Newport station is to the hotel front door. Organized by Doug Burnell-Higgs, Isca Fairs, 10 Norman Street, Caerleon Nr. Newport, Gwent, NP6 1BB, Wales, telephone (0633) 421527.

Cambridge, Cambridgeshire

Cambridge book market last Wednesday of every month from 10 a.m. to 5 p.m. at Fisher Hall. Only used and antiquarian books may be sold at this fair. Organized by the Provincial Booksellers Fairs Association, P.O. Box 66, Cambridge, CB1 3PD, telephone (0223) 240921.

Canterbury, Kent

Antiques and crafts market every Saturday year round from 9:30 a.m. to 5 p.m. at the Sidney Cooper Centre on St. Peters Street in the town center. This indoor market is where about 40 local dealers show off small items, such as silver, porcelain, ceramics, glass, coins, and books. There isn't much furniture. There is no admission charge. The market is easily accessible by rail from the British Rail Canterbury West station. Parking is difficult; the nearest is on Pound Lane (20p per hour). Organized by the Markets Department, Canterbury City Council, Military

Road, Canterbury, Kent, CT1 1YW, telephone
(0227) 451755, extension 4704.

Antiques market first and third Saturday of
every month from 8 a.m. to 4:30 p.m. at the Red
Cross Hall, Lower Chantry Lane, about a block
toward Dover from the city walls and bus station.
Dealers offer porcelain, silver, jewelry, and scales
with weights. Dateline 1930; no reproductions or
modern works are allowed. Admission is free.
Free parking is available in front of the building
and on some surrounding streets. For information, contact the organizer, Mr. A.W. Garratt, The
Old Court House, Upper Hardres, Canterbury,
Kent, telephone (0227) 70437.

Worsfold Fine Art Auctioneers
Monthly auctions of antiques, furniture, fine arts,
and clocks once a month, usually on a Thursday.
Sales with special interests, particularly books,
pictures, and paintings, are held irregularly in
addition to the monthly sales. Viewing is held the
day before the sale. Sales site and information
from Worsford Fine Art Auctioneers, 40 Station
Road West, Canterbury, Kent, telephone (0227)
68984.

Cardiff, South Glamorgan (Wales)

Antiques markets every Thursday and Saturday
year round. One is in the city center on St. Mary
Street, and the other is Jacob's Market on Canal
Wharf. These two are among the better markets
in Wales, offering antiques and lots of collector's
items. There is no admission charge.

Antiquarian book fair second Saturday of April
and November from 10 a.m. to 5 p.m. at St.
Davids Hall in The Hayes.
   Only used books and related items may be sold.
Organized by the Provincial Booksellers Fairs
Association, P.O. Box 66, Cambridge,
Cambridgeshire CB1 3PD, telephone (0223)
240921.

Phillips Fine Art Auctioneers

Auctions are held on two Wednesdays per month at 11 a.m. at the auctioneer's office on Westgate Street. Sales are specialized, with topics such as Victoriana (a frequent classification), silver and jewelry, furniture, etc. Catalogues are issued at least one week before the sale, price between £1 and £2. Viewing is Monday from 9 a.m. to 5 p.m., Tuesday from 9 a.m. to 6:30 a.m. and from 9 a.m. on sale day. A free schedule of yearly sales is available upon request. Bidders must register at the office before bidding. Bids may be left or made by mail or telephone. Access by road on M4 to A48 to Junction 29,then follow signs to City Centre. Phillips is just west of the castle. No parking is available on site, but there is a parking lot at the Cardiff Arms Park on off Westgate Street. Access by rail to Central Station, then walk about 300 yards. Sales are held at and further information is available from Phillips in Wales, 9-10 Westgate Street, Cardiff, South Glamorgan CF1 1DA, telephone (0222) 396453.

Cark, Cumbria

"The Lake District and Interior Design Fair" the first weekend of November (Friday are from 11 a.m. to 9 p.m., Saturday and Sunday from 10 a.m. to 6 p.m.), at Holker Hall, (telephone (044853) 328), a stately home originally built in the 17th century but almost totally rebuilt since. In addition to the hall, there are about 200 acres of grounds and several museums. This event mixes antiques with a few modern items for interior design purposes. All types of antiques are sold, including furniture, silver, clocks, paintings and prints, and other items. All items are vetted. The general dateline is 1880. Admission is £2, accompanied children free. Access by car from Grange-over-Sands on B5277 to Cark, and then north on B5278 for about one mile. Free parking is available at the grounds. Access by public transit is by rail to Cark and then by taxi to Holker Hall. For exact dates and further information, contact Robert Soper, Castle Fairs, Bowcliffe Road, Bramham, Wetherby, Yorkshire, telephone (0937) 845829.

Carmarthen, Dyfed (Wales)

John Francis, Auctioneer

Auctions are held every six weeks on Tuesday at 11 a.m. "precisely" either at the Curiosity Sale Room, King Street (antiques, catalogue issued, price £1), or the White Elephant Auction Room, Old Station Road. Antique auctions include paintings, prints, some carpets, silver, some silver plate, clocks, large quantities of (mainly Victorian) furniture, porcelain, and miscellaneous other items. Catalogues are published at least two weeks in advance, price £1 (postpaid £1.40). Viewing is held the day before the sale from 3 to 6 p.m. and the morning of the sale from 9 a.m. Bidders must register before their first bid. Bids may be left, made by mail, or by telephone if confirmed in writing. Parking is available, for which a charge is made. Access by train to Carmarthen, then walk from the station. For exact sale dates and further information, contact John Francis, Curiosity Sale Room, King Street, Carmarthen, Dyfed, Wales, telephone (0267) 233456.

Castle Combe, Wiltshire

(Please also see Chippenham.)

Car boot sales every three weeks on Sunday from the end of April through October from 10 a.m. to 3 p.m. at Castle Coombe Circuit. This large boot sale takes place inside the main entrance. All types of used goods and some antiques can be found here. This is often a good place to make true finds—the dealers come early and look. Access by car is on B4039 between Bristol and Chippenham. Admission is 20p (donated to charity). For exact dates and further information, contact Castle Combe Circuit, Chippenham, Wiltshire SN14 7EY, telephone (0249) 782417.

Chard, Somerset

Antique and collectors market every Thursday from 8 a.m. to 4 p.m. at the Guildhall. This is a small, regional market. No admission is charged; parking is available nearby. Organized by Mr. Gill, Illminster, telephone (04605) 2873.

Charnock Richard, Lancashire

(Please also see Preston.)

"Park Hall Charnock Richard Antique and Collectors' Fair" every Sunday from dawn or 6 a.m. (whichever comes first) to 4 p.m. at Park Hall Leisure Centre. This is one of the largest and best antique fairs in Britain, and richly rewards the early bird. In the middle of one of the regions richest in antiques, dealers from all over Britain converge here to buy and sell. All types of antiques and other collectable items are sold, ranging from silver, porcelain, glass, and jewelry, to furniture, old machinery, flatirons, and hip baths. Outdoors, over a hundred vans, station wagons, and cars operate more or less in boot sale fashion until about 9:30, though the quality is far higher than the typical boot sale. Inside, as many as 300 dealers and other sellers offer all types of antiques and collectables. (More than a few dealers buy outside, and bring their purchases inside at double the price.) There is no admission charge to the outside portion, but 50p is charged for the indoor fair. All items are supposed to older than 1950, but this doesn't seem to be closely monitored. Access by car is easy: take the M6 to the Charnock Richard Service Area, and drive out through the open gate that says "no entry except for service" (really!), and turn right on the road at the bridge. Follow it for about half a mile, and turn into the Park Hall Leisure Centre. Follow the road all the way to the far end (about 500 yards) until you see cars parked on the gravel. There is no public transport to this fair. For further information, contact Unicorn Fairs Ltd., P.O. Box 30, Hereford, Hereford & Worcester HE2 8SW, telephone (098987) 339.

Chatham, Kent

Baldwin and Partners Auctions
This general sale of antiques and other odds and ends is held the first Wednesday of every month. Previews are the Saturday and Tuesday before the sale. Auction site and information is available from Baldwin & Partners, 26 Railway Street, Chatham, Kent, telephone (0634) 400121.

Cheam, Surrey

(A suburb of London)

Parkins Auctioneers & Valuers
Auctions are held at least once a month, often on Friday evenings at 7 p.m., at the auction rooms. Auctions include all types of antiques and collectables. Viewing is held the day of the sale from 2 to 7 p.m. There is no buyer's premium. For exact sale dates and further information, contact Parkins Auctioneers & Valuers, 18 Malden Road, Cheam, Surrey, telephone 01-644 6127.

Chelmsford, Essex

(Please also see Ipswich.)

Cooper Hirst, Auctioneers
Weekly auctions are held every Friday at 10 a.m. at the Granary Sale Room, Victoria Road, Chelmsford. These are auctions of all types of used goods and household items. In addition, there are special sales of antiques and collectables, usually held on Wednesdays. For further information, contact Cooper Hirst, Goldlay House, Parkway, Chelmsford, Essex CM2 7PR, telephone (0245) 58141.

Cheltenham, Gloucestershire

Antiques fair second Sunday of each month year round from 10 a.m. to 4.30 p.m. in the Golden Valley Hotel two miles west of the town center on Gloucester Road (A40). This is a regional fair with about 50 dealers selling. Parking is available on the site. Organized by Somerset & Avon Antique Fairs, telephone (0278) 784912; the hotel telephone is (0242) 32691.

Antiques and collectors fair the third Sunday of every month from 10 a.m. (members of the antiques trade 9 a.m.) to 5 p.m. in the Prestbury Suite at the Cheltenham Racecourse. These are local fairs, with not more than 80 vendors. Admission is 30p. Most vendors are dealers.

In addition, the same organizers sponsor the "Midsummer Magnet" the last Tuesday of June at the same location, and all over the racecourse grounds. The midsummer fair has over 500 vendors. Admission is £1, but members of the antiques trade is admitted for free at 8 a.m. Access from M5 Junction 10, through Cheltenham on A435 to the racecourse. Access by public transport is difficult. There is plenty of free parking at this fair. Organized by Westfairs, P.O. Box 43, Weston-super-Mare, Avon BS23 2DS, telephone (0934) 33596.

Antiques fair the second weekend of February, last weekend of May, and in mid-September at the Town Hall, Imperial Square. These are regional fairs.

Chettle near Blandford Forum, Dorset

"Dateline Antique Fair" on one Sunday per month from July through October (schedule subject to change in 1988) from 10 a.m. to 5 p.m. at Chettle House, a Queen Anne house dating from about 1700. The small regional fair requires that most antiques be older than 1920 and the balance "top quality collectables" with no new or reproduction items. Admission is 50p, which includes admission to the house and garden. Access by car is on A354 between Blandford Forum and Salisbury. Parking is free; there is no convenient public transit. Organized by Mrs. S. J. Lunn, Lunn Antique Fairs, Flat 2, Stanton Court, 11 Greenhill, Weymouth, Dorset DT4 75W, telephone (0305) 789193.

Chester, Cheshire

Phillips in Chester, Auctioneers
Auctions are usually held the last Friday of every
month, except in March, April, July and November,
when they continue for three days, Wednesday through Friday. Most sales begin at 12 noon.
Contact any Phillips office (including in New
York, N.Y.) for the exact schedule. Catalogues are
available several weeks in advance for all antiques sales, and cost between £1 for one-day sales
and £4 for the three-day sales. Auctions are
usually specialized; antique furniture, paintings,
silver and jewelry, etc. Each specialized sale
takes one day. Special sales here include fishing
tackle, golfing memorabilia, and automobiles. In
addition, sales of less spectacular household
goods are held once a month on Monday. Viewing
is the day before the sale from 10 a.m. to 4 p.m.
and the morning of the sale. Buyer's premium is
10% of the hammer price. Bids may be left,
mailed, or telephoned; however, telephone bids
must be made at least one hour before the beginning of the sale. Access by public transit from the
Chester rail station on bus lines 4 or 5. Access by
car is on A41 about two miles east of the rail station. Free parking is available on the site. Sales
are held at and further information is available
from Phillips in Chester, New House, 150
Christleton Road, Chester, Cheshire CH3 5TD,
telephone (0244) 313936.

Chichester, West Sussex

(Please also see Fontwell.)

Street market every day except Sunday in the
town center. A small number of antiques dealers
offer odds and ends of mainly collectables and
some small antiques.

"The South East Counties Antique Dealers' Fair"
held three weekends a year: the second weekend
of February, the third weekend of June, and the
last weekend of November. Hours on Friday are
from 11 a.m. to 9 p.m. and Saturday and Sunday
from 10 a.m. to 6 p.m. at Goodwood House, a fine

17th- and 18th-century stately home (telephone (0243) 774107. This event mixes antiques with a few modern items for interior design purposes. All types of antiques are sold, including furniture, silver, clocks, paintings and prints, and other items. All items are vetted. The general dateline is 1880. Admission is £2, accompanied children free. These are some of the top antiques fairs in Britain. Access by car from Chichester 3 miles north east on A27, then follow signs north to Waterbeach. Free parking is available at the grounds. Access by public transit is by rail to Chichester and then by taxi to Goodwood House. For exact dates and further information, contact Robert Soper, Castle Fairs, Bowcliffe Road, Bramham, Wetherby, Yorkshire, telephone (0937) 845829.

Stride & Son, Auctioneers
Auctions are held the last Friday of every month at the auction room at the auctioneer's offices. Auctions consist of antiques, miscellaneous items, and household furniture. Previews are held on the day before the sale. Information and sales are held at Stride & Son, Southdown House Saleroom, St. John's Street, Chichester, West Sussex, telephone (0243) 782626.

Wyatt & Son, Auctioneers
Auctions are held monthly on Tuesdays and Thursdays (call for exact schedule) at the sale rooms at Baffins Hall or St. Martin's Hall, Chichester. Almost any type of items can be found at this auction, including antiques. Sales usually consist of over 500 lots. Previews are the day before the sale. For information and schedule, contact Wyatt & Son, 59 East Street, Chichester, West Sussex, telephone (0243) 787548.

Chippenham, Wiltshire

(Please also see Castle Combe.)

Street market including antiques vendors is held as the general market on Fridays and Saturdays.

Only a few vendors (usually less than 20) sell antiques, collectables, and junk.

Antiques and collectors fair the last Sunday of every month from 10 a.m (9 a.m. to members of the antiques trade) to 5 p.m. at Neald Hall. These are regional fairs, with odds and ends of antiques and collectables. Admission is 30p, but is free to members of the antiques trade and children. Organized by Westfairs, P.O. Box 43, Weston-super-Mare, Avon BS23 2DS, telephone (0934) 33596.

Christchurch, Dorset

(Please also see Bournemouth, Brockenhurst, and Lyndhurst.)

Antique and collector's fair every Monday from 9 a.m. to 3:30 p.m. at Druitt Hall, High Street. This is a local fair about 20 stands, and free admission. Street parking is available but can be difficult to find. Organized by Linda Forster, Forest Fairs, 28 Glenwood Road, West Moors, Dorset, telephone (0202) 875167.

Antique and collectors' fair the last Sunday of most months at the Kings Arms Hotel, Castle Street (hotel telephone (0202) 484117). This is a fair of local interest. Organized by and further information is available from Kingston Promotions, 157 Plymouth Drive, Hill Head, Fareham, Hampshire PO14 3SN, telephone (0329) 661780.

Cirencester, Gloucestershire

Antique market every Friday from 9 a.m. to 3 p.m. at the Corn Hall in the town center. This is a small market in a provincial town in the well-touristed Cotswolds. This hall is also used the first through fourth Saturday of every month for crafts markets from 9:30 a.m. to 4 p.m.

Antiques fairs are held every three or four weeks on Friday from 10 a.m. (9 a.m. for members of the antiques trade) to midafternoon at Bingham Hall, on King Street. All types of items are sold, including furniture, various antiques, and collectables. These are small, local fairs, with less than 40 sellers. Fairs are also held at this location on the second Sunday of every month. Admission is 30p, but is free to members of the antiques trade and children. Organized by Westfairs, P.O. Box 43, Weston-super-Mare, Avon BS23 9DS, telephone (0934) 33596.

Hobbs & Chambers, Auctions

Auctions are held monthly at Bingham Hall, King Street. These are country auctions; all types of items are sold, both antiques and all other types of items. Exact schedule and further information is available from Hobbs & Chambers, Cirencester, telephone (0285) 4736.

Fraser, Glennie, & Partners

Auctions are held monthly at Bingham Hall, King Street. Auctions include all types of items, both antiques and used goods. For further information, contact Fraser, Glennie & Partners, Cirencester, telephone (0285) 3938.

Cleeve, Avon

(Please also see Bristol.)

Antique and bric-a-brac fair usually the first Sunday of every month from 10 a.m. to 4 p.m. at Cleve Village Hall, about eight miles from Bristol on A370. The sales are held indoors, and are small country sales of collectables and some antiques. Admission is 20p, but free to members of the antiques trade. Free parking is available. Organized by Evergreen Promotions, 118 Main Road, Cleeve, Bristol, Avon BS19 4PN, telephone (0934) 833629.

Clitheroe, Lancashire

(Please also see Hurst Green and Burnley.)

Street market with a number antique stalls every Tuesday and Saturday from early morning to just after noon on New Market Street. In addition to collectables and small antiques, several dealers offer used books and related items. Access to is Clitheroe is easiest by car on A59.

Cobham, Kent

"Dateline Fair" antiques fair fourth Sunday and Monday of May at Cobham Hall in Cobham, a historic house near Rochester. Organized by Wakefield Antiques Fairs, 1 Fountain Road, Rede Court, Rochester, Kent, telephone (0634) 723461.

Cobham, Surrey

(Please also see Bletchingly, Dorking, Epsom, Guildford, and Woking.)

Antiques and collectors' fair last Saturday and Sunday of September at the Ladbroke Seven Hills Hotel, one and half miles south of the town on A245 (hotel telephone (09325) 4471). This is a good regional fair, with all types of small antiques and collectables. The dateline is 1930. For further information, contact Kingston Promotions, 157 Plymouth Drive, Hill Head, Fareham, Hampshire PO14 3SN, telephone (0329) 661780.

Colwyn Bay, Clwyd (Wales)

Phillips Auctioneers
Auctions are held the last Thursday of most months at 10 a.m. Sales at this relatively small auction house include a wide variety of antiques and collectables, including quantities of furniture, paintings and drawings, and small quantities of silver and other metalware. Sales consist of at least 200 lots. Catalogues are issued at least two weeks before the sale, price from 50p to £1. Viewing is the day before the sale. The buyer's premium is 10%, but there is no premiums on coins. Parking is 20p per day. Access by train to Colwyn Bay station, then walk. Sales are held at and further information is available from Phillips Colwyn Bay, 9 Conwy Road, Colwyn Bay, Clwyd LL29 7AF, telephone (0492) 533406.

Crayford, Kent

Albert Andrews Auctions and Sales
Auctions of all types of used goods and antiques
are held every Wednesday at 10 a.m. at the auction offices. Not all items are antiques; nor are
antiques separated from other items in the sale's
organization. For example, consecutive lots in a
recent sale included "bosun's whistle, gilded
brooch, porcelain desk set, George III silver
punch ladle, model boat in glazed case," etc.
Catalogues are issued the day before the sale.
Viewing is Tuesday from 4:30 to 8:30 p.m. and
Wednesday from 9 a.m. until the sale begins.
There is no buyer's premium. Telephone bids may
be made. Payment must be made and all items
removed by Thursday afternoon. Parking is available on the road outside the salesroom. Access by
train to Crayford, then take the local bus. Sales
are held at and further information is available
from Albert Andrews Auctions and Sales, Farm
Building, Maiden Lane, Crayford, Kent, DA1
4LX, telephone (0322) 528868.

Crowborough, East Sussex

(Please also see Tunbridge Wells.)

Black Horse Agencies—Geering & Colyer
Fine art and antiques auctions are held every two
months on Wednesdays in the Ballroom at the
Winston Manor Hotel on Beacon Road (telephone
(08926) 2772). All types of antiques are offered in
every sale, including furniture, porcelain and
glass, art objects, and silver, plate, and jewelry.
Catalogues are issued two weeks before the sale,
price £1 plus postage. Viewing is held Tuesday
from 11 a.m. to 5 p.m. and Wednesday from 9 a.m.
until the sale begins. There is no buyer's
premium. Payment must be made the day of the
sale and removed by 11 a.m. on the next day. Free
parking is available at the hotel or in the public
Car Park near the hotel. Further information is
available from the auctioneer's offices, Black
Horse Agencies—Geering & Colyer, 22/24 High
Street, Tunbridge Wells, Kent TN1 1XA,
telephone (0892) 515300.

Croydon, Surrey

Antiques and collectors fair first Saturday of every month from 8 a.m. to 4 p.m. at the Parish Hall at Reeves Corner. There are at least 50 stalls every month, with odds and ends of antiques and collectables. Information from telephone 01-657 7414.

Cullompton, Devon

"Devon & Somerset Antiques & Collector's Fair & Book Fair" third Sunday of every month from January through June and first Sunday from October through December from 11 a.m. to 5 p.m. at Verbeer Manor. This is a good regional fair. Admission is 50p. Parking is available. Access by car is easy from M5 Junction 28. There is no easy access by rail; the nearest station is Tiverton Junction Station, several miles to the north. Organized by West Country Antiques & Collectors Fairs, The Dartmoor Antiques Centre, Off West Street, Ashburton, Devon TQ13 7DV, telephone (0364) 52182.

Deal, Kent

(Please also see Dover.)

Easter Monday Boot Fair and Bank Holiday Boot Fair on Easter Monday and the August Bank Holiday at the Deal Town Centre, Astor Theatre, and St. George's Hall. This is a large boot sale with antiques, crafts, and odds and ends. Admission is free to all. Organized by East Kent Fairs, 201 London Road, Dover, Kent CT17 0TF, telephone (0304) 201644.

Deal Collector's Centre stamp, postcard, and book market, first Saturday of every month from 9:30 a.m. to 1 p.m. at the Landmark Centre on High Street. Organized by East Kent Fairs, 201 London Road, Dover, Kent CT17 0TF, telephone (0304) 201644.

Derby, Derbyshire

"The Pennine Hotel Antiques Fair" two weekends a year, in late June and mid October (Friday from 1 to 9 p.m., Saturday from 11 a.m. to 6 p.m., and Sunday from 11 a.m. to 5 p.m.) at The Pennine Hotel on Macklin Street (hotel telephone (0332) 41741). This is a major regional fair, offering all types of good quality antiques, including Persian rugs, glass, porcelain, jewelry, silver, and other objets d'art. All items are vetted by outside experts. The dateline is 1885 to 1920 depending on the particular type of item (for example, furniture 1885, paintings 1920). Admission is £2.50. Parking is available, both at the hotel and also at city Car Parks nearby. Access by public transit to Midland Station, then walk or take a taxi past the Shopping Centre to Macklin Street. For exact dates and further information, contact Robert Bailey Antiques Fairs, 1 Roll Gardens, Gants Hill, Ilford, Essex IG2 6TN, telephone 01-550 5435.

Devizes, Wiltshire

Antique market every Tuesday from 9 a.m. to 4 p.m. in the Shambles. This small market is in a long-established country market town, but offers only a small to moderate selection of antiques and collectables. The same location is used Tuesdays and Thursdays for a general street market.

"Devizes Annual Antiques Fairs" the fourth Friday and Saturday of January, and May at the Bear Hotel in the Market Place. Hours on Friday are 2 to 8 p.m.; on Saturday are from 10 a.m. to 5 p.m. Organized by West Country Antiques & Crafts Fairs, The Dartmoor Antiques Centre, Off West Street, Ashburton, Devon TQ13 7DV, telephone (0364) 52182.

Doncaster, South Yorkshire

Antiques and collectables section of the general market every Wednesday from early morning to noon at the Corn Market in the city market area.

This is a local market for antiques and collectables.

"Giant Indoor Event" four Saturdays per year (May, July, August, and November) from 9:30 a.m. to 4 p.m. at the Doncaster Racecourse Grandstand. Since the dates are subject to change, please confirm them in advance. All types of antiques and collectables are offered by 150 to 200 vendors, most of whom are dealers. The dateline is 1930; no new items or reproductions may be offered. Admission is 60p for adults, 25p for persons over 65, and accompanied children are admitted free. Access by car on M1 to Junction 4, then west on A18 to the racecourse. Free parking is available at the racecourse. For exact dates and further information, contact Bowman Antiques Fairs, P.O. Box 37, Otley, West Yorkshire LS21 3AD, telephone (0943) 465782 or (0532) 843333.

Dorking, Surrey

(Please also see Epsom, Guildford, and Godalming.)

Crow, Watkin, & Watkin Auction Rooms
Auctions are held every Monday year round at the Auction Rooms at Dorking Market off High Street, Dorking. Sales include antiques and household items. Viewing is held the morning of the sale. For information contact Crow, Watkin, & Watkin, 16 South Street, Dorking, telephone (0306) 888080.

P.F. Windibank Auctions
Auctions are held every month to six weeks on Saturdays at the Dorking Halls. Previews are the Friday before the sale. This sale consists of antiques and reproductions (reproductions are identified as such), plus occasional offers of paintings and books. The buyer's premium is 10%. For further information contact: P.F. Windibank Auctions, 18-20 Reigate Road, Dorking, telephone (0306) 884556.

Dover, Kent

(Please also see Deal.)

Summer Sunday Boot Fairs every Sunday from June through September from 9:30 a.m. to 3 p.m. at the Plough Inn on A20. Free admission and free parking. Organized by East Kent Fairs, 201 London Road, Dover, Kent CT17 0TF, telephone (0304) 201644.

"Dover Antiques Fair" third Thursday of July (may vary) from 10 a.m. to 5 p.m. at the Dover Town Hall on Ladywell Park Street. This is a small but long-established fair. Admission is 25p. Parking can be difficult. Access by public transit: train station, then walk. Organized by East Kent Fairs, 201 London Road, Dover, Kent CT17 0TF, telephone (0304) 201644.

"Dover Annual Boot Fair" last Monday of August at the Crabble Athletic Ground in the inland River district from 8:30 a.m. (admission £1 until 10 a.m., then 25p). This is a large holiday boot fair, with all types of items both used and antique. Antique dealers search this fair. Access by car on the London Road, parking can be difficult. Organized by East Kent Fairs, 201 London Road, Dover, Kent CT17 0TF, telephone (0304) 201644.

Eastbourne, Kent

Edgar Horn Auction Room
A regional auction house of antiques and used goods. Three-day sales are held every five weeks on Tuesday, Wednesday, and Thursday. Viewing is held on the Monday before the sale. For exact sale dates and further information, contact Edgar Horn, Auctioneer, 47 Cornfield Road, Eastbourne, Kent, telephone (0323) 22801. Auctions are held at 46-50 South Street, Eastbourne.

Ely, Cambridgeshire

"The Annual Fenland Antiques Fair" third Friday through following Sunday from 11 a.m. to 5 p.m. at the Riverside Maltings in Ely. All items are supposed to be older than 1890. Access to Ely rail station and walk, or by car. Organized by Antiques in Britain Fairs, Hopton Castle, Craven Arms, Shropshire SY7 0QJ, telephone (05474) 356.

Epping, Essex

(Please also see Hatfield, Harlow, Hertford, London, and Ware.)

Antique and collectors fair the second Sunday of December, March, July, and December, (dates subject to change) at The Blacksmith Arms, Thornwood Common. This is a small market, with about 35 to 50 stands of antiques and collectables, including silver, porcelain, coins, and other types of items. Modern items and reproductions are prohibited. Organized by Bartholomew Fayres, Executive House, The Maltings, Station Road, Sawbridgeworth, Hertfordshire CM21 9JX, telephone (0279) 725809 or (0279) 725699.

Epsom, Surrey

(Please also see Cheam, Esher, London and Redhill.)

Antique and collector's fair the last Sunday of every month year round from 10 a.m. to 5 p.m. at the Drift Bridge Hotel on Reigate Road, Epsom. This is a middle-sized but regular fair in the London suburbs. Organized by Ray Ratcliff, telephone 01-764 3602.

Esher, Surrey

(Please also see Epsom, London, and Woking.)

"Sandown Park Antique Fair" four times (February, April, June, October) on a Tuesday from 3 p.m. to 8 p.m. at Exhibition Centre at Sandown Park Racecourse. This is a large quarterly indoor fair; up to 550 dealers offer all types antiques and collectables. New work or reproductions are prohibited. Long aisles have everything from silver and porcelain to bric-a-brac and small pieces of furniture. Access by car to Esher on A3, then right to the racecourse, where there is free parking. Access by train to Esher station (main line from Waterloo to Guildford), then by free (courtesy) bus to the show. Access by charter bus leaving Marble Arch at about 11 a.m. for £3; call the organizer for details. Admission for the antiques trade begins at 1 p.m. for £10; the public is admitted at 3 p.m. for £3 and at 5 p.m. for £1.50. For exact dates and further information contact Alan Kipping, Wonder Whistle Enterprises, 1 Ritson Road, London E8 1DE, telephone 01-249 4050.

Exeter, Devon

(Please also see Cullompton and Exmouth.)

"Exeter Antique Fairs" the second Wednesday and Thursday of March, Thursday and Friday of November at St. George's Hall, Fore Street, Exeter. The first day of each show is open from 2 to 8 p.m., the second 10 a.m. to 5 p.m. This is a regional show, and only dealers may sell. Organized by West Country Antiques & Crafts Fairs, The Dartmoor Antiques Centre, Off West Street, Ashburton, Devon TQ13 7DV, telephone (0364) 52182. This hall is also used occasionally for other antique and collectable events.

Antiquarian book fair first Saturday of March, June, September, and December from 10 a.m. to 5 p.m. at the Arts Centre on Gandy Street. Only used and antiquarian books and related items may be sold. Organized by Provincial Booksellers

Fairs Association, P.O. Box 66, Cambridge, Cambridgeshire CB1 3PD, telephone (0223) 240921.

Phillips Fine Art Auctioneers

Auctions of antiques and collectables are held every other Thursday at 11 a.m. at the auction offices. Each auction is limited to specialized areas, such as Victoriana (frequently), antique furniture, paintings, silver and jewelry, or similar categories. Catalogues are issued in about 10 days before each auction, cost from £1 to £2. An annual schedule of sales is available upon request. Viewing is Tuesday and Wednesday from 9 a.m. until at least 5 p.m. (sometimes 7 p.m.) and the day of the sale from 9 to 11 a.m. The buyer's premium is 10%. Bids may be left or made by telephone or mail. All purchases must be paid for and removed by the end of the second working day after the sale. Access by car from M5 exit 31, then right at the each of two roundabouts, then left at Alphin Brook Road. Free parking is available at the salesroom. Sales are held at and further information is available from Phillips in Exeter, Alphin Brook Road, Alphington, Exeter, Devon EX2 8TH, telephone (0392) 39025.

Exmouth, Devon

(Please also see Budleigh Salterton and Exeter.)

"Sunday Antiques & Collectors Bazaars" second Sunday of every month except December and every Sunday from July through the end of September from 10:30 a.m. to 5 p.m. at the Pavilion. The market in summer is larger but caters to the tourists. Organized by West Country Antiques & Collectors Fairs, The Dartmoor Antiques Centre, Off West Street, Ashburton, Devon, TQ13 7DV, telephone (0364) 52182.

"Antiques & Collector's Fairs" during a number of holidays: May Bank Holiday, first Friday, Saturday, and Sunday of May; Whitsun, usually in late May; Annual Antiques, mid September; Christmas, usually the second Sunday in December, from 2 p.m. to 8 p.m. the first day of multiday fairs, or 10 a.m. to 5 p.m. at the Pavilion in the town center. Access by train to Exmouth. Organized by West Country Antiques & Crafts Fairs, The Dartmoor Antiques Centre, Off West Street, Ashburton, Devon TQ13 7DV, telephone (0364) 52182.

Farnham, Surrey

(Please also see Aldershot, Godalming, Guildford, and Hook.)

"The Farnham Antiques Fair" third Saturday and Sunday of May at the Church House, Farnham. Parking is available at the car park, the first right turn past the house. Organized by Gamlins Exhibition Services, telephone (045) 285 2557 or (0272) 621424.

Antiques and collectors' fair the last Sunday of February, May, August, and November at the Maltings. These are local fairs of local interest. Exact dates and further information is available from Kingston Promotions, 157 Plymouth Drive, Hill Head, Fareham, Hampshire PO14 3SN, telephone (0329) 661780.

Folkestone, Kent

(Please also see Hythe.)

Michael Shortall Auction Rooms (Phillips Folkestone)
Monthly auctions of antiques, arts, and furniture are held on irregular dates. Call or write for exact dates since they vary. Previews are held the day before and the morning of the sale before it begins. For further information, contact Michael Shortall, Phillips Fine Art Auctioneers & Valuers, Bayle Place, Bayle Parade, Folkestone, Kent CT20 1SQ, telephone (0303) 45555.

Fontwell, Sussex

"Drive-in Antiques Market" several Wednesdays in the summer (usually the first or second) at the Fontwell Racecourse about four miles east on A27 from Chichester. Outdoor, admission free, free parking, not accessible by public transit. Organized by Mostyn Fairs, 64 Brighton Road, Lancing, Sussex, telephone (0903) 752961.

Glastonbury, Somerset

(Please also see Wells.)

Monthly antiques market the last Saturday of the month from 9 a.m. to 4 p.m. at Glastonbury Town Hall. This is a small, local market. For further information, contact Mr. Holley, Stalbridge, telephone (0963) 62478.

Godalming, Surrey

(Please also see Dorking and Guildford.)

"The Charterhouse Antiques Fair" in early April (Friday from 1 to 9 p.m., Saturday from 11 a.m. to 6 p.m., and Sunday from 11 a.m. to 5 p.m.) at the Charterhouse. This is a major regional fair, offering all types of good quality antiques, including Persian rugs, glass, porcelain, jewelry, silver, and other objets d'art. All items are vetted by outside experts. The dateline is 1885 to 1920 depending of the particular type of item (for example, furniture 1885, paintings 1920). Admission is £2.50. Parking is available. Access by public transit to Godalming Station, then walk or take a taxi. For exact dates and further information, contact Robert Bailey Antiques Fairs, 1 Roll Gardens, Gants Hill, Ilford, Essex IG2 6TN, telephone 01-550 5435.

Messenger May Baverstock Auctions
Auctions of household goods (which may include old furniture and collectables) are held the first and third Saturday of every month beginning at 9:30 a.m. at the Bridge Street Salesroom.

Catalogues, not illustrated, are 30p. At these sales, previews are the day of the sale and there is a buyer's premium of 10%. Payment must be made and all items removed on the day of the sale; items not removed by Monday are stored at £1 per lot per day.

Auctions of true antiques are held once or twice a month at 10 a.m., usually on Wednesday or Thursday, at the auction room at 93 High Street, Godalming. Previews are held the day before the sale from 10:30 a.m. to 7 p.m. and the morning of the sale. Sales include antiques, silver, paintings and fine arts, and jewelry. Usually each sale is limited to one to three types of items. Illustrated catalogues are available about two weeks before sales; cost is £1.50 to £2. The buyer's premium is 10%. Bids may be left, mailed, or made by telephone. Payment must be made within three days of the sale, and items left longer will be stored at least £1 per day at the auctioneer's discretion. Parking is available at the Council Car Park across the street. Access is by train to Godalming, then walk. Information and exact dates are available from Messenger May Baverstock, 93 High Street, Godalming, Surrey GU7 1AL, telephone (04868) 23567.

Grantham, Lincolnshire

"The Harlaxton Manor Antiques Fair" two weekends a year near the end of May and beginning of October (Friday from 1 to 9 p.m., Saturday from 11 a.m. to 6 p.m., and Sunday from 11 a.m. to 5 p.m.) at Harlaxton Manor, near the village of Harlaxton. This is a major regional fair, offering all types of good quality antiques, including Persian rugs, glass, porcelain, jewelry, silver, and other objets d'art. All items are vetted by outside experts. The dateline is 1885 to 1920 depending of the particular type of item (for example, furniture 1885, paintings 1920). Harlaxton Manor is one mile west of the Grantham rail station on A607, about one half mile west of the roundabout at A1. Admission is £2.50. Parking is available. Access by public transit to Harlaxton station, then take a taxi. For exact dates and further information, contact Robert Bailey Antiques Fairs,

1 Roll Gardens, Gants Hill, Ilford, Essex IG2 6TN, telephone 01-550 5435.

Greenwich, Greater London

(Please also see Crayford and London.)

"Greenwich Antique Market" every Saturday and Sunday from early morning to mid afternoon in the old Fruit and Vegetable Market on High Street, near the Cutty Sark museum ship. This market expands to High Street across the street from St. Alpmage Church in the summer. Antiques and collectables of all types are sold. (Above the entrance to the market hall is a beautiful saying lettered in 18th-century wrought iron, "A FALSE BALANCE IS ABOMINATION TO THE LORD, BUT A JUST WEIGHT IS HIS DELIGHT.") Access by car to Greenwich Park; you must find street parking. Access by train on British Rail to Greenwich. But perhaps the most pleasant means of access is by river boat from Charing Cross Pier, along the Embankment near Charing Cross Station. It is only a short walk from the pier at Greenwich to the antiques market. Organized by Sherman & Waterman Associates, 12/13 Henrietta Street, Covent Garden, London WC2E 8LH, telephone 01-240 7405.

Guildford, Surrey

(Please also see Godalming and Farnham.)

"Surrey Antiques Fair" first Friday through second Saturday of November at the Civic Hall on London Road. This is a long-established regional fair. Items offered include furniture, glass, ceramics, silver, and other types of items. Only antiques may be sold; all items are vetted, with an 1840 dateline. Admission is charged to all and includes a catalogue. Organized by Roger Heath Bullock, Cultural Exhibitions Ltd., 8 Meadrow, Godalming, Surrey GU7 3HN, telephone (04868) 22562.

Clarke-Gammon Auctioneers
Auctions are held on one Tuesday of the month
(the Tuesday varies) at the Auction Rooms on
Bedford Road, Guildford. Previews are the Saturday morning and all day Monday before the auction. These sales consist of fine arts, including old
paintings. The buyer's premium is 10%. For exact
sale dates and further information contact
Clarke-Gammon, 45 High Street, Guildford, Surrey, telephone (0483) 572266.

Harlow, Essex

(Please also see Epping, Hertford, and Ware.)

Antiques and collectable fair the first Sunday of
every month from 10:30 a.m. to 5 p.m. at the Moat
House Hotel on Southern Way (hotel telephone
(0279) 22441). About 60 dealers and collectors
offer all types of antiques, including porcelain,
silver, and prints. Few large items such as furniture are offered. Admission is 50p. Organized by
Bartholomew Fayres, Executive House, The
Maltings, Station Road, Sawbridgeworth,
Hertfordshire CM21 9JX, telephone (0279)
725809.

"Mammoth Antique & Collectors Fair" on the
Sunday nearest to the first day of February, May,
August, November, and January from 10 a.m.
(antiques trade only) to 5 p.m. at the Harlow
Sportcentre on Hammarskjold Road (telephone
(0279) 635100). These are major regional fairs,
with over 200 vendors of all types of antiques and
collectables, including toys, linen, porcelain,
postage stamps, silver, and some furniture. Admission is £1 from 10 to 11 a.m., 70p from 11 a.m.
to 5 p.m. Accompanied children are free. Access
by car from Junction 7 on M11, and follow signs
to the fair. Free parking is available at the
Sportcentre. Access by train from London to Harlow Town Station (Liverpool Street Station), and
walk about half a mile to the Sportcentre. Organized by Bartholomew Fayres, Executive
House, The Maltings, Station Road,
Sawbridgeworth, Hertfordshire CM21 9JX,
telephone (0279) 725809.

Halifax, West Yorkshire

Flea market and collector's fair four or five times
a year on Sunday from 9:30 a.m. to 5 p.m. at the
Civic Theatre. At this local show, over 60 vendors
offer all types of antiques and bric-a-brac. For
exact sale dates and further information, contact
Panda Promotions, 24 Westgate, Honley, Huddersfield, West Yorkshire HD7 2AA, telephone
(0484) 666144.

Harrietsham, Kent

B.J. Norris, Auctioneers
Auctions are held every other Thursday at 10:30
a.m. at the Agricultural Hall at Maidstone
Market (Hall telephone (0622) 58705). This is an
auction of all types of items: antiques and newer
furniture, collectables, and other odds and ends.
No catalogues are issued in advance of the sale.
Viewing is held the morning of the sale from 8 to
10 a.m. For further information, contact B.J. Norris, Auctioneers, The Quest, West Street, Harrietsham, Kent, telephone (0622) 859515.

Harrogate, North Yorkshire

Antiques fair ten Sundays per year (about every
five or six weeks) from 9:30 a.m. to 4 p.m. at the
Crown Hotel (telephone (0423) 67755) on Crown
Place near the Tourist Information Office. About
60 to 60 dealers show antiques and collectables.
The dateline is 1930, and reproductions and new
work are forbidden. Admission for adults is 50p,
for persons over 65 is 25p, and accompanied
children are free. For exact dates and further information, contact Bowman Antiques Fairs, P.O.
Box 37, Otley, West Yorkshire LS21 3AD,
telephone (0943) 465782 or (0532) 843333.

Flea market and collector's fair several times a
year on Sunday from 9:30 a.m. at the Conference
and Exhibition Centre on Ripon Road. All types of
antiques, collectables, and bric-a-brac are offered
by over 100 vendors at this indoor location. Parking is available at the north end of the site. For

exact sale dates and further information, contact
Panda Promotions, 24 Westgate, Honley, Huddersfield, West Yorkshire HD7 2AA, telephone
(0484) 666144.

"The Pavilion of Yesteryear" first Friday, Saturday, and Sunday, and Monday of May (Bank
Holiday), from 10 a.m. to 6 p.m. at Ripley Castle
(telephone (0423) 770152), in the village of
Ripley. This is an 18th-century stately home,
with large grounds and a 1410 gatehouse. This
event mixes antiques with a few modern items for
interior design purposes. All types of antiques are
sold, including furniture, silver, clocks, paintings
and prints, and other items. All items are vetted.
The general dateline is 1880. This is a huge fair,
held at the same time and place as "The British
Homes & Gardens Exhibition." Admission is £2,
accompanied children free. Access by car on A61
four miles north of Harrogate rail station on A61.
This is one of the larger regional fairs and worth
attending. Organized by Castle Fairs, telephone
(0937) 845829. For exact dates and further information, contact Robert Soper, Castle Fairs,
Bowcliffe Road, Bramham, Wetherby, West
Yorkshire, telephone (0937) 845829.

"The Old Swan Hotel Antiques Fair" two
weekends a year in early February and mid
November (Friday from 1 to 9 p.m., Saturday
from 11 a.m. to 6 p.m., and Sunday from 11 a.m.
to 5 p.m.) at the Old Swan Hotel (telephone
(0423) 500055). This is a regional fair, offering all
types of good quality antiques, including Persian
rugs, glass, porcelain, jewelry, silver, and other
objets d'art. All items are vetted by outside experts. The dateline is 1885 to 1920 depending of
the particular type of item (for example, furniture
1885, paintings 1920). The Old Swan Hotel is
about a block west of the Conference and Exhibition Centre on Swan Road. Admission is £2.50.
Free parking is available. Access by public transit
to Harrogate station, then walk or take a taxi. For
exact dates and further information, contact
Robert Bailey Antiques Fairs, 1 Roll Gardens,
Gants Hill, Ilford, Essex IG2 6TN, telephone 01-
550 5435.

"The Royal Bath Assembly Rooms Antiques Fair" the first weekend of June (Friday from 1 to 9 p.m., Saturday from 11 a.m. to 6 p.m., and Sunday from 11 a.m. to 5 p.m.) at the Royal Bath Assembly Rooms. This is a regional fair, offering all types antiques. All items are vetted by outside experts. The dateline is 1885 to 1920 depending of the particular type of item (for example, furniture 1885, paintings 1920). The Royal Bath Assembly Rooms are easy to find, since the Tourist Information Office is in the building. Admission is £2.50. Free parking is available. Access by public transit to Harrogate station, then walk or take a taxi. For exact dates and further information, contact Robert Bailey Antiques Fairs, 1 Roll Gardens, Gants Hill, Ilford, Essex IG2 6TN, telephone 01-550 5435.

"Northern Antiques Fair" the last week of September to be beginning of October at the Royal Baths Assembly Rooms. This is a long-established quality fair. About 50 dealers have stands. All antiques are vetted; dateline 100 years old. Admission is £5 on the first day and £4 on subsequent days; admission includes an illustrated fair handbook. Parking is available at the fair, but is not free. For information, contact Robert Aagaard, Secretary, Northern Antiques Fair, Manor House, High Birstwith, Harrogate, North Yorkshire HG3 2LG, telephone (0423) 770385.

"The Christmas County Antique Dealers' Fair" the first weekend of December (Friday from 11 a.m. to 9 p.m., and Saturday and Sunday from 10 a.m. to 6 p.m.) at Rudding Park House village of Ripley. All types of antiques are sold, including furniture, silver, clocks, paintings and prints, and other items. All items are vetted. The general dateline is 1880. Admission is £2, accompanied children free. This event mixes an antiques fair with a Christmas Gift and Fashion fair. This is one of the larger regional fairs and worth attending. For exact dates and further information, contact Robert Soper, Castle Fairs, Bowcliffe Road, Bramham, Wetherby, West Yorkshire, telephone (0937) 845829.

Harrow

(Northwest suburbs of London.)

Antiques, crafts, and collectables market every Thursday at Centre Crafts, 308A Station Road. Organized by Centre Crafts, telephone (0923) 46559.

Antiques, crafts, and collectables market every Thursday from 10 a.m. to 4:30 p.m. at Victoria Hall, Sheepcote Lane at the junction of Station Park Road. Access by tube to Harrow-on-the-Hill, then walk. Organized by M & S Enterprises, telephone 01-440 2330.

Hatfield, Hertfordshire

(Please also see Hatfield House, Hertford, and Ware.)

Antiques and collectors' fair the third Wednesday of every month (except second Sunday of April and December) at The Red Lion on Great North Road from 10:30 a.m. to 5 p.m. This regional fair attracts about 60 vendors of all types of antiques and collectables. Free parking is available at the hotel. Organized by Bartholomew Fayres, Executive House, The Maltings, Station Road, Sawbridgeworth, Hertfordshire CM21 9JX, telephone (0279) 725809.

Hatfield House, Hertfordshire

(Please also see Hatfield, Hertford, and Ware.)

"Living Crafts Exhibition," a crafts fair and antique show the second weekend of May (Friday, Saturday, and Sunday) at the well known stately home, Hatfield House. It is near Hatfield, about 1-1/2 miles west of Hatfield railway station. Ample parking (for a fee) is available on the grounds. Information from Mrs. Jean Younger, Harpenden, telephone (05827) 61235.

Haywards Heath, West Sussex

(Please also see Ardingly and Lewes.)

T. Bannister & Company, Auctioneers
Auctions are held approximately every six weeks, always on Wednesdays at the salesroom on the Market Place. This auction specializes in antique furniture. Viewing is held the day before the sale. Most auctions consist of about 300 to 500 lots. For exact schedule and further information, contact T. Bannister & Company, Market Place, Haywards Heath, telephone (0444) 412402.

Sussex Auction Galleries
Auctions are held on many Tuesdays and the following Wednesdays at the salesroom on Perrymount Road. Antiques of all types are offered; each sale has over 600 lots. Antiques of all types are offered; each sale has over 600 lots. Previews are held the Saturday mornings and all day Monday, and Tuesday before the sale begins. For exact dates and further information, contact Sussex Auction Galleries, 59 Perrymount Road, Haywards Heath, West Sussex, telephone (0444) 414935.

Heathfield, East Sussex

Street market every Tuesday and Saturday from early morning to early afternoon in the town center. This general market has a number of dealers of antiques and collectables as well as used items.

E. Watson & Sons Auctions
This monthly auction of Victorian and more recent furniture is held on one Tuesday (varying) during every month. Viewing is the day Monday before the auction and the morning of the sale. Catalogue are not issued. Information and exact dates are available from the auctioneer, E. Watson & Sons, Heathfield Furniture Salerooms, The Market, Heathfield, East Sussex, telephone (04352) 2132.

Hemel Hempstead, Hertfordshire

Antique market at every Wednesday year round at the market place. Up to 100 dealers offer antiques and collectables of all types. Organized by Antique Forum, Flat 2, 98 Maida Lane, London W9, telephone 01-624 3214.

Henley-on-Thames, Oxfordshire

"Henley Antiques Fair" first or second weekend of May (beginning Friday for members of the antiques trade and Saturday for the public) at the Town Hall. Organized by LaChaise Antiques, telephone (0367) 20427.

Antiques and junk market, third Thursday of May from 10 a.m. to 3:30 p.m. at the Town Hall. Organized by Granny's Attic, telephone (06284) 3658.

Simmons & Lawrence, Auctioneers
Auctions are held eight times a year, almost always on a Friday, beginning at 10:30 a.m. at the salesrooms, which are not always at the auction offices. Items for sale include glass and crystal, porcelain and pottery, rugs, costumes, prints, paintings, silver and silver plate, jewelry, furniture, household items, and other miscellaneous items. While most of them are antiques and collectables, since most of these items are from estates, modern items may be offered as well. Catalogues are issued about two weeks before each sale, price is usually £1. Viewing is held the day before the sale from 10 a.m. to 5:30 p.m., and the day of the sale from 9 a.m. until the sale begins. Bids may be left or telephoned. There is no buyer's premium. Buyers must register and receive a bidder's number before their first bid. All items must be paid for and removed the day of the sale or next morning. For exact sale dates and further information, contact Simmons & Lawrence, 32 Bell Street, Henley-on-Thames, Oxfordshire RG9 2BHH, telephone (0491) 571111.

Hereford, Hereford and Worcester

"Hereford Antiques Fair" second week of October
(often Tuesday through Thursday) from 11 a.m.
to 8 p.m. at the Green Dragon Hotel on Broad
Street in the town center (telephone 0432)
272506). This is a long-established regional fair.
About 60 dealers fill the exhibit hall of the hotel
with antiques. The dateline is 1890. Organized by
Antiques in Britain Fairs, Hopton Castle, Craven
Arms, Shropshire SY7 0QJ, telephone (05474)
356.

Hertford, Hertfordshire

*(Please also see Epping, Harlow, Hatfield,
Sawbridgeworth, and Ware.)*

Flea Market first and third Saturday of every
month from 10 a.m. to 4 p.m. at the Corn Exchange on Fore Street in the town center. Admission is 10p, free to persons over 65. All types of
used items and antiques are offered at this rather
general market: furniture, bric-a-brac, tools,
clothes, jewelry, brass, and other similar items.
Parking is available at the Gascoyne Way Car
Park. Access by public transit by train to Hertford
East Station and by bus to the Bus Station, both
within walking distance of the Corn Exchange.
Organized by Alan J. Barrett Fairs, Glenroy,
Paynes Lane, Nazeing, Waltham Abbey, Essex
EN9 2GU, telephone (0992) 460929.

Norris & Duval, Fine Art Auctions
Auctions of fine arts and antiques are held once
every month on a Thursday at 9:30 a.m. at Castle
Hall, Hertford, a large, relatively new hall on the
grounds of Hertford Castle (hall telephone (0992)
59024). An annual schedule of auctions is available upon request. Catalogues are issued at least
one week before the sale. Viewing is held the
Wednesday before the sale from noon to 7 p.m.
and the morning of the sale. Bids may be left or
mailed, or made by telephone. All bidders not
present must call the afternoon of the sale to see
if they have won. There is no buyer's premium.
All lots must be removed by 6 p.m. on the day of

the sale; if unable to this, arrange this before sale day with the auctioneers.

This auction house also holds weekly auctions of all types of used goods, furniture, and household items at its salesroom at Caxton Hill, Hereford. No catalogues are issued for these weekly sales. For exact sale dates and further information, contact Norris & Duval, 106 Fore Street, Hertford, Hertfordshire SG14 1AH, telephone (0992) 582249.

Hitchin, Hertfordshire

Antiques and collectable market every Thursday from about 8:30 a.m. until noon at the Market Place in the town center. This is a small regional market, with about 30 vendors of odds and ends, used items, and collectables. In addition, the 20-stand West Alley Antiques Market takes place every Tuesday, Thursday, and Bank Holiday Monday. Access by car to the center of Hitchin. Access by train from Kings Cross (London), or by bus on the London Country bus lines to Hitchin. Organized by the Market Office, 22 Churchgate, Hitchin, Hertfordshire, telephone (0462) 56202.

Holmfirth, West Yorkshire

(Please also see Uppermill.)

Flea market and collector's fair several Saturdays a year (dates vary) from 9:30 a.m. to 5 p.m. at the Civic Hall. At least 60 vendors offer all types of collectables, bric-a-brac, and antiques. For exact sale dates and further information, contact Panda Promotions, 24 Westgate, Honley, Huddersfield, West Yorkshire HD7 2AA, telephone (0484) 666144.

Horsham, West Sussex

(Please also see Haywards Heath.)

Denham Auction Galleries
Auctions are held the first and third Wednesday of every month at the galleries. On the first Wednesday, lower quality antiques are offered, plus pine furniture. On the third Wednesday, good antique furniture plus silver, pictures, and clocks, and other good antiques are offered. Most sales have over 500 lots. Previews are the Tuesday before the sale. The buyer's premium is 10%. The sales site and further information is available from Garth Denham & Associate, Horsham Auction Galleries, The Carfax, Horsham, West Sussex, telephone (0403) 43837.

Hove, East Sussex

(Please see Brighton, East Sussex.)

Huntingdon Near Brampton
Cambridgeshire

Antiques fair third Friday through following Sunday of May at Huntingdon Racecourse (racetrack) along A1 about one mile west of Huntingdon rail station. Ample parking for cars. This fair prohibits all reproductions and items made after 1920. Organized by Christina Page Fairs, telephone (0223) 211736.

Antiques fair fourth Saturday through following Monday of May from 10 a.m. to 5 p.m. at Hitchingbrooke House, a major stately home southwest of the town on A141. About 110 dealers and a few collectors (including much furniture) show their wares. In the vicinity, follow the yellow AA signs to the fair. Parking is available on the grounds. Organized by Crown Antiques Fairs, 55 Barton Road, Cambridge, Cambridgeshire CB3 9LG, telephone (0223) 353016.

Hurst Green, Lancashire

(Please also see Preston.)

"The Lancashire Antiques and Interior Design Fair" the first weekend of November first (Friday from 11 a.m. to 9 p.m., Saturday and Sunday from 10 a.m. to 6 p.m. at Stonyhurst College, just north of the village. This event mixes antiques with a few modern items for interior design purposes. All types of antiques are sold, including furniture, silver, clocks, paintings and prints, and other items. All items are vetted. The general dateline is 1880. This is a good regional fair. Admission is £2, accompanied children free. Access by car on A59 east from Junction 31 on M6, then to Billington, north on B6246 for three miles, then west on B6243 to Hurst Green. Free parking is available. There is no convenient public transit. Organized by Castle Fairs, telephone (0937) 845829. For exact dates and further information, contact Robert Soper, Castle Fairs, Bowcliffe Road, Bramham, Wetherby, West Yorkshire, telephone (0937) 845829.

Hythe, Kent

(Please also see Folkestone.)

Butler & Hatch Waterman, Auctioneers
This country auction house hold monthly auctions, usually on a Wednesday (call for exact date and time). Auctions include antiques, silver, and miscellaneous items. For further information contact Butler & Hatch Waterman, 86 High Street, Hythe, Kent, telephone (0303) 66023.

Ilkley, West Yorkshire

(Please also see Harrogate and Leeds.)

"The Kings Hall & Wintergardens Antiques Fair" held at the last weekend of August at Kings Hall. This regional fair offers good quality antiques, including Persian rugs, glass, porcelain, jewelry, silver, and other objets d'art. All items are vetted by outside experts. The dateline is 1885 to 1920 depending of the particular type of item (for example, furniture 1885, paintings 1920). Admission is £2.50. Free parking is available. Access by public transit to Ilkley station, then walk or take a taxi. For exact dates and further information, contact Robert Bailey Antiques Fairs, 1 Roll Gardens, Gants Hill, Ilford, Essex IG2 6TN, telephone 01-550 5435.

Dacre, Son & Hartley Auctions

Auctions are held every other Wednesday at 9:30 a.m. at The Victoria hall Saleroom, Little Lane, Ilkley. Each sale includes between 400 and 500 lots antique and used goods, including pottery and porcelain, miscellaneous items and books, silver, silver plate, and jewelry, rugs,clocks, and furniture. Viewing is held the Tuesday before the sale. Bidders must register with the office before bidding. No smoking permitted on the premises. There is no buyer's premium. Purchases must be paid for and removed within two days of the sale. Catalogues (which often include some photographs of the best items) are available about two weeks before the sale, cost £1.50. A free auction schedule is available upon request. Telephone and mail bids can be left with the management by known bidders. Access is from London (King's Cross) to Leeds, change at Leeds to Ilkley, and walk from the station. Parking is available near the sale room. For further information and exact schedule, contact Dacre, Son & Hartley, 1-5 The Grove, Ilkley, West Yorkshire LS29 9HS, telephone (0943) 600655.

Ipswich, Suffolk

Phillips in Ipswich

Auctions are held on Thursdays approximately every three to four weeks at the saleroom. Most auctions are specialized (for example "Silver and Jewellery" or "Victoriana"). Inspections are held the day before and morning of the sale. Catalogues are issued approximately two weeks before every sale, and cost from £1 to £2. Bids may be left or mailed or made by telephone. The buyer's premium is 10%. Sales are held at Phillips in Ipswich, Dover House, Wolsey Street, Ipswich, telephone (0473) 55137. Information can be obtained from Phillips in Ipswich, 50 St. Nicholas Street, Ipswich, Suffolk IP1 1TP, telephone (0473) 54664.

Kendal, Cumbria

Street market every Monday, Wednesday, and Saturday from early morning to early afternoon in the center of this town at the entrance to the beautiful Lake District. A number of dealers offer small antiques, collectables, and junk on Monday, where they congregate in the Market Hall. Other days offer all types of new and used goods as well as food in the Market Square as well as the hall. A book fair is held in mid-July at the same location.

Kettering, Northamptonshire

Antiques market every Wednesday at the Market Place in the town center. This market is long-established, and a good number of dealers and collectors regularly buy and sell all types of antiques, collectables, and bric-a-brac. Parking in the immediate area can be difficult.

Kinver, West Midlands

(Please also see Birmingham.)

Antique fairs first Sunday of every month from 10 a.m. to 5 p.m. at the Kinver Community Centre in the center of Kinver village. Approximately forty dealers and amateurs sell antiques and collectables of all types, plus modern painters. The third Sunday of the month, ths same site is a large book fair with books, postcards, postage stamps, and records. No early admission for dealers is allowed. Access by car only; no public transit is convenient. Organized by Waverly Fairs, Boreley Cottage, Boreley Near Ombersley, Worcester, telephone (0205) 620697.

Knowle, West Midlands

(Please also see Birmingham.)

Phillips Knowle
Auctions are held at least two or three Wednesdays per month at 10:30 a.m. Sales are specialized into subjects such as "Paintings and Drawings," "Victoriana," and "Fine Furniture."
Catalogues are issued at least two weeks before
each sale, and cost £1 to £2. Viewing is held the
day before and morning of the sale. Bids may be
left, or mailed or telephoned. The buyer's
premium is 10%. Access by car on M42 to Junction 2, then on A41 to Knowle. For exact sale
dates and further information, contact Phillips
Knowle, The Old House, Station Road, Knowle,
Solihull, West Midlands B93 0HT, telephone
(05645) 6151.

Knutsford, Cheshire

"The Tatton Hall Antiques Fair" held twice a
year, four days early in March and near the end
of September at Tatton Park, an 18th century historic estate. Only the finest quality antiques are
shown. All items are vetted by Sotheby's,
Christie's, and Phillips specialists, or officials
from BADA or LAPADA. The dateline is 1860.
These are major antique fairs. Admission is
£2.50. Access by car on Motorway M6 to Junction
19, then north on A530 past Mere village, then
right on A50. Access by public transit is inconvenient at best. For exact dates and further information, contact Robert Bailey Antiques Fairs, 1
Roll Gardens, Gants Hill, Ilford, Essex IG2 6TN,
telephone 01-550 5435.

Lamport Hall, Northamptonshire

Antiques fair last weekend of May at Lamport
Hall, a stately historic house. Access by A 508
about nine miles north of Northampton, then follow signs to the hall. Organized by Prestige
Promotions, telephone (0533) 56045.

Lancing, Sussex

(Please also see Brighton.)

Collectables market most Thursdays from 8:30 to 10 noon at the Parish Hall. This is a regular, local market in an antiques-rich area. Organized by Shirley Mostyn, Mostyn Fairs, 64 Brighton Road, Lancing, Surrey, telephone (0903) 752961.

"Drive-in Antiques Market" usually the third Wednesday of May, August and September from 8 a.m. to 2:30 p.m. at Lancing Beach Green. Outside spaces only—no indoor area. Admission free, parking 50p, bus stop on line from Brighton across the street.

Lavenham, Suffolk

Antique and collectors fair several times per year on Saturday in May, June, September from 10:30 a.m. to 5 p.m. in the Church Rooms in the village. This small fair offers all types of antiques and collectables. Organized by Lorna Quick, Fourseason Fairs, 6 Post Office Lane, Glemsford, Suffolk CO10 7RA, telephone (0787) 281855.

Leeds, West Yorkshire

Flea market and collector's fair several times per year on Saturdays from 9:30 a.m. to 5 p.m. at Queens Hall. All types of antiques and bric-a-brac is offered. This is a large indoor regional fair with as many as 500 vendors. Admission is 50p. Parking is available at a charge. Organized by Panda Promotions, 24 Westgate, Honley, Huddersfield, West Yorkshire HD7 2AA, telephone (0484) 666144.

Phillips in Leeds
Auctions are held most (but not all) Wednesdays at the salerooms on East Parade. Auctions are specialized into various subjects, such as "Silver and Jewellery," "Clocks and Watches," and "Art Nouveau and Art Deco." Catalogues are issued at least two weeks before each sale, and are usually

£1. Bids may be left or made by mail or telephone. The buyer's premium is 10%. Sales are held at and further information is available from Phillips in Leeds, 17a East Parade, Leeds, West Yorkshire LS1 2BU, telephone (0532) 448011.

Leicester, Leicestershire

"Annual Leicester Antiques Fair" third Thursday through Saturday of February at the Wigston Stage Motel in the Wigston district of Leicester, about three miles south of the city on A50. This is a long-established regional fair. All vendors are antiques dealers, and most items are small to medium- sized. The dateline is 1890. Organized by Antiques in Britain Fairs, Hopton Castle, Craven Arms, Shropshire SY7 0QJ, telephone (05474) 356.

Letchworth, Hertfordshire

(Please also see Hitchin and Luton.)

Antique and collectors' fair five Sundays per year (usually but not always the last Sunday of the month) from 10:30 a.m. to 5 p.m. in the Functions Suite at The Broadway Hotel on The Broadway (hotel telephone (04626) 685661. This is a small regional fair, with about 60 stalls at each fair. Admission is 40p, 20p for children, but this fair is free to members of the antiques trade. Access by car from the M1 to Letchworth, then follow the signs to the fair. Parking is free at the hotel. For exact fair dates and further information, contact Bartholomew Fayres, Executive House, The Maltings, Station Road, Sawbridgeworth, Hertfordshire CM21 9JX, telephone (0279) 725809.

Lewes, East Sussex

(Please also see Brighton.)

Gorringes Auction Galleries
This general auction house sells all types of antiques and bric-a-brac at three-and-four day sales

(Tuesday through Fridays) held about every six weeks. Previews of sales items is held the Friday and Saturday before the sale from 10 a.m. to 5 p.m. Information and sale site is Gorridges Auction Galleries, 15 North Street, Lewes, East Sussex, telephone (0273) 472503.

Lewes Auction Rooms

Another auction house offers antiques twice a month on Thursday, and bric-a-brac, furniture, and used goods every Monday at the sale rooms. Information and sale site is Julian Dawson, Lewes Auction Rooms, 56 High Street, Lewes, East Sussex, telephone (0273) 478221.

Wallis & Wallis

This specialist auction house has nine auctions per year of militaria, arms, armor, and coins and medals. Information is available from Wallis & Wallis, 7-9 West Street, Lewes, East Sussex, telephone (0273) 473137. The sales are held at the West Street Auction Gallery, also on West Street.

Liverpool, Merseyside

"Paddy's Market," common name for St. Martin's Market, Monday through Saturday (Friday and especially Saturday best) from early morning until early afternoon on Great Homer Street, about half a mile north of the Lime Street rail station. This boisterous street market is a combination of new and used, collectables, clothes, furniture, and other odds and ends. Access by public transit from the city center on Bus 101; free parking is available but sometimes difficult on street surrounding the market. Organized by Liverpool City Council Markets Department, St. Martin's Market, Great Homer Street, Liverpool, Merseyside L5 3LQ, telephone (051) 207 0601.

Llangefni, Gwynedd (Wales)

Morgan Evans & Co. Ltd., Auctioneers

Auctions are held on the last (or occasionally next to last) Wednesday of each month at 10:30 a.m. at the salerooms. Previews are held on the Monday before the sale from 10:30 a.m. to 12:30 p.m. and 2 to 6 p.m., and the morning of the sale. Auctions consist of several hundred lots, including furniture, china and pottery, glassware (including crystal), paintings and prints, rugs, metalware (all types—silver, silver plate, gold, brass, iron) and miscellaneous items. Catalogues are issued several weeks before the sale. Bids may be left, mailed, or made by telephone (saleroom direct line is (0248) 355). Buyers receive the next six catalogues free, postpaid. There is no buyer's premium. All purchases must be paid for and removed by the end of the second working day after the sale. This new saleroom is in a far corner of Britain; as a result, Welsh woodwork and other items can be found. Access by car across on A5 toward Holyhead; then take A6114 toward Llangefni. Free parking is available at the saleroom. Access by public transport can be difficult; the nearest main rail stations are at Bangor and Holyhead, though the nearest one is at Llanfair. Sales are held at and further information is available from Morgan Evans & Co. Ltd., 28/30 Church Street, Llangefni, Gwynedd, telephone (0248) 723303.

Llangybi near Usk, Gwent

Antiques fair, third Sunday of every month from 11 a.m. to 5 pm. at the Cwrt Bleddyn Hotel in the village of Llangybi. This regional fair is of good quality; several dozen dealers show wares. Reproductions must be clearly marked. Items offered include small furniture, brass, coper, postcards, and other miscellaneous items. Admission is 30p, trade free. Free parking is available at the hotel; no public transit is available (no service to this location on Sunday). Organized by Doug Burnell-Higgs, Isca Fairs, 10 Norman Street, Caerleon nr. Newport, Gwent NP6 1BB, Wales, telephone (0633) 421527.

London

*(Please also see Beaconsfield, Beckenham, Bex-
leyheath, Crayford, Croydon, Epping, Epsom,
Greenwich, Harlow, Harrow, Loughton, Redhill,
Romford, Waltham Abbey, and Windsor.)*

Dozens of markets of all types exist throughout
London; fruit and vegetable markets, wholesale
markets, clothes markets, even a gardening
market. They do not have any items of interest to
antique collectors and dealers, or only a very few
such items. These markets are not discussed in
this book even though, such as Petticoat Lane,
theymay be world-famous for other reasons.

These markets include: Bayswater Road,
Balham, Battersea High Street, Berwick Street,
Brixton, Chapel Market, Broadway, Chiswick,
Chrisp Street, Church Street, Columbia Road,
Exmouth, Hampstead, Hoxton Street, Lansbury,
Leadenhall, Leather Lane, London Bridge,
Middlesex Street (Petticoat Lane), Mile End
Waste, Queens Market, Roman Road, Shepherd's
Bush, Southwark, Strutton Ground, Tower
Bridge Road, Watling, Whitechapel Road,
Whitecross Street, and Woolwich.

*Note: The number in parentheses immediately
after the market, fair, or auction pinpoints its
location on the London city maps on pages 162-
165 or London region map near the end of the
book. Numbers 1-30 are regularly-held markets
on the city map, 40-60 are major antiques fairs on
the city map, and 60-99 are auction houses on the
city map. All numbers over 100 are on the London
Home Counties map on pages 246 and 247, since
they lie outside the central part of the city.*

Regularly Held Antiques and Flea Markets

The Arches (15) stamp, coin, and militaria
market every day except Sunday but especially
on Thursday from 8 a.m. until 1 p.m. under the
British Rail tracks off Villiers Street at Charing
Cross Station, WC2, under the viaduct between
the station and the Thames. Though easy to find,

in order to get to the market, walk on the east side of the viaduct from Charing Cross toward the Embankment. The Arches is through a small passageway, and consists of stalls in the large brick barrel-vaults holding up the tracks. The main passage has shops, but if you go into the main passage, a side passage leads to the tables with dozens of day merchants. Access by car is to Charing Cross Station; the nearest car parks are on St. Martin's Lane and at Trafalgar Square. Access by Underground, British Rail, or many busses to Charing Cross station, and walk.

Bell Street Market (1) every Saturday from 9 a.m. to mid afternoon on Bell Street, just off Edgware Road and Marylebone Road, NW1. This is a small market with assorted odds and ends, including old clothes, broken-down furniture, bric-a-brac, and junk. Access by car to Marylebone (don't go up on the motorway) and look for parking on the side streets. Access by Underground to Edgware Road (District, Metropolitan, and Bakerloo lines) or bus lines 6, 7, 8, 15, 16, 18, 27, 36, and 136.

Bermondsey Street Antiques Market (2) every Friday morning year round beginning about 2 a.m. (furniture) and 5 a.m. (most other items) and going until 2 p.m. It takes place on a square at the corner of Bermondsey Street and Long Lane, SE1. This is London's best antiques market and offers the best selection of good-quality items. There are no reproductions or modern craft work. Items offered include lots of silver, furniture, odds and ends, some pottery, some porcelain, glass and crystal. Get there early, and bring a flashlight! The antique- dealer buyers have picked over the market by about 7:30 a.m. Several permanent indoor antiques markets face the square. Access by Underground from London Bridge Station (Northern Line), south on Bermondsey Street, or Borough Station (Northern Line), east on Long Lane to the market, or by night bus N47 to Tower Brige Road, or N89 to London Bridge Station. For further information, contact the Consumer Services Division, London Borough of Southwark, 23 Harper Road, London SE1 6AW, telephone 01-403 5867.

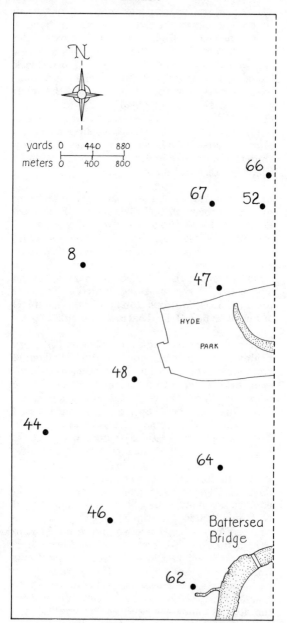

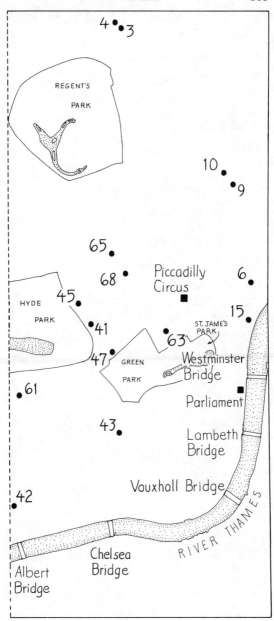

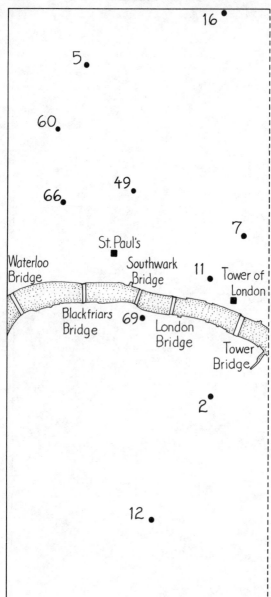

16

5

60

49

66

7

St. Paul's

Waterloo
Bridge

Southwark
Bridge

11

Tower of
London

Blackfriars
Bridge

69

London
Bridge

Tower
Bridge

2

12

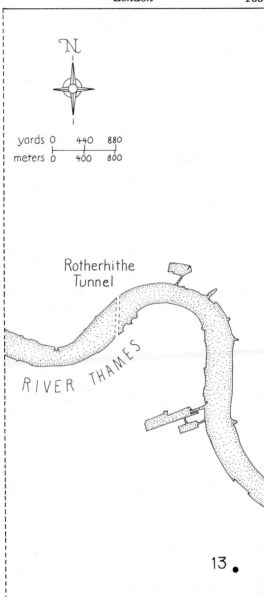

Rotherhithe
Tunnel

RIVER THAMES

13

Camden Antiques Market (3) every Thursday from 7 a.m. to 1 p.m. at the corner of Camden High Street and Buck Street in Camden Town, NW1. This market offers antiques and collectables, as well as new and used clothes. Access by car to Camden Town. Parking can be very difficult in this area. Access by Underground to Camden Town (Northern or Piccadilly Lines) or any of the many busses to Camden Town. Information from ABC, 15 Flood Street, Chelsea, London SW3, telephone 01-351 5353.

Camden Lock and The Stables (4) every Saturday and Sunday from 8 a.m. to late afternoon at Camden High Street and the Grand Union Canal, NW1. The Camden Lock part of this market is one of the best bric-a-brac and crafts fairs in London. As you cross the bridge over the canal, on the left is a jumble of hundreds of stands. Behind them, old mill buildings are the locations of craftsmen and some antique dealers. Jugglers and musicians entertain in one of the most pleasant and touristy London markets. The Stables, a five-minute walk further on Camden High Street past where it turns into Chalk Farm Road, is a major source of collectables, Victoriana, and some of the best Art Deco items found in Britain. In these old converted stables, several hundred vendors offer all types of items, but few new items or reproductions. Access by car to Camden Town; parking is easier to find along Chalk Farm Road and the Stables than near Camden Lock. Access by car to Camden Town. Parking can be very difficult in this area. Access by Underground to Camden Town Station (Northern or Piccadilly Lines) or any of the many busses to Camden Town.

Camden Passage (5) every Wednesday from 7 a.m. to mid afternoon and every Saturday from 7 a.m. to 5 p.m. (some dealers open later) on Camden Passage, N1. Camden Passage is a narrow pedestrian-only lane (actually named Islington High Street) behind Upper Street from Duncan Street to Essex Road.

A number of vendors offer all types of small antiques, collectables, and bric-a-brac on tables along the lane and its warren-like side alleys, and in some of the buildings converted into semi-permanent markets. In addition, a number of full-time shops and galleries offer some of the finer pieces of furniture, paintings, and objets d'art to be found. This is one of the more exclusive and most expensive markets in London. Access by car to Islington. Parking in the area can be almost impossible, though the car park on Duncan Street offers a large number of spaces. Access by Underground to Angel Station (Northern Line), or on bus lines 4, 19, 30, 43, 73, 171, 171A, 277, and 279.

Clapham Collectors Fair (100) first Saturday of every month from 10 a.m. to 5 p.m. at the Contact Centre, Hambalt Road, Clapham Park, SW4. This is a small fair of bric-a-brac and odds and ends. For information contact 01-622 4200.

Covent Garden antiques fair (6) every Monday from 6:30 a.m. to 4:30 p.m. on the east and south side of Covent Garden and the Jubilee Market, also on the south side, WC1. This is one of the best weekly fairs in London, and many regulars at the Bermondsey Street market can be found here Monday. Many are situated in the cavernous open building on the south side of the Covent Gardens market buildings. Most tourists don't arrive until about 9 a.m., but the bustle begins among the dealers at dawn. Organized from Sherman & Waterman Associates, 12/13 Henrietta Street, Covent Garden, London WC2E 8LH, telephone 01-240 7405.

Maridale Fairs also has an indoor antiques fair every Sunday from 10 a.m. to 5 p.m. and every Monday from 7:30 a.m. to 4:30 p.m. at 38 King Street, to the west of the Covent Gardens buildings. Information from Maridale Antique & Collectors Fairs, 9 Mill Ridge, Edgware, Middlesex, England, telephone 01-958 8354.

Access by car to Covent Garden area is easy before 7:30 a.m.,and some free parking is available on the surrounding streets, but cars must be removed by 9 a.m. Access by Underground to Covent Garden station, on the Victoria line. Any bus to Cambridge Circus or Holborn is within walking distance of Covent Garden.

Cutler Street Antiques Market (7) every Sunday from 6 a.m. to 2 p.m. on Goulston Street (near Aldgate), EC1. This market specializes in silver, gold, jewels, and coins. The early hours are when a large number of dealers come to buy; many of the items later turn up at the Silver Vaults, Portobello Road, or Camden Passage. By 8:30 or 9 a.m., the dealers are set up for the tourists. Prices increase, though the best items have long gone. This long-established market moved in 1985 from a courtyard off Cutler Street. Parking is difficult in this neighborhood after about 7 a.m. since the large Petticoat Lane and other markets take place in this area. Access by Underground to Aldgate East, and walk to the north. A large number of bus lines pass nearby, but few operate during the early hours of this market. Organized by ABC, 15 Flood Street, Chelsea, London SW3, telephone 01-351 5353.

Deptford market (13) every Friday from 8 a.m. to about noon on High Street and Douglas Way, SE8. The antiques and bric-a-brac are at the west end of the market on Douglas Way, past the fruit and vegetable vendors. While most of the items are junk, occasional treasures can be found, such as early 19th- century crystal port decanters, battered but solid oak chairs, and similar types of used items. This market is totally away from the tourist and antiques orbit and is refreshingly unpretentious. Access by Underground to New Cross Station (Metropolitan Line), walk north one block to Douglas Way, then turn right. The market is halfway down the street.

Kingsland Waste market (16) every weekday but really worthwhile only early on Saturday morning from dawn to about 9:30 a.m. along Kingsland Road, E8. This market offers all types of merchandise—food and new items as well as antiques and junk—but on Saturdays, the used-furniture merchants and used-bicycle sellers arrive in force. True bargains can be found to those who are both early and knowledgeable. Access by car to Kingsland Road; early arrivals will be rewarded by nearby street parking, but later arrivals will have to walk several blocks. Access by British Rail to Dalston Junction from Camden

Road or on bus lines 22, 22A, 30, 38, 48, 67, 78, 149, 243, 243A, and 277.

Portobello Road market (8) every Saturday from 6 a.m. to 5 p.m. on Portobello Road and some side streets, W10 and W11. Without doubt, this is the most famous antique market in Britain. The market stretches for almost a quarter of a mile from Chepstow Villas under the Westway motorway to Monroe Mews and takes in several side streets, numerous warren-like warehouses and buildings, and any nook that is available. Unfortunately, though it is the most famous and there are hundreds of dealers offering immense quantities of all types of items, it is over-touristed, and prices sometimes seem to be significantly higher for equivalent items than at other markets. In fact, a number of Portobello Road dealers can be found bidding at various auctions during the week and at Bermondsey on Friday morning to obtain stock to resell to the tourists on Saturday. Also, at this market, reproductions and some arts-and-crafts items are offered. During the week and on Saturdays as well, a fruit, vegetable, fish, and meat market takes place about midway through the antiques market—which then picks up on the other side of the fish. Access by Underground to Notting Hill Gate Station (Central, Circle, and District lines) and walk one block up Pembridge Road, then to the left along Portobello Road until arriving at the market, or to Ladbroke Grove Station (Metropolitan Line), walk east under the Westway to Portobello Road. Most but not all of the market is to your right. Access by bus to 7, 15, 15A, 28, 31,52, and 52A.

Putney Flea Market (101) every Saturday from 8:30 a.m. to mid afternoon on Putney Hill near Upper Richmond Road, SW15. This small market has about 30 vendors of old clothes, mismatched china, bric-a-brac, and junk. Parking in the area can be difficult, since the Lacey Road Car Park is a general Saturday market as well. Access by Underground to East Putney Station (District Line), or by bus lines 13, 30, 37. 74, and 85.

Sclater Street market (14) every Sunday from 4:30 a.m. (5 a.m. in winter) until mid afternoon on

Sclater Street, Cheshire Street, and surrounding lanes, E1. This market is also called Brick Lane, Club Row, or Cheshire Street. This is the quintessential Sunday market to make true finds of antiques, collectables, and other items. Beginning at 4:30 a.m., all types of antique and collectables come out of battered doctors' bags, cars, cardboard boxes, and other anonymous containers. This market seems to be one of the places that antiques and other interesting items first surface, and at a lower price than later. Because of its rather early hour, only dealers looking for stock and dedicated collectors come to this market. The main part of this early market is on Cheshire Street, which is a continuation of Sclater Street. Later in the morning, a regular market with cheap clothes, car parts, food, and other items engulfs this early morning market. Street parking is easy until about 7 a.m. After that, it rapidly becomes difficult, then almost impossible. Access by Underground (after 6 a.m. only) to Shoreditch Station (Central Line), then walk north over the tracks on Brick Lane to Sclater Street and Cheshire Street. Access by bus on lines 8, 8A, and 78 after 6 a.m., or night bus N83 or N11 to Bethal Green Road.

Streatham Antiques Market (102) every Tuesday from 8 a.m. to 2 p.m. at the United Reformed Church Halls on Streatham High Road, Streatham, SW16. This is a smaller but regular market for minor antiques and collectables. Access by Underground to Tooting Bec Station (Northern Line) and walk east on A214. Organized by Ray Ratcliff, London, telephone 01-764 3602.

Antiquarian book fair (9) second Sunday of every month except June in the assembly rooms of the Russell Hotel on Russell Square (telephone 01-837 6470). The fair is open on Sunday from 2 to 7 p.m. and Monday from 10 to 7 p.m. Once a year, in June the fair is the third Monday through Wednesday from 10:30 a.m. to 7 p.m., and is much larger than usual (about 150 vendors) and includes a third day. Access by Underground to Russell Square Station (Piccadilly Line), walk one block to the hotel at Russell Square. Access by bus on lines 68, 77, and 77A. Parking is difficult and expensive, though there are some parking meters on surrounding streets and cars may be parked at the hotel. Organized by the Provincial Booksellers Fairs Association, P.O. Box 66, Cambridge, Cambridgeshire CB1 3PD, telephone (0223) 240921.

"Bloomsbury Fair" (10) postcard, cigarette card, and printed ephemera fair the last Sunday of every month from 10 a.m. to 4 p.m. at the Bloomsbury Crest Hotel on Coram Street, one block north of Russell Square, W1 (hotel telephone 01-837 1200). This is a long-established specialists' fair; more than 100 dealers offer all types of ephemera. Admission is 35p. Parking is available at the hotel or in a car park across the street. Access by Underground to Russell Square Station (Piccadilly Line) and walk left to Russell Square and then right along Woburn Place, or on busses 77, 77A, and 188. Organized by IPM Promotions, 2 Frederick Gardens, Brighton, Sussex BN1 4TB, telephone (0273) 675757 or in London at 62 Greyhound Hill, Hendon, London NW4, telephone 01-203 1772.

"London City Book Market," (11) an antiquarian book fair the third Tuesday of most months at St. Olaves Parish Hall from 10:30 a.m. to 6 p.m., in Mark Lane, EC4. Access by car is difficult at best and parking is almost impossible. A parking garage is near the Tower of London. Access by Underground to Tower Hill Station, then walk west to Mark Lane. Organized by the Provincial Booksellers Fairs Association, P.O. Box 66, Cambridge, Cambridgeshire CB1 3PD, telephone (0223) 240921.

Westmoreland Road (12) used goods and bric-a-brac market every Sunday from 8 a.m. to noon on Westmoreland Road, SE17. About 70 vendors offer all types of used goods and junk. This is a market at which finds can be made, including beat-up Victorian furniture and other neglected but restorable or salvageable items. It is also a good market for those unwilling to arrive by dawn. Access by car to Elephant and Castle, then southeast along Walworth Road to Westmoreland Road (Walworth Road changes its name to Cam-

berwell Road near the market). Street parking is
available to early arrivals. Access by Underground to Elephant and Castle Station (Northern
and Bakerloo Lines), or by bus lines 12, 35, 40, 42,
45, 46, 68, 171, 176, 184, and 185A.

Antiques Fairs

These markets are held irregularly, but are often
the largest specialized markets in the London
area, and some include museum-quality antiques
offered by the top dealers as well as large markets
with all types of bric-a-brac, antiques, and collectables.

"The Alexandra Palace Antique and Collectors
Fair" (103) five times a year (mid January, mid
May, mid September, mid September, and mid
November) from noon (members of the antiques
trade 10:30) until 6 p.m. at the Alexandra
Pavilion (until March 1988) and Alexandra
Palace (after March 1988), Wood Green, N22. Admission at 10:30 is £3 and an antiques trade business card required; at noon the general public is
admitted for £1. All children with adults are free.
This is one of the largest fairs in London; more
than 500 stands offer all types of items, specializing in small items rather than large pieces of furniture. No reproduction or new work may be offered. Free parking is available on the grounds.
Access by British Rail from Kings Cross to
Alexandra Palace station, then by free bus to the
fair. Organized by Pig & Whistle Promotions, 53
Muswell Ave., London N10 2EH, telephone 01-
883 7061 and 01-249 4050.

"West London Antiques Fair" (48) held the second
Wednesday through following Sunday of January
and August from 11 a.m. to 8 p.m. (Sunday 11
a.m. to 6 p.m.) at Kensington Town Hall on
Hornton Street, W8. This is a good fair, with
about 90 stands. All types of items are offered,
from small pieces of jewelry to large furniture.
However, coins, medals, stamps, and militaria
are prohibited. The dateline is 1870, except jewelry, textile, and collectables 1900, and paintings
1920. All items are vetted, and reproductions and
modern works are prohibited. Admission is £2.50,

which includes a catalogue. Members of the antiques trade are admitted free. Access by car to Kensington High Street. Parking on the street is often difficult, but there is a car park under the library in the Kensington Town Centre. Access by Underground to Kensington High Street, and then walk across the street past the library to Kensington Town Hall. Many busses from all over London stop in front of the Underground station and library. For further information, contact Penman Fairs, P.O. Box 114, Haywards Heath, West Sussex, RH16 2YU, telephone (04447) 2514, or Mobilphone (0860) 515101 during fairs.

"The London Decorative Arts Fair" (40) four times a year, usually the end of March, June, September, and December from 11 a.m. (trade 9.30) to 4.30 p.m. at the Westminster Exhibition Centre, Vincent Square, SW1. About 150 dealers of Art Nouveau, Art Deco, and modern works show their items, for one day only. Organized by Bagatelle Fairs, London, telephone 01-391 2339.

"The International Silver & Jewellery Fair & Seminars" (41) held four days during January (dates vary) at the Dorchester Hotel, Park Lane, W1 (hotel telephone 01-629 8888). This fair includes not only excellent examples of vetted sterling silver and jewelry, but also seminars and lectures by well-regarded experts. Entry to the sale is £5, which includes and illustrated catalogue. Entry to each seminar is at extra cost. Access by car is to Park Lane; street parking is difficult to nonexistent, but cars may be parked at the hotel. Access by Underground to Marble Arch and then walk along Park Lane to the hotel. Organized by Brian & Anna Haughton, ICF&S, 3B Burlington Gardens, Old Bond Street, London W1X 1LE, telephone 01-734 5491.

"The Chelsea Antiques Fair" (42) second Tuesday through third Saturday (11 days) of March and September from 11 a.m. to 8 p.m. (5 p.m. Saturday and closed Sunday) at Chelsea Old Town Hall, Kings Road at Sydney Street, SW3 (Old Town Hall telephone 01-351 9152). These fairs are some high points of the British antiques fair circuit and are one of the older, established fairs.

All types of items are shown, from small items such as jewelry, glass, coins, and medals, through paintings and a large selection of furniture. The dateline for furniture is 1830; for most other items 1851; and for paintings, jewelry, and rugs, 1888. All vendors are professional dealers. All items are vetted, and new work, reproductions, and over-restored items are prohibited. Admission is £3, which includes an illustrated catalogue. There is no reduction or free admission for the trade. Access by car is easy, and the fair is AA signposted. Parking, however, is difficult, since there is no on-site parking, and unoccupied street spaces are scarce. Access by Underground to Sloane Square or South Kensington, then walk. Bus lines 11, 19, 22, and 49 stop in front of the exhibition hall. For further information, contact Penman Antiques Fairs, P.O. Box 114, Haywards Heath, West Sussex RH16 2YU, telephone (04447) 2514.

"The Westminster Spring Antiques Fair" (43) held in late April. This is a new antiques fair (first one is April 21-24, 1988), held near Victoria Station. All antiques will be vetted, and furniture has an 1830 dateline and most other items have an 1860 dateline. Admission is £2.50, which includes a catalogue, but members of the antiques trade are admitted free. Contact the organizer to find the exact location and for further details. Organized by Penman Fairs, P.O. Box 114, Haywards Heath, West Sussex RH16 2YU, telephone (04447) 2514.

"The Syon Park Antiques Fair" (105) held twice a year at May Bank Holiday and during the first week of November at Syon Park in west London near Kew Bridge. This is a major antiques fair. Only the best antiques may be offered; items found include clocks, furniture, silver, porcelain and pottery, paintings, and other items too numerous to mention. All items are vetted before the sale by experts from Christie's, Phillips, or Bonhams. Admission is £2.50. (In addition to the fair, Syon Park also has an excellent transport museum and an Adam-designed house.) Access by car to Syon Park along A315 (follow Kew Bridge Road west from Kew Bridge) to the park.

Parking is available. Access by bus lines 117, 203, 237, 267, and E2 to Syon Park stop.

"The Fine Arts & Antiques Fair" (44) for two weeks from the end of May to mid-June at the Olympia Exhibition Centre, Hammersmith Road, W14. This is a major antiques event; all items are vetted. Access by Underground to Olympia Kensington and walk south one block to Hammersmith Road, then west to the Centre. Pay parking available in a car park behind the Centre. Organized by Philbeach Events Ltd., Earls Court Exhibitions Centre, Warwick Road, London SW5, England, telephone 01-385 1200.

"The Grosvenor House Antiques Fair" (45) for 10 days in early to late June (usually about the 10th to 20th) at the Grosvenor House Hotel in the Great Room. Hours vary: opening night is 5 to 8 p.m., others are 11 a.m. to 8 p.m. or ll a.m. to 6 p.m. These fairs are some the very highest peaks of the British antique fair circuit; well worth attending. All items are vetted and all sellers are antique dealer members of the British Antique Dealers Association. Only the finest antiques, almost all of museum quality, are shown and offered. Admission and catalogue are £3. Held at the Grosvenor House Hotel, Park Lane, in Mayfair a block east of Hyde Park and between Mount Street and Grosvenor Street. Pay parking is available on Reeves Mews across the street. Access by Underground to Marble Arch Station on Central line, then walk, or any bus to Marble Arch/Oxford Street and walk. Organized by Ann Rudd and Elaine Dean, British Antique Dealers Association, 20 Rutland Gate, London SW7 1BD, telephone 01-581 0373.

"The International Ceramics Fair and Seminar" (41) the second weekend of June (Friday through following Monday) from 11 a.m. to 8 p.m. at the Dorchester Hotel, Park Lane, W1, telephone 01-629 8888. This fair not only has vetted ceramics of all types (Chinese, European porcelain, other types of ceramics) but also lectures by internationally known specialists in the field of ceramics. Entry for the public and antiques trade as well is £4, which includes an illustrated catalogue; lectures are £8 for the first and £5 for following ones. Access by car to Park Lane; street parking is difficult to nonexistent, but cars may be parked at the hotel. Access by Underground to Marble Arch and then walk along Park Lane to the hotel. Organized by Brian & Anna Haughton, ICF&S, 3B Burlington Gardens, Old Bond Street, London W1X 1LE, telephone 01-734 5491.

"The London Arms Fair" (46) last Friday and Saturday of September at the London West Hotel, Lillie Road, SW6. This is one of the oldest regular fairs for antiques, armor, assorted militaria, and books. Admission is £3 on Friday and £2 on Saturday. Access by Underground to West Brompton (District Line) then walk west one block on Lillie Road. Access by car to the hotel, where limited parking is available. Access by bus on lines 30, 264, and 283. Hotel telephone is 01-385 1255.

"The National Antique & Collectors' Porcelain, Pottery, and Glass Fair" (47) the third Sunday of September from 11 a.m. to 6 p.m. at the Park Court Hotel, 75 Lancaster Gate, Bayswater W2. The title of this specialists' fair is self-descriptive. Programs and admission is 75p or £1. Organized by London House, 271-273 King Street, London W6, telephone 01-741 8011. This hotel is occasionally used for other one-day fairs. Information is available from the hotel 01-402 4272. The site is halfway between the Queensway and Lancaster Gate Underground Station on the north side of Bayswater Road. Access by bus on any line along Bayswater Road (12, 28, 88). Parking in this area can be difficult.

"The Park Lane Hotel Antiques Fair" (47) first week of October. This is another of the famous fairs held in posh hotels. Only beautiful, perfect antiques are shown at this exclusive fair. Organized by the Park Lane Hotel Antiques Fair, London House, 271-273 King Street, London W6 9LZ, telephone 01-741 8011.

This hotel is frequently used by other organizers for one-day antique fairs. Examples include a fair the third weekend of September, sponsored by Century Antiques Fair Ltd., 58 Mill

Lane, London NW6 1N3, telephone 01-794 3551. The schedule of coming events can also be obtained from the hotel, telephone 01-499 6321. Access by Underground to Green Park, then walk along Piccadilly toward Hyde Park to Park Lane.

"Kensington Antiques Fair" (48) first Saturday through following Sunday of November at the New Town Hall, Hornton Street, Kensington W8. All antiques are vetted and must be older than 1840. Admission is charged to all and includes a catalogue. Parking, for which a charge is made, is available in the Town Hall buildings. Access by Underground to Kensington High Street, then walk north on Hornton Street. Access by bus to Kensington High Street. Organized by Roger Heath-Bullock, Cultural Exhibitions Ltd., 8 Meadrow, Godalming, Surrey GU7 3HN, telephone (04868) 22562.

"The Chingford Antiques and Collectors' Fair" (106) is a relatively new antiques fair, held on the third Saturday of September from 10 a.m. to 4 p.m. at the Chingford Assembly Rooms at the Green, Station Road in the northeast part of London. About 80 dealers of antiques and collectables offer all types of items. Admission is 50p, but accompanied children and members of the antiques trade are free. Access by car from A104 to Woodford, then left to Chingford. This fair is signposted. Access by train to Chingford Station from Liverpool Street (only about 10 miles). Access by bus on lines 69, 97, 235, and 313 to Chingford Station. Chingford Station is on Station Road. For exact dates and further information, contact Bartholomew Fayres, Executive House, The Maltings, Station Road, Sawbridgeworth, Hertfordshire CM21 9JX, telephone (02779) 725809.

"The City of London Antiques Fair" (49) held the last Wednesday through Saturday of November from 11 a.m. to 8 p.m. (Saturday closing at 4 p.m.) at the Barbican Centre Exhibition Hall, across Beech Street from the Barbican Centre, EC2. This is a large, quality fair of more than 150 dealers of furniture, clocks, textiles, glass and crystal, silver, and quantities of furniture. The dateline for furniture is 1850; for some other items 1860; jewels, textiles, and collectables 1900, and paintings 1920. All items are vetted. Admission, which includes an illustrated catalogue, is £2 in 1987, and £4 in future years. Readmission is free. There is no discount or free admission for members of the antiques trade. Access by car is easy: follow signs to Barbican Centre, and use Barbican Car Parks 2 and 3 off Silk Street, or 4 and 5 off Beech Street. A charge is made for parking, and street parking is virtually unavailable. Access by Underground to Barbican (the nearest), Moorgate, or St. Paul's station. Many busses stop in front of the Exhibition Hall, including 4, 9, 11, 21, 43, 76, 141, 279a, and 502. Organized by Penman Fairs, P.O. Box 114, Haywards Heath, West Sussex RH16 2YU, telephone (04447) 2514.

Auctions

London is the auction center of Britain; the major houses are listed here in alphabetical order. Be sure to contact them before planning to attend a sale, both to obtain catalogues (where one is issued) and to be sure that the auction will be held as scheduled.

Bainbridges Auctioneers and Valuers (160)

Auctions of all types of items, including but not limited to antiques and art, are held irregularly at the salerooms on Mattock Lane, Ealing. For further information and sales calendar, contact Bainbridges Auctioneer, St. Johns Yard, St. Johns Parade, Mattock Lane, Ealing, London W13, telephone 01- 579 2966.

Bloomsbury Book Auctions (60)

This auctioneer, a specialist in books and other papers, holds 22 auctions per year, with at least 400 lots in each auction. Auctions are held on Thursdays at 11 a.m. in their salesrooms and offices. Catalogues are available about two to three weeks before the sale for £3.50 each. (Annual airmail subscription in the U.S. and Canada: U.S. $112.50.

Viewing is held on Tuesday from 9:30 a.m. to 5 p.m., Wednesday from 9:30 a.m. to 8 p.m., and the morning of the sale. Bids may be left, mailed, or telephoned. Bidders should register with the office before bidding. The buyer's premium is 10%. All bids must be paid for and purchases removed within five days. Access by car to Finsbury on Rosebery Avenue; the Finsbury Car Parks are nearby, for which a charge is made. Access by Underground to Angel (Black line) and walk south on St. John Street, then left on Rosebery Avenue to Hardwick Street, or by busses 19, 38, 153, 171, 171A, 196, all of which run on Rosebery Avenue. Sales are held at and exact dates and further information is available from Bloomsbury Book Auctions, 3/4 Hardwick Street, London EC1R 4RY, telephone 01-833 2636 and 833 2637.

Bonham's Montpelier Galleries (61)
This is one of the most active auctioneers of antiques and collectables in London. Two to five sales per week are held at 11 a.m. at the salerooms on Montpelier Street, Knightsbridge. This Bonham's usually offers better items than at Bonham's Chelsea (please see next entry). A free monthly schedule of sales is available upon request. All sales are specialized categories of antiques. Every other Tuesday, sales of Silver and Plate are held. Every thursday a sale of Oil Paintings is held, and every other week Thursday a sale of furniture is held. In addition other sales are held from time to time. Catalogues are issued for all sales, and cost from £1 to £3. Viewing is held several days before the sales from 9 a.m. to 5 p.m. (and until 7 p.m. on Tuesdays). Bids may be left, telephoned, or mailed. All bids must be on hand by the beginning of the sale. The buyer's premium is 10%. Sales are held at and further information is available from Bonham's, Montpelier Galleries, Montpelier Street, Knightsbridge, London SW7 1HH, telephone 01-584 9161. Access by car to Brompton Road, on the south side of Hyde Park. Street parking is difficult, but several Car Parks are located on Sloane Street. Access by Underground to Knightsbridge, then walk along Brompton Road to Montpelier Street, on the right.

Bonham's Chelsea (62)

This is Bonham's workaday auction gallery. Two to three sales a week are held at this slightly run-down gallery, one of several auction houses on Lots Road. Sales are specialized, and usually start on Tuesday at 10 a.m. for furniture and carpets, and every other Friday at 10:30 a.m. for ceramics and at 2 p.m. for pictures. Catalogues are issued in advance of every sale, and often cost 80p to £1. Viewing is held the day before the sale during normal business hours, and on Mondays until 7 p.m. The buyer's premium is 10%. All items must be paid for and removed by 6 p.m. on the day after the sale to avoid storage charges of £1 per lot per day. Sales are held at and further information is available from Bonhams New Chelsea Galleries, 65-69 Lots Road, Chelsea, London SW10 0RN, telephone 01-351 0466. Access by car to Chelsea Bridge, then continue along the north bank of the Thames until the main road turns north. Lots Road is straight ahead, and when it turns north, the auction houses are found 100 yards on. A car park is between Lots Road and Upcerne Road. Access by Underground to Fulham Broadway, walk to King's Road, then east to Lots Road, or take busses 11 or 22 to King's Road, then walk south on Lots Road to the auction site.

Christie's St. James's (63)

This is the head office of Christie's, where the best items are offered, such as Old Master paintings that sometimes are sold at record prices, which are recorded as newspaper headlines. However, not all items sold here are that expensive. Sales are specialized by category. A schedule of sales, which are held frequently, is available upon request.

Catalogues are issued in advance of all sales, and cost from £1 to £4. Bidders are required to register before bidding. Bids may be left, or made by telephone or mail.

Sales are held at and further information is available at Christie's St James, 8 King Street, St. James's, London SW1Y 6QT, telephone 01-839 9060. Access by car is difficult, and is just south of Piccadilly, off St. James's Street. Parking is difficult to impossible in this area. Access by

Underground to Green Park or (with a longer walk) Piccadilly Circus. St James's Street is across the street from the Royal Academy.

Christie's South Kensington (64)
This is Christie's workaday auction house. While the grand sales of famous art take place in the St. James' location, almost every day (except Sunday) at least one sale takes place. Many days, there are three or four. A catalogue is issued at least a week before every sale (charges vary, never free), viewing is the day before the auction and just before the auction. A calendar of forthcoming sales is issued by the Press Office, and is available free upon request. The buyer's premium is 10% of the hammer price. Bids may be left, or made by telephone, or mail. Buyers have up to two days after the sale to pay for purchases and remove them.

While exceptions to the following schedule take place, and there are many special sales, in general the schedule is as follows:

Monday: 2 p.m. Silver, 5:30 p.m. Wine
Tuesday: 2 p.m. Jewelry, 2 p.m. Pictures
Wednesday: 10:30 a.m. Carpets, 1 p.m. Furniture, 2 p.m. Watercolors and Drawings, Prints,
Thursday: 10:30 a.m. Glass and Ceramics, 2 p.m. Oriental Art, or Ceramics of various origins
Friday: 2 p.m. Books and Maps

Sales are informal, though bidders should register and obtain a bidder's number before bidding.

The auction is located at 85 Old Brompton Road, London SW7 3LD, telephone 01-581 7611. Access by car to Old Brompton Road. Some street parking with meters is available on the surrounding streets, or for £1 per hour at the National Car Park nearby. Access by Underground to South Kensington Station (Circle, District, or Piccadilly Lines), then walk several blocks down Old Brompton Road, or bus 30, which travels on Old Brompton Road.

Glendining & Co. (65)
This Phillips-affiliated auction house has auctions every month or two, usually on Tuesday. This house specializes in items such as coins,

medals, and jewelry. Catalogues are issued several weeks before the sale, and cost from £1 to £4. The buyer's premium is 10%. Sales are held at and further information can be obtained from Glendining & Co., 7 Blenheim St., New Bond Street, London W1Y 9LD, telephone 01-493 2445. (This is the same location as Phillips Blenstock House.)

Hatton Gardens Auctions (66)

This auction house specializes in jewelry and silver. Auctions of are held every Thursday; jewelry and watches at 1:30 p.m., and silver and silver plate later in the afternoon, usually at 3:15 p.m. The sale of general items begins at 2:30 p.m. Auctions of specialized classes of items are held occasionally. Catalogues are issued at least one week before the sale; the usual price is £2. Viewing is held the day of the sale. Bids may be left, or mailed or made by telephone. The buyer's premium is 10%. Auctions are held at and further information can be obtained from Hatton Garden Auctions, 36 Hatton Garden, London EC1N 8HP, telephone 01-242 6452. Access by

auto is difficult and parking almost impossible except at the Car Park on Hatton Gardens near Clerkenwell Road. Access by Underground to Chancery Lane Station (Central Line) or Farringdon (Circle or Metropolitan Lines), or British Rail to Holborn Viaduct station. Hatton Gardens is a street running between Holborn Circus and Clerkenwell Road; the auction house is almost exactly at the midpoint.

London Bridge Auctions (69)

Weekly auctions of odds and ends are held at 2 p.m. at the saleroom at 6 Park Street, SE1. Almost anything can turn up at these sales: furniture, silver, porcelain, clocks and watches, jewelry, pictures, and other odds and ends. Each auction includes over 500 lots, and the auction moves quickly. There are no catalogues issued in advance of the sale. Viewing is the Sunday of the sale from 10 a.m. to 2 p.m. There is no buyer's premium. All purchases must be paid for and removed on the day of the sale. Sales are held at and further information is available from London Bridge Auctions, 6 Park Street, off Stoney Street,

Southwark, London SE1, telephone 01-407 9577. Access by car to Southwark Bridge; Park Street is the second cross street. Access by Underground (Northern Line) and British Rail to London Bridge Station, walk upstream along the viaduct to Park Street. Access by bus on 17, 44, 70, 95, 149, 184, and any bus to London Bridge Station.

Lots Road Galleries (62)
The most hurly-burly of the several auction houses on Lots Road, hold auctions every Monday at 6 p.m. Auctions are not specialized and consist all types of antiques and used items. The auction moves at a *very* rapid pace, with a new item approximately every thirty seconds. Register with the office and obtain a bidder number before bidding. Viewing on Fridays, Saturday, Sundays from 10 a.m. to 1 p.m. and 10 a.m. to 6 p.m. on Monday. Telephone bids and left bids can be made; if so, bidding is started at half the left bid. Buyer's commission is 12%. Catalogues are free. Buyers have 24 hours to pay for and remove their purchases. Lots Road Galleries is located at 71-73 Lots Road, Worlds End, Chelsea, London, SW10 0RN, telephone 01-351 7771 or 351 5784. Access by car to Chelsea Bridge, then continue along the north bank of the Thames until the main road turns north. Lots Road is straight ahead, and when it turns north, the auction houses are found 100 yards on. Access by Underground to Fulham Broadway, walk to King's Road, then east to Lots Road, or take busses 11 or 22 to King's Road, then walk south on Lots Road to the auction site.

Newington Green Auctions (161)
Auctions are held every Thursday evening at 6:30 p.m. at the auction salesroom in the northern suburb of Stoke Newington. All types of antiques, including gold, silver, clocks, paintings, and furniture, and some modern furniture (if in good condition) is auctioned. Catalogues are issued the day before the sale, consisting of conditions of sale and simple listing of two hundred or more lots; there is no charge for the catalogue. Viewing takes place on Wednesday from 10 a.m. to 8 p.m. and Thursday before the sale. Bids may be left, mailed or telephoned. The buyer's premium is £2 per lot. No items may be removed before the end

of the sale. Payment and removal must be completed by the close of business the following Tuesday. Access by Underground isn't convenient (nearest station is Manor House) and walk down Green Lanes. Access by bus to Stoke Newington is on lines 141 and 171A. Parking is on the street, sometimes difficult to find. Sales are held at and further information is available from Newington Green Auctions, 55 Green Lanes, London N16 4TD, telephone 01-246 4222.

Phillips at Blenstock House (65)

The headquarters of one of the largest auction houses in Britain is a true delight for the collector, since regular auctions are held every day from Monday through Friday at 11 a.m., plus numerous special sales of specialized categories. The weekly sales include: Monday, antique furniture, rugs, ceramics, glass, and art objects; Tuesday, antique furniture, carpets, bronzes, and works of art; Wednesday, alternating between porcelain, pottery, and glass one week and Oriental art the next; Thursday, postage stamps and sometimes paper money; Friday, silver. Viewing for the regular sales is two days before the sales. Catalogues for regular sales are £1. Special occasional sales include prints, paintings, clocks, jewelry (Tuesday), miniatures (Wednesday), Art Nouveau (Thursday), armor (Thursday), furs (Thursday), books and music (usually held on Thursdays), and Art Nouveau (Thursday). A collector's sale of items from lead soldiers, dolls, postcards, and scientific instruments to war medals and rock n roll memorabilia are held Wednesday at 12 noon. Blenstock house is at the end of Blenheim Street, a small alley off New Bond Street one block north of Oxford Street. Catalogues for special sales are sold, minimum price £1, but for some sales may be more. Buyer's premium is 10%. Bids may be left or made by mail or telephone. Payment and removal of purchases must be made within two working days. Access by auto is difficult, and parking is virtually impossible. The nearest underground parking is at Cavendish Square. Access by Underground to Bond Street or Oxford Circus (Central or Jubilee Lines), or any bus going to Oxford Street. Sales are held at and further information is available from Phillips Blenstock House, 7 Blenheim Street, New Bond Street, London W1Y 0AS, telephone 01-629 6602.

Phillips Marylebone (66)

This is another Phillips auction house, which has weekly sales every Friday of antique and modern furniture, ceramics, and pictures at 10 a.m. and pictures and paintings at 1 p.m. Viewing is Thursday from 9 a.m. to 5 p.m. Occasional sales of pianos and organs are held here as well. Catalogues (including estimated sale price) are issued for all sales about one week before the sale, price £1. Buyer's premium is 10%. Street parking is difficult in the neighborhood; the nearest parking lot is on Broadley Street, off Edgware Road. Access by Underground to Marylebone Station then walk west two blocks to Lisson Grove (a street) or by bus to Marylebone station and walk, or bus 159 to Lisson Grove. Sales are held at and further information is available from Phillips Marylebone, Hayes Place, Lisson Grove, London NW1 6UA, telephone 01-723 2547.

Phillips West 2 (67)

Another of the Phillips houses has sales every Thursday at 10 a.m. The sales include furniture, ceramics, and works of art, and special sales of "vintage" cars. Viewing is Wednesday from 9 a.m. to 7 p.m. Catalogues are issued before the sale, price usually £1. Buyer's premium is 10%. Access by public transit to Paddington Station, then walk. Sales are held at and further information is available from Phillips W2, 10 Salem Road, London W2 4BU, telephone 01-221 5303.

Sotheby's (68)

This is the headquarters of the Sotheby's auction house, specializing in fine arts and the best antiques. This is the location of some of the sales that shatter world records for paintings. A free schedule of sales is available upon request. Viewing is held several days before every sale. Catalogues are issued before every sale, and cost £1 to £6. The buyer's premium is 10% in most cases. Parking in this area is almost impossible at any time. Access by Underground to Bond Street (Central or Jubilee lines) or any of the busses along Oxford Street. Sales are held at and further information is available from Sotheby's, 34 New Bond Street, W1A, telephone 01-493 8080.

Southgate Antique Auction Rooms (163)
This auction of antiques and collectables, and a bit of modern work, takes place in the northern suburbs of London every Friday at 6:30 p.m. Catalogues (which are simple descriptions of the items) are issued the day before the sale. Viewing is held Friday from 10 a.m. until the sale begins. Sales consist of over 500 lots, and they move very rapidly through jewelry and silver, then bric-a-brac, glass, ands porcelain, then paintings and drawings, and last, furniture. Bids may be left or telephoned, but winning bids be paid for within two days of the sale. There is no buyer's premium. All items must be paid for within two days and removed within seven days. Access by car north of London on Green Lanes (A105) to Southgate Town Hall. Free parking is available at the auction. Access by bus on lines 29, 123, green bus 735, and at night on bus N29. Sales are held at and further information is available at Southgate Antique Auction Rooms, Rear of Southgate Town Hall, Green Lanes, Palmers Green, London N13, telephone 01-886 7888.

Indoor, Permanent Antiques Markets

A number of antiques markets are open most weekdays, and include large collections of dealers with all types of items. They're included because they are indoors, open most days, though not antiques fairs as generally understood. These markets' location market are not shown on the maps.

Alfie's Antique Market, 13-25 Church Street, NW8, telephone 01-723 6066. Open Tuesday through Saturday from 10 a.m. to 6 p.m. About 90 dealers. Nearest Underground Station: Edgware Road or Marylebone.

Antiquarius Antiques Market, 135 Kings Road, Chelsea, SW3, operated by ABC, 15 Flood Street, Chelsea, London SW3, telephone 01-351 5353, open Monday through Saturday from 10 a.m. to 6 p.m. About 200 stands. Nearest Underground Station: Sloane Square.

Bermondsey Antique market and Antique Hypermarket, Long Lane at Bermondsey Street, SE1, operated by ABC, 15 Flood Street, Chelsea, London SW3, telephone 01-351 5353, open Monday through Friday 7 a.m. to 5 p.m. (note: Bermondsey Antique Market only open Friday from 5 a.m. to 2 p.m.). Nearest Underground Station: Tower Bridge.

Bond Street Antique Centre, 124 New Bond Street, W1, operated by ABC, 15 Flood Street, Chelsea, London SW3, telephone 01-351 5353, Open Monday through Saturday from 10 a.m. to 5:45 p.m. About 25 dealers. Nearest Underground Station: Bond Street.

Chelsea Antiques Market, 253 Kings Road, SW3, telephone 01-352 1424 or 352 9695. Open Monday through Saturday from 10 a.m. to 6 p.m. Nearest Underground Station: Sloane Square.

Chenil Galleries, 181 Kings Road, SW3, operated by ABC, 15 Flood Street, Chelsea, London SW3, telephone 01-351 5353. Open Monday through Saturday from 10 a.m. to 6 p.m. About 45 dealers. Nearest Underground Station: Sloane Square.

Earlham Street, WC2. Open Monday through Saturday from 9 a.m. to 5 p.m. Nearest Underground Station: Covent Garden.

Grays Antique Market, 58 Davies Street, W1, telephone 01-629 7034. Open Monday through Friday from 10 a.m. to 6 p.m. Several hundred dealers. Nearest Underground Station: Bond Street.

Grays Mews Antique Market, 1-7 Davies Mews, W1, telephone 01-629 7034 and 629 7036. Open Monday through Friday from 10 a.m. to 6 p.m. Nearest Underground Station: Bond Street

London Silver Vaults, Chancery Lane, WC2, telephone 01-242 3844. Open Monday through Friday from 9 a.m. to 5:30 p.m. and Saturday from 9 a.m. to 12:30 p.m. The most amazing and largest quantity silver for sale. Nearest Underground Station: Chancery Lane. For further information, contact the London Silver Vaults, telephone 01-242 3844.

Long Ashton, Avon

(Please see Bristol.)

Lostwithiel, Cornwall

Jefferys, Auctioneers & Estate Agents
Auctions are held every other Wednesday at 10:30 a.m. at the salerooms at 5 Fore Street. Auctions include antiques, collectables, and other used goods. These can be good country auctions, since this is in an out-of-the-way corner of Britain. No catalogues are issued. Inspection is held on Tuesday before the sale during normal business hours, and on Wednesday morning. The buyer's premium is five per cent. Bids may be left, mailed, or telephoned, but references (such as a banker) are required. Access by car is on A390 to Lostwitheil. Free parking is available all around the town. Access by train to Lostwithiel, then walk across the bridge and take the first left. The auction rooms are almost straight ahead. Auctions are held at and further information is available from Jefferys, The Auction Rooms, 5 Fore Street, Lostwithiel, Cornwall PL22 0BP, telephone (0208) 872245.

Loughton, Essex

(Please also see Epping, Harlow, and London.)

Antique and collectors' fair held four Bank Holiday Mondays per year (third Monday of April, first and fourth Monday of May, and last Monday of August) from 10 a.m. to 5 p.m. at the

Loughton Methodist Hall on High Road. This is a small fair with about 30 dealers offering mainly small items on tables. Access by car on High Road (A104) directly to the hall. Access by bus on line 20 and Green Lines 201, 250, and 501 from London, or by British Rail to Loughton Station from Liverpool Street Station, also in London. For further information, contact Bartholomew Fayres, Executive House, The Maltings, Station Road, Saw-bridgeworth, Hertfordshire CM21 9JXZ, telephone (0279) 725809.

Luton, Bedfordshire

(Please also see Hatfield, Hitchin, Letchworth, and Tring.)

Antique and collectors' fair the last Sunday of May, September, and November from 10:30 a.m. to 6 p.m. at the Putteridge Recreation Centre on Putteridge Lane, Stopsley, along A505. This is a good-sized regional fair with about 100 stands. Admission is 60p, but accompanied children are free. Entrance is free to members of the antiques trade who enter between 9 and 10:30 a.m. Access by car is on A505 north two miles north from Luton toward Cambridge. The fair is signposted, and there is free parking. This fair is not easily accessible by public transport. For further information, contact Bartholomew Fayres, Executive House, The Maltings, Station Road, Sawbridgeworth, Hertfordshire CM21 9JX, telephone (0279) 725809.

Lyndhurst, Hampshire

(Please also see Brockenhurst, Ower, and Southampton.)

Antiques and collectors' fair two weekends (Saturday and Sunday) per year at the Lyndhurst Park Hotel. This is a good regional fair with all types of antiques and collectables shown. The dateline is 1930. Admission is 50p. Free parking is available at and near the hotel. For exact dates and further information, contact Kingston

Promotions, 157 Plymouth Drive, Hill Head, Fareham, Hampshire PO14 3SN, telephone (0329) 661 780.

Manchester, Greater Manchester

(Please also see Stretford.)

Capes Dunn & Company Fine Art Auctioneers
Specialized antiques auctions are held most Wednesdays of the year, with each auction focusing on a particular type of goods, such as antique furniture, bronzes and small sculpture, paintings and watercolors, jewelry, sterling, glass, ceramics, carpets, musical instruments, and books. Catalogues are issued for the antique sales, priced £1. In addition, used and household goods are held every other Tuesday year round. Previews are held the Monday before the sale from 10 a.m. to 4 p.m. Most auctions consist of 300 to 1 000 lots. There is a 10% buyer's premium. Bids may be left or telephoned if the bidder is known to the auctioneers. Access by public transit by rail to Oxford Road or Manchester Piccadilly Road stations, or by bus on Oxford Road or Princess street. There is no on-site parking, and street parking may be difficult to find, since the auctions are in central Manchester. Sales are held at and additional information can be obtained from Capes Dunn & Company, the Auction Galleries, 38 Charles Street, Manchester, M1 7DB, telephone (061) 273 1911.

Margam, West Glamorgan (Wales)

"Antique Dealers' Fair of Wales" third weekend of May (Friday 11 a.m. to 8 p.m., Saturday and Sunday 11 a.m. to 6 p.m.) at Margam Castle in the Orangery, a stately home. This is one of the best antique fairs in Wales. All items are vetted. The dateline is 1880, though a very few more recent pieces are accepted. Food is available on the site. Access by car on M38 to Junction 49, then south to the castle on A48. Free parking is available on the grounds. Nearest rail station is three miles away in Port Talbot. For further information and

exact sale dates, contact Robert Soper, Castle
Fairs, Bowcliffe Road, Bramham, Wetherby,
North Yorkshire, LS23 9JS, telephone (0937)
845829.

Margate, Kent

Stewart, Gore, Auctioneers and Valuers
Auctions every four to six Thursdays (varies),
starting at 9 a.m., are held at the Salerooms, Clifton Place, Margate. All types of items are offered—modern, antique, and in between. For
exact sale dates and further information, contact
Stewart, Gore, 102 Northdown Road, Margate,
Kent, telephone (0843) 221528.

Marlborough, Wiltshire

"Oxfam Antiques Fair" second Friday and Saturday of May at the Town Hall in the Marlborough
town center. Saturday the hours are 11:30 a.m. to
5:30 p.m., and Sunday hours are 10 a.m. to 6 p.m.
No train service is available; parking is available
on nearby streets. Organized by the Mrs. L.
Smith, Marlborough & District Oxfam Committee, 27 Oxford Street, Ramsbury, Marlborough,
Wiltshire, telephone (0672) 20871.

Dennis Pocock & Drewett Auctioneers
Auctions of antiques are held the first Wednesday
of every month at 10 a.m., and of used goods in
general and garden furniture on the second Wednesday of every month at 10 a.m. at the
Marlborough Salerooms at the auctioneer's
premises. Catalogues are issued about two weeks
before the antiques sale, no charge. Previews are
held the Tuesday before the auction from 9 a.m.
to 7 p.m. and from 9 a.m. on the sale day. Auctions consist of up to 1000 lots. There is no buyer's
premium. Bids may be left or telephoned if the
bidder is known to the auctioneers. Purchases
must be removed by 7 p.m. Thursday after the
sale, or storage charges of £1 per day will accrue.
There is no easy access by public transit to
Marlborough. Free parking is available on High
Street, the George Lane parking lot, or in the

Waitrose Supermarket lot in front of the saleroom. Sales are held at and further information can be obtained from Dennis Pocock & Drewett, Marlborough Salerooms, 20 High Street, Marlborough, Wiltshire SN8 1AA, telephone (0672) 53471.

Matlock, Derbyshire

(Please also see Bakewell.)

Antiques fair several times per year (mid-March, early June, early September, and early November) at the Imperial Rooms. These relatively small, local fairs, offer antiques and collectables. Parking is available nearby. Access by public transit is difficult. For exact dates and further information, contact Peak Fairs, Hill Cross, Ashford, Bakewell, Derbyshire DE4 1QL, telephone (062981) 2008.

Merstham, Surrey

(Please also see Dorking, Godalming, and Guildford.)

Harold Williams Bennet & Partners, Auctioneers
Auctions are held monthly on a Thursday at the Village Hall on Station Approach North. Access from by train is to the Merstham station, by car to Exit 7 on M23 (just north of the M25 ring road), then south to the Merstham station. This auction offers all types of items and collectables, as well as household goods. Previews are held the Wednesday before the sale. For information and sale dates, contact Harold Williams Bennett & Partners, 1-3 South Parade, Merstham, Surrey, telephone (07374) 2234.

Middlesbrough, Cleveland

Flea market and collector's fair several times per year on several Saturdays at the Town Hall on Albert Road. This is a large indoor regional fair in an out-of-the-way part of England. All types of antiques, collectables, and bric-a-brac are offered. Parking (charge) is available several blocks east on Corporation Road. Admission is 50p. Access by rail to Middlesbrough, then walk about 200 yards out the front on Albert Street. Exact dates and further information is available from Panda Promotions, 24 Westgate, Honley, Huddersfield, West Yorkshire HD7 2AA, telephone (0484) 666144.

Midhurst, West Sussex

G. Knight & Son Auctions
Auctions are held every two months on a Thursday (call for exact schedule) at the saleroom on Bepton Road, Midhurst. The sales include antiques, reproductions, miscellaneous collectables, and ordinary household items. For information and exact dates, contact G. Knight & Son, West Street, Midhurst, West Sussex, telephone (073081) 2456.

Mundford Near Brandon, Suffolk

Antiques fair first Saturday, Sunday and Monday of May (Bank Holiday) from 10 a.m. to 4 p.m. at Lyford Hall in Mundford, about two miles north of Brandon and five miles northwest of Thetford. This regional fair has about 70 stands, mostly dealers. In the area, follow the yellow AA signs to the fair. Organized by Crown Antiques Fairs, 55 Barton Road, Cambridge, Cambridgeshire CB3 9LG, telephone (0223) 353016.

Nately Scures Near Hook, Hampshire

Antiques fair last Sunday of every month at the Basingstoke Country Hotel on A30 west of Hook. This show has about 40 dealers, mostly of small items including silver, linens, crystal, porcelains, and prints. Organized by Stagecoach Antique Fairs, telephone (0628) 23970.

Newark, Nottinghamshire

Antique & Collectors Fair the last Tuesday of February, second Tuesday of June, third Tuesday of August and last Tuesday of October at the Newark & Nottinghamshire Showground from 8 a.m. (7 a.m. with an antique dealer business card). (1988 dates: 23 February, 7 June, 16 August, 25 October.) More than 1000 stands are at every show, as many as 2000 in October, making these some of the largest one-day shows in Britain. Tens of thousands of visitors crowd the grounds. Access by car: follow yellow AA signs to the free car parking area, or take chartered busses from London (call 01-249 4050 for information). These shows offer shipping services from small consignments to shipping containers. All types of items, including a lot of furniture, are represented at this show. Admission is £2 before 9 a.m., £1 after. Organized by Geoffrey Whitaker Antique Fairs, 25B Portland Street, P.O. Box 100, Newark, Nottinghamshire NG24 1LP, England, (0636) 702326.

Newcastle-upon-Tyne, Tyne and Wear

Tynemouth Flea and Antique Market, held every Saturday from April to October at the Tynemouth Metro station, in Tynemouth, five miles east of the city center. This market is a general market with a fair representation of antiques, bric-a-brac, collectables, and just plain junk. Access by Metro to the Tynemouth station; free parking is available in the area. Organized by Newcastle City Council, Estate & Property Department, Civic Centre, Newcastle-upon-Tyne, Tyne and Wear, telephone (091) 232 8520.

Flea market every other Saturday, year round, at the Guildhall, Quayside, Newcastle-upon-Tyne. This is a general market with good quantities of antiques, bric-a-brac, and other miscellaneous odds and ends. This indoor market is accessible by public transit, but parking in the area is difficult. Information available from the Newcastle City Council, Estate & Property Department,

Civic Centre, Newcastle-upon-Tyne, Tyne and Wear, telephone (091) 232 8520.

"The Gosforth Park Antiques Fair" during the first week in August for four days at Gosforth Park, northeast of the city on the Great North Road. This is one of the major fairs of top-quality antiques in northern England. All types of antiques are offered, including furniture, silver, porcelain and pottery, paintings, and other items. All items are vetted by Phillips and Bonham's experts. The dateline is 1860. Admission is £2.50. Parking is available in the park. For exact dates and further information, contact Robert Bailey Antiques Fair, 1 Roll Gardens, Gants Hill, Ilford, Essex 1G2 6TN, telephone 01-550 5435.

Newcastle-under-Lyme, Staffordshire

Antique and junk market every Tuesday from 8 a.m. until early afternoon in the town center. All types of items are available, with an emphasis on small items. Most markets have from 40 to 70 stands. Information from Alan Kipping, Wonder Whistle Enterprises, 1 Ritson Road, London E8, telephone 01-249 4050.

Antiques Fair one day twice a year at the end of April and beginning of September from 10 a.m. to 5 p.m. at the Sports Centre at Keele University west of the city on A525. This site is also used for crafts fairs. For exact dates and further information, contact the Sports Centre, Keele University, Newcastle-under-Lyme, Staffordshire, telephone (0782) 621111.

Newmarket, Suffolk

(Please also see Bury St. Edmunds and Cambridge.)

"Annual Newmarket Antiques Fair" first Thursday through following Saturday of December at the White Hart Hotel on High Street (hotel telephone (0638) 663051). Only antiques may be shown and all items are sold with a money-back guarantee should they prove other than as described. This is a good regional fair. Admission is charged. Organized by Antiques in Britain Fairs, Hopton Castle, Craven Arms, Shropshire SY7 0QJ, telephone (05474) 356.

Newton Abbot, Devon

"Giant Antiques & Collector's Fair" last Thursday and Friday of March, June, and August at the Racecourse along the river. This is a regional fair. Admission is charged, but parking is free. Organized by West Country Antiques & Crafts Fairs, The Dartmoor Antiques Centre, Off West Street, Ashburton, Devon, telephone (0364) 52182.

Michael J. Bowman, Auctioneer
Auctions are usually held on the third or fourth Friday of every month at 11 a.m., often at the Chudleigh Town Hall. Auctions include antiques and used goods, including appliances(!), books, pictures, glass, ceramics and porcelains, clocks and jewelry, furniture, and miscellaneous items. Catalogues are available before the sale, price 40p. No items can be taken until the sale is over, but all items must be paid for and removed the day of the sale. Buyer's premium is 5%. Bids can be left, mailed, or telephoned, but a banker's reference or deposit may be required. For further information and exact sale dates, contact Michael J. Bowman, Auctioneer, 6 Haccombe House near Netherton, Newton Abbot, Devon TQ12 4SJ, telephone (0626) 872890.

Orsett, Essex

"Bank Holiday Antiques Drive-in and Country Fair" first weekend of May (Bank Holiday) at Orsett Hall near Orsett. Access from A13 east from London to Orsett. Organized by Stephen Charles, Basildon, telephone (0268) 774977.

Northampton, Northamptonshire

"The Castle Ashby Antiques Fair" held one weekend in late August (Friday from 1 to 9 p.m., Saturday from 11 a.m. to 6 p.m., and Sunday from 11 a.m. to 5 p.m.) at Castle Ashby, and Tudor historic home east of the city. Only top-quality antiques are offered, including furniture, silver, porcelain and pottery, paintings, and other items. All items are vetted by experts from BADA or LAPADA. The dateline from is 1885 (furniture) to 1920 (artwork). Admission is £2.50. Access by car on A428. Free parking is available on the grounds. For exact dates and further information, contact Robert Bailey Antiques Fair, 1 Roll Gardens, Gants Hill, Ilford, Essex 1G2 6TN, telephone 01-550 5435.

Norwich, Norfolk

Antiques and collectables market most (but not every) Wednesdays from 9:30 a.m. to 3:30 p.m. in the cloisters at St. Andrews Hall on George Street in the city center. The number of vendors varies; all types of antiques are offered. There is no admission fee, but there is access for the disabled. Parking (pay) is available behind the hall off Elm Hill. For information, contact Mr. A. Bailey, Cloisters Antique Market, St. Andrews Hall, Norwich, Norfolk, telephone (0603) 628477.

"Annual Norwich Antiques Fair" second week of January (1988: Thursday January 7 from 2 to 8 p.m.; Friday from 11 a.m. to 8 p.m., and Saturday from 10:30 a.m. to 5 p.m.) at Blackfriars Hall, St. Andrew's Plain. This fair is a long- established show, where only antiques and items older than the dateline (usually 1899) may be offered. All vendors are dealers. All items are guaranteed, with a money-back guarantee should they not be as represented. Admission is charged. For further information, contact Antiques in Britain Fairs, Hopton Castle, Craven Arms, Shropshire SY7 0QJ, telephone (05474) 356.

Ower, Hampshire

(Please also see Brockenhurst, Lyndhurst, and Southampton.)

Antiques and collectors' fairs one Sunday of every other month (exact day varies) at the New Forest Moat House Hotel on A31 in Ower. This is a small, regional fair. Most items are small; there's not much furniture. The dateline is 1930. Free parking is available on the grounds. For exact dates and further information, contact Kingston Promotions, 157 Plymouth Drive, Hill Head, Fareham, Hampshire PO14 3SN, telephone (0329) 661780.

Oxford, Oxfordshire

Phillips in Oxford
Auctions of all types of antiques and collectors items take place almost every week at 11 a.m. at the salerooms. Sales of Victoriana take place about every three weeks (usually on Tuesday), furniture (usually on first Thursday of every month except January), and paintings, rugs, silver, jewelry, books, and wine at irregular intervals, but usually every three months or so. A free schedule of sales is available upon request. Catalogues are issued before every sale; usual price is £1. Viewing is held the day before for Victoriana sales and for two days before the sale on all other sales from 9 a.m. to 4 p.m. and the day of the sale from 9 to 11 a.m. Bids may be left or made by mail or telephone. The buyer's premium is 10%. All purchases must be paid for and removed within two days. The salerooms are on the west side of Oxford, a few hundred yards toward the city center from the British Rail station. Some free parking is available on the street in front of the saleroom, and more is available (for a charge) at the Car Park at the east end of Park End Street. Sales are held at and further information is available from Phillips in Oxford, 39 Park End Street, Oxford, Oxfordshire OX1 1JD, telephone (0865) 723524.

Par, Cornwall

Phillips in Cornwall
Auctions are held the second Tuesday of every month at 10 a.m. at the saleroom and offices. Auctions are somewhat specialized; for example, many sales consist solely of ceramics. Catalogues are issued several weeks before the sale and usually cost £1. Viewing is held the day before and morning of the sale. Bids may be left, or made by mail or telephone. The buyer's premium is 10%. For further information, contact Phillips in Cornwall, Cornubia Hall, Eastcliffe Road, Par, Cornwall PL24 2AQ, telephone (072681) 4047.

Peterborough, Cambridgeshire

"International Antiques and Collectors' Fair" last Tuesday of September at the East of England Showground along the A1 road. Hundreds of stands inside, plus trucks and outdoor spaces. This large fair is one of the largest fall fairs and has many services, including food, packing and shipping services, and money exchange. Open at 8 a.m. (trade 6.30) to 4 p.m. Admission is £1. Parking is free. Organized by Crown Antiques Fairs, 55 Barton Road, Cambridge, Cambridgeshire CB3 9LG, telephone (0223) 353016.

Petworth, West Sussex

(Please also see Billingshurst.)

"The Seaford College Antiques Fair" New Year's weekend and the first weekend of September at Seaford College near Petworth village. This is a good regional fair of good-quality antiques, including furniture, silver, jewelry, porcelain, paintings and prints, and other items. All items are vetted. The dateline is from 1885 (furniture) to 1920 (paintings and ceramics). Admission is £2.50. Access is only by car. Parking is available at the fair. For exact dates and further information, contact Robert Bailey Antiques Fair, 1 Roll Gardens, Gants Hill, Ilford, Essex 1G2 6TN, telephone 01-550 5435.

Plymouth, Devon

Plymouth flea market every Bank Holiday
Weekend at the Guildhall at Royal Parade and
Armada Way. This is a regional fair with all types
of collectables, some antiques, and a bit of junk.
Admission 35p. Organized by P. Smith, 87
Pembroke Street, Sevon Port, Plymouth,
telephone (0752) 668837. Another organizer uses
this location at irregular but approximately
monthly intervals. For further information, contact A. Robins, Chapel Cottage, Cubert near New-
quay, Cornwall, telephone (0637) 830566. Parking at this location is available in the adjoining
Council Car Park.

Portishead, Avon

(Please also see Bristol and Yatton.)

Antiques and collector's fair at usually on the last
Sunday of five months of the year and Bank
Holiday Monday in May and August from 10 a.m.
(9 a.m. for members of the antiques trade) to 5
p.m. at Somerset hall. This is a local fair, with
some antiques and collectables. Admission is 25p,
but is free to accompanied children. Access from
M5 Junction 19, then on A369 to Portishead. A
large car park is available at the fair. Access by
rail to Portishead, then walk. For further information, contact the organizer at Yatton (0934)
838187.

Portsmouth and Southsea, Hampshire

*(Please also see Botley, Chichester and
Southampton.)*

Antiques and collectors' fair the third Sunday of
March, May, July, September, and November
from 11 a.m. to 6 p.m. at the Guildhall in the city
center. This is a regional fair of antiques and collectables. Admission is 30p, but accompanied
children are free. Access by car to the any of the
car parks in the city center. Access by train to the
Portsmouth station, then walk about 100 yards

south to the Guildhall. (The Tourist Information Centre is also in the Guildhall Square.) For further information, contact Kingston Promotions, 157 Plymouth Drive, Hill Head, Fareham, Hampshire PO14 3SN, telephone (0329) 661 780.

Antiques and collectors' fair the first, second, or (most often) third Sunday of February, April, June, August, October, and December from 11 a.m. to 6 p.m. at the Crest Hotel on Pembroke Road in Southsea, about half a mile east of the Hoverport (hotel telephone (0705) 827651. This is a fair of regional interest. There is a good amount of silver, porcelain, and pottery, but little furniture or other large items. Admission is 30p, but accompanied children are free. Parking is available at or near the hotel. For exact dates and further information, contact Kingston Promotions, 157 Plymouth Drive, Hill Head, Fareham, Hampshire PO14 3SN, telephone (0329) 661 780.

Preston, Lancashire

(Please also see Charnock Richard and Hurst Green.)

"Collector's Market and Boot Sale" every Tuesday and Thursday from 8 a.m. to early afternoon (official closing 4 p.m.) under the old but open-air covered markets in the town center. Up to 300 sellers of used goods and miscellaneous items sell all types of items. No new items are allowed in the Car Boot section of the market. Don't confuse this with the new items on the Monday, Wednesday, Friday, and Saturday market in the same location or the new, adjacent indoor marketplace just to the north! Access by public transit: walk to the City Centre to the Head Post Office. Street parking is difficult or almost impossible, though there are pay car parks on Lancaster Road and Ringway. Organized by Hoyle's Markets, telephone (0153) 725788.

"The Houghton Tower Antiques Fair" first weekend of March and last weekend of December. This is a good- quality regional fair in a relatively depressed area. Only antiques dealers may sell, and all items are vetted. The dateline is from 1885 (furniture) to 1920 (pottery and paintings). Admission is £2.50. Parking is available at the fair. For exact dates and further information, contact Robert Bailey Antiques Fairs, 1 Roll Gardens, Gants Hill, Ilford, Essex 1G2 6TN, telephone 01-550 5435.

Redhill (Near Reigate), Sussex

(Also please see Epsom.)

Antiques and collector's fair the second Sunday of every month from 10 a.m. to 5 p.m. at Lakers Hotel, Redstone Hill, Redhill, Surrey. Access by train to Redhill, or drive. Organized by Ray Ratcliff, telephone 01-764 3602

Retford, Nottinghamshire

(Note: this town is shown on some maps as "East Retford.")

Henry Spencer & Sons Ltd., Fine Art Auctioneers Auctions are held almost every Wednesday, and occasional Tuesdays and Fridays at 10 a.m. at the company's saleroom. A free schedule is available upon request. Most sales are specialized; for example, silver, silver plate, jewelry, and watches, or furniture, or pictures and paintings. Catalogues are issued at least one week before the sale, price from £1 to £3, and by annual subscription. Viewing is held the day before the sale from 10 a.m. to 3 p.m. Bids may be left, mailed, or telephoned. The buyer's premium is 10%. Cars may be parked for £1 per day. Access by train to Retford from Kings Cross in London, then walk to the saleroom. Sales are held at and further information is available from Henry Spencer & Sons Ltd., 20 The Square, Retford, Nottinghamshire DN22 6DJ, telephone (0777) 703331.

Ringwood, Hampshire

Antique and Collectors Fair last Sunday of every month (except June, July, and August) from 10:30 to 5 p.m. at the Crown Hotel. This small regional fair of approximately 20 stands offers small antiques and bric-a-brac. Parking is free; admission is 20p. Organized by Linda Forster, Forest Fairs, 28 Glenwood Road, West Moors, Dorset, telephone (0202) 875167.

Antique and collectors' fair on Easter Monday, Spring Bank Holiday (last Monday of May), August Bank Holiday Monday (last Monday of August) at the Avon Country Club. This is a moderately sized regional fair with antiques and collectables. The dateline is around 1930, but this is not always monitored by the organizers. For further information, contact Kingston Promotions, 157 Plymouth Drive, Hill Head, Fareham, Hampshire PO14 3SN, telephone (0329) 661780.

Ripon, North Yorkshire

Flea market and collector's fair on several Sundays (about six to eight weeks apart) from 9:30 a.m. to 5 p.m. at the racecourse southeast of town on B6265. This is a large regional fair, offering all types of collectables. Admission is 50p. Exact dates and further information is available from Panda Promotions, 24 Westgate, Honley, Huddersfield, West Yorkshire HD7 2AA, telephone (0484) 666144.

Romford, Essex

(Please also see London.)

Antique market as part of a gigantic market held on Wednesday, Friday, and especially Saturday from early morning until mid afternoon at the Market Place. This large market draws people from a large area. The general market is held in the Market Place, but the antiques market is held on North Street, outside the main market area. Dealers offer antiques, bric-a- brac, and reproductions in abundance. Access by car from London on A12. Parking is available in four large car parks. Access by British Rail to Romford Station from Bethnal Green, or bus lines 66, 66A, 248, and 252.

Rotherham, South Yorkshire

Flea market and collector's market on several Saturdays from 9:30 a.m. to 5 p.m. at Clifton Hall. This is a regional fair with all types of items. Admission is 50p. Exact dates and further information is available from Panda Promotions, 24 Westgate, Honley, Huddersfield, West Yorkshire, HD7 2AA telephone (0484) 666144.

"The Ridings Antiques and Interior Design Fair" the third weekend of September (Friday 11 a.m. to 8 p.m., Saturday and Sunday 11 a.m. to 6 p.m.) at Wentworth House, a palatial 18th-century stately home. This is a very good regional antiques fair. All items are vetted. The dateline is 1880, though a very few more recent pieces are accepted. Access by car on M1 to Junction 35, then north on local roads to Wentworth House. Free parking is available on the grounds. Nearest rail station is three miles away in Rotherham. For further information and exact sale dates, contact Robert Soper, Castle Fairs, Bowcliffe Road, Bramham, Wetherby, North Yorkshire LS23 9JS, telephone (0937) 845829.

Royal Tunbridge Wells, Kent

(Please see Tunbridge Wells, Kent.)

Rye, East Sussex

Vidler & Company, Auction & Estate Offices
Auctions of antiques and fine art are held the first Friday of each month at 10 a.m. Previews are held the afternoon before the sale from 1 to 6 p.m. The sales are held at the Rye Auction Galleries, Cinque Ports Street. For information, contact Vidler & Company Auction & Estate Offices, Cinque Ports Street, Rye, East Sussex, telephone (0797) 222124.

St. Ives, Cambridgeshire

(Please also see Huntingdon.)

Antiques and collectors' fair several holidays and weekends (January 1 and 2, Easter Sunday and Monday, both May Bank Holidays, August Bank Holiday Sunday and Monday, and the last weekend of November, most days from 11 a.m. to 5 p.m.) at St. Ivo recreation center (telephone (0480) 63028). These are good regional fairs. All types of collectables and other items are offered. The dateline is 1930. Admission is 50p, but free to the antiques trade. Parking is available nearby. Organized by Herridge's Antiques & Collectors Fairs, Tickencote Mill, Tickencote near Stamford, Lincolnshire PE9 4AE, telephone (0780) 57163.

Prudential Fine Arts Auctioneers
Antique Auctions are held every four weeks on Tuesday at 10 a.m.; previews are held the Saturday before the sale from 9 a.m. until noon, and Monday from 9 a.m. to 5 p.m. Catalogues are issued and usually cost £1. Auctions include all types of antiques, including silver, paintings, furniture, glass, and ceramics. There are also sales of household items and used items every other Saturday at 10 a.m.; no catalogues are issued and viewing is the morning of the sale from 9 a.m. There is no buyer's premium. Bids may be left or mailed but must be in writing. No personal cheques are accepted without a bank guarantee or a credit card. Sales are held at and further information is available from Prudential Fine Arts Auctioneers, St. Ives Auction Rooms, The Market, St. Ives, Huntingdon, Cambridgeshire PE17 4JA, telephone (0480) 68144.

Salisbury, Wiltshire

Antique market every Tuesday in the hall of the United Reformed Church in Fisherton Street only a few blocks from the famed cathedral. This market is as much a rummage sale as an antique market; therefore, finds can be made, but lots of uninteresting items must be looked at as well. Parking is available in the car park north of the church, more easily accessible from Churchill Way West.

"Salisbury Summer Antiques Fair" the third weekend of June from 11 a.m. until 8 p.m. at the Red Lion Hotel on Milford Street in the city center. This is a good regional fair. Parking may be very difficult. Organized by Antiques in Britain Fairs, Hopton Castle, Craven Arms, Shropshire SY7 0QJ, telephone (05474) 356.

Sandwich, Kent

(Please also see Deal.)

Riverside Annual Bank Holiday Boot Fair, held on Bank Holiday Monday from 10 a.m. to 5 p.m. at Gazen Salts. This is a large regional boot fair. Admission is 25p per person. Thousands of cars can be parked in the nearby lot. Organized by East Kent Fairs, 201 London Road, Dover, Kent CT17 0TF, telephone (0304) 201644.

Sawbridgeworth, Hertfordshire

(Please also see Epping, Harlow, Hatfield, Hertford, and Ware.)

Antiques and collectors' fair four Sundays per year (second Sunday of February, May, September, November, but subject to change) from 10:30 a.m. to 5 p.m. at the Memorial Hall. This is a local fair, with about 60 dealers of antiques, collectables, and other odds and ends. Admission is 50p. Parking is available near the hall. For further information, contact Bartholomew Fayres, Executive House, The Maltings, Station Road, Sawbridgeworth, Hertfordshire CM21 9JX, telephone (0279) 725809.

Sevenoaks, Kent

Parsons, Welch, & Cowell, Auctioneers
Fine arts and antique auctions are held every six
weeks on Wednesdays at the Argyle Salerooms,
Argyle Road, Sevenoaks. Each sale contains
about 1000 lots. Buyers premium is 10%. For further information, contact Parsons, Welch, &
Cowell, 49 London Road, Sevenoaks, Kent,
telephone (0732) 451211.

Sheffield, South Yorkshire

Flea market and collector's fair several Saturdays
per year from 9:30 a.m. to 5 p.m. at Roxy's Disco.
All types of antiques and collectables are offered
at this indoor fair, for which admission is
charged. Over 150 vendors usually offer their
goods. Admission is 50p. Exact dates and further
information is available from Panda Promotions,
24   Westgate,   Honley,   Huddersfield,   West
Yorkshire HD7 2AA, telephone (0484) 666144.

Shepton Mallet, Somerset

(Please also see Wells.)

"Antiques Drive-in and Collectors Fairs" usually
last weekend of July from 10 a.m. to 5 p.m., third
Tuesday of July from 8 a.m. to 4 p.m. and second
weekend of November (third weekend in 1988)
from 10 a.m. to 5 p.m at the Royal Bath & West
Showground south of the town on A371. These
are good indoor regional fairs, with all types of
antiques and collectables. Dateline is 1930. Admission is £1, free to members of the antiques
trade. Free parking is available on the grounds,
but this fair is not accessible by public transit. Organized by Ms. A. Stroud, Merlin Fairs, Will o'
the Wisp, Moorland Near Bridgwater, Somerset,
telephone (027869) 616.

Sherborne, Dorset

Phillips in Sherborne
Auctions are held every other Tuesday at 10 a.m.
at the salerooms. Each auctions is a specialized
category, such as "Victorian Furniture,"
"Ceramics," or "Victoriana." A catalog is
published several weeks before each sale, and
usually costs £1 to £2. Viewing is held the day
before the sale and on the morning of the sale.
Bids may be left, mailed, or telephoned. The
bidder's premium is 10%. For further information, contact Phillips in Sherborne, Long Street
Sale Rooms, Long Street, Sherborne, Dorset DT9
3BS, telephone (0935) 815271.

Shrewsbury, Shropshire

"Annual Shropshire Antiques Fair" second Tuesday through Thursday of February from 11 a.m.
to 9 p.m. at the Lion Hotel, Wyle Cop (hotel
telephone (0743) 52107). Only antiques (dateline
1890) may be sold and all purchases carry a
money-back guarantee of authenticity. Admission is charged. This is a well-established antiques fair. Organized by Antiques in Britain Fairs,
Hopton Castle, Craven Arms, Shropshire SY7
0QJ, telephone (05474) 356.

"The Lord Hill Hotel Antiques Fair" the second
weekend of September (Friday from 1 to 9 p.m.,
Saturday from 11 a.m. to 6 p.m., and Sunday
from 11 a.m. to 5 p.m.) at the Lord Hill Hotel, 131
Abbey Foregate (hotel telephone (0743) 52601).
This is a good quality regional fair. Only antiques
may be sold and all items are vetted. The dateline
is from 1885 (furniture) to 1920 (paintings and
pottery). Admission is £2.50. Access to the hotel
by car on A49, which is Abbey Foregate. Parking
is available at the hotel. Access by train is to
Shrewsbury Station, and take a taxi. Organized
by Robert Bailey Antique Fairs, 1 Roll Gardens,
Gants Hill, Ilford, Essex IG2 6TN, telephone 01-
550 5435.

Southampton, Hampshire

(Please also see Winchester.)

"Annual Stamp and Postcard Fair" first Sunday of May from 11 a.m. to 5 p.m. at Southampton Guildhall. This is the largest stamp and postcard fair in the region, with more than 60 vendors. Free parking is available next door in the car park. For further information, contact Rom Emmott Productions, 2 Fourways, Church Hill, West End, Southampton, Hampshire SO3 3AU, telephone (0703) 474862.

"Special Summer Antique Event" second Sunday of June from 11 a.m. to 5 p.m. at Southampton Guildhall. This is a large indoor event with antiques of all types, including silver, brass, clocks, porcelain and pottery, and other items, but not much furniture. Admission is 35p. Free parking is available next door in the Car Park. For further information, contact Rom Emmott Productions, 2 Fourways, Church Hill, West End, Southampton, Hampshire SO3 3AU, telephone (0703) 474862.

"Antique and Bric-a-Brac Marquee" first weekend of July (Friday, Saturday, Sunday) from on the Southampton Common about one mile north of the city center on The Avenue. This is a large regional fair, with hundreds of vendors of antiques, collectables, and just bric-a-brac and junk. Parking is available nearby. For further information, contact Rom Emmott Productions, 2 Fourways, Church Hill, West End, Southampton, Hampshire SO3 3AU, telephone (0703) 474862.

"Collectorama" second Sunday of October from 11 a.m. to 5 p.m. at Southampton Guildhall. This is an event for collectors of all types of things, from antiques to corkscrews. Admission is 35p. Parking is available next door in the Car Park. For further information, contact Rom Emmott Productions, 2 Fourways, Church Hill, West End, Southampton, Hampshire SO3 3AU, telephone (0703) 474862.

Stafford, Staffordshire

Antique and collector's fairs held six times per year (Good Friday through Easter Monday, first weekend of July, third weekend of August, first weekend of October, third Wednesday of October, and second weekend of December) from 9:30 a.m. to 4 p.m. at Bingley Hall at the Country Showground near Junction 14 on the M6 motorway. These are large regional fairs, with between 300 and 350 vendors at each, and as many as 500 for the Wednesday sale in October. All types of items are available, except that the one-day shows don't have much large furniture. The dateline is 1930; new items and reproductions are prohibited. Admission is £1, or 50p for people over 65. Shipping company representatives are available at these fairs. Access by car on motorway M6 to Junction 14, then to the Showgrounds. A large free car park is on the showgrounds. This fair is not easily accessible by public transport. Organized by Bowman Antiques Fairs, P.O. Box 37, Otley, West Yorkshire LS21 3AD, telephone (0943) 465782 or (0532) 843333.

Stamford, Lincolnshire

"Antiques and Collectors' Fair" second Saturday and Sunday of April, third Saturday and Sunday of August, and last Saturday and Sunday of October (Saturday from 10 a.m. to 5 p.m. and Sunday from 11 a.m. to 5 p.m.) at the Stamford Boys School. This is a good regional fair, with all types of small antiques and collectables. The dateline is 1930. Admission is 50p, but free to members of the antiques trade. Organized by Herridge's Antiques and Collectors Fairs, Tickencote Mill, Tickencote near Stamford, Lincolnshire PE9 4AE, telephone (0780) 57163.

Stockport, Cheshire

(Please also see Manchester.)

Burlings St. Mary's Auction Rooms
Auctions are held every other Tuesday at 11 a.m. at the Auction Rooms. Auctions include antiques,

secondhand goods, and bric-a-brac of all types. Viewing is Monday before the sale from noon to 7 p.m. Buyer's premium is 10% including VAT. Free parking is available on the site. Access by train to Disley rail station. Sales are held at and further information is available from Andrew McCann, Burlings St. Mary's Auction Rooms, Buxton Old Road, Disley, Stockport, Cheshire SK12 2BB, telephone (0663) 64854.

Stockbridge, Hampshire

(Please also see Salisbury.)

"Antique and Collector's Fair" occasionally on Saturday from 2 p.m. to 6 p.m. at Marsh Court School. This is a very small local sale, with 15 to 20 stands. Free parking is available. Organized by Linda Forster, Forest Fairs, 28 Glenwood Road, West Moors, Dorset, telephone (0202) 875167.

Stratford-upon-Avon, Warwickshire

Colliers, Bigwood, & Bewlay, Auctioneers
Auctions are held every Monday at 11 a.m. at the salerooms. These sales are specialized: silver, furniture, and books are some categories. Catalogues are issued in advance of all sales and cost £1. Viewing is held the two days before each sale from 9 a.m. to 5:30 p.m. Sales are held at and further information is available from Colliers, Bigwood, & Bewlay, The Old School, Tiddington, Stratford-upon-Avon, Warwickshire CV37 7AW, telephone (0789) 69415.

Stretford, Greater Manchester

(Please also see Manchester.)

Antiques fair first Friday, Saturday, and Sunday of May (Bank Holiday) at the Stretford Sports Centre, near Exit 7 of the M63 motorway, along Chester Road, A5067. Organized by Dualco Promotions, telephone (061) 766 2012.

Sudbury, Suffolk

Antiques fair second Saturday and Sunday of May at the Sudbury Town Hall. Follow the yellow AA signs to the fair. Organized by Crown Antiques Fairs, 55 Barton Road, Cambridge, Cambridgeshire CB3 9LG, telephone (0223) 353016.

Swindon, Wiltshire

Allen & Harris—The Planks Salerooms
Auctions of used items and other odds and ends, including quantities of furniture, are held every Saturday at 10 a.m. The last Thursday of every month, an antique and collector's auction is held at 10:30 a.m. Viewing for all sales is held on the day before the sale from 1 to 7 p.m. Catalogues are available (usually £1) for antique and collector's sales only. A free schedule of all auctions is available upon request. Bids may be left, mailed, or telephoned if you're known to the auctioneers. Buyer's premium is 5%. Items must be paid for and removed by 4 p.m. on the day of the sale. The auction rooms are in the center of the Old Town; parking is available across the street in a car park. Information is available from and sales are held at the Planks Salerooms, Old Town, Swindon, Wiltshire SN3 1QP, telephone (0793) 615915.

Tatton Hall Near Knutsford, Cheshire

"The Tatton Park Antiques Fair" first week of October at Tatton Park (a historic house). On most days, the fair is open from 11 a.m. to 9 p.m. This is a good regional fair, with approximately 120 dealers. This fair prohibits new work and reproductions. Access by car: M6 to Junction 19, then follow yellow AA signs to the fair. Parking is available on site. Organized by Robert Bailey Antiques Fairs, 1 Roll Gardens, Gants Hill, Ilford, Essex IG2 6TN, telephone 01-550 5435.

Tenterden, Kent

Butler & Hatch Waterman, The County Group, Auctioneers
The second Thursday of most months, this auction house sells between 500 and 700 lots of antiques of all types, including furniture, silver, and other miscellaneous items. The auction room is behind the firm's offices. Previews are held the Sunday from 10:30 to 4 p.m. and Tuesday from 9:30 a.m. to 4 p.m. before the sales. Catalogues are sold (price varies), available the Friday before the sale. Mail bids and left bids may be made. Information is available from and sales are held at the County Group, Auctioneers, 102 High Street, Tenterden, Kent, telephone (05806) 3233.

Tisbury, Wiltshire

(Please also see Billingshurst and Petworth.)

"The New Wardour Castle Antiques Fair" the second weekend of August (Friday from 1 to 9 p.m., Saturday from 11 a.m. to 6 p.m., and Sunday from 11 a.m. to 5 p.m.) at this country estate. This is a good quality fair. Only antiques may be sold and all items are vetted. The dateline is from 1885 (furniture) to 1920 (paintings and pottery). Admission is £2.50. Parking is available at the hotel. Access by train to Tisbury Station. Organized by Robert Bailey Antique Fairs, 1 Roll Gardens, Gants Hill, Ilford, Essex IG2 6TN, telephone 01-550 5435.

Tonbridge, Kent

(Please also see Sevenoaks and Royal Tunbridge Wells.)

"The Penshurst Place Antiques Fair" late in March on a weekend (Friday from 1 to 9 p.m., Saturday from 11 a.m. to 6 p.m., and Sunday from 11 a.m. to 5 p.m.) at the historic 14th-century historic house (telephone (0892) 870307). This is a good quality regional fair. Only antiques may be sold and all items are vetted. The dateline is from 1885 (furniture) to 1920 (paintings and pottery). Admission is £2.50. Access to the house by car east of Tonbrige on B2027. Parking is available at the hotel. Access by train is to Penshurst Station, and walk half a mile to the fair. Organized by Robert Bailey Antique Fairs, 1 Roll Gardens, Gants Hill, Ilford, Essex IG2 6TN, telephone 01-550 5435.

Torquay, Devon

Antiques and collectors fair the first Sunday of every month at the Belgrave Hotel on Seafront (hotel telephone (0803) 28566). These are regularly held regional fairs. All vendors are dealers. Admission is charged. Organized by Westfairs, P.O. Box 43, Weston-super-Mare, Avon BS23 2DS, telephone (0934) 33596.

Bearnes Auctioneers & Valuers
Auctions are held two or three times per month, either on Wednesdays or Thursdays, beginning at 10:30 a.m. "precisely," at the saleroom and offices. Auctions consist of specialized items, such as paintings and prints, jewelry and silver and silver plate, furniture and miscellaneous items, or ceramics and glass. A free schedule of sales is available upon request. Catalogues are issued several weeks before the sale, cost from £1 to £3. Viewing is held the three (business) days before the sale from 10 a.m. to 5 p.m. and the morning of the sale. Bids may be left, or made by mail or telephone. The buyer's premium is 10%. All purchases must be paid for and removed within two working days of the sale, but no purchases can be taken until the end of the sale. Access by car is on A380 from Newton Abbot. On Avenue Road, take the second right past the Torre Station, and then go to "Rainbow," which is at the end of the road. Free parking is available at the salerooms. Access by train to Torquay Station, then left along Falkland Road to Avenue Road, then left past Mill Lane. (While it can be walked, it is much quicker by taxi.) For exact schedule and further information, contact Bearnes Auctioneers & Valuers, Rainbow, Avenue Road, Torquay, Devon TQ2 5TG, telephone (0803) 26277.

Tring, Hertfordshire

Brown & Merry Ltd., Auctioneers
Auctions are held twice monthly on Saturdays at 10 a.m. at the Saleroom, Castle Market, Brook Street, Tring. All types of items are offered, including antiques, silver, porcelain, painting, furniture, and used goods that are not antique. Formal catalogues aren't issued, but printed sheets of items are available a few days before the auction. Viewing is the Friday before the sale from 2 to 6 p.m. and Saturday from 8:30 until the sale begins. Bids may be made by telephone if you leave your name, address, and a telephone number where you can be reached. Payment must be made by Monday after the sale. Free parking is available at the site. Further information and exact sale dates are available from Brown & Merry Ltd., 41 High Street, Tring, Hertfordshire HP23 5AP, telephone (044282) 6446.

Truro, Cornwall

Antiques and collectors' fairs in mid-August and first Thursday, Friday, and Saturday of October at the conference hall in City Hall. Hours on the first day are 2 to 8 p.m., other days 10 a.m. to 5 p.m. This is a local fair, but sometimes interesting pieces surface. All vendors are dealers. Organized by West Country Antiques & Crafts Fairs, The Dartmoor Antiques Centre, Off West Street, Ashburton, Devon, telephone (0364) 52182.

Tunbridge Wells, Kent

Bracketts Auctions
Weekly auctions are held on Friday at the Royal Sussex Assembly Rooms, The Pantiles, Tunbridge Wells. All types of items are sold in rapid succession, many for only a few pounds. Both antiques and modern items are sold. Previews are held Thursday and early Friday morning before the sale. For information contact Bracketts, 27-29 High Street, Tunbridge Wells, Kent, telephone (0892) 33733.

Messrs. Geering & Coyer, Auctioneers
Every two months, always on a Wednesday, this
firm auctions off more than 400 lots of fine art, including painting, sculpture, prints, and similar
items. Since this is a specialized auction house,
no other items are offered. Previews and sales are
held at the Crest Hotel, Crowborough (telephone
(08926) 2772). For information and catalogues,
contact Messrs. Geering & Coyer, 22-24 High
Street, Tunbridge Wells, telephone (0892) 25136.

Wakefield, Kent

"Ceramics Fair" first weekend of May (Bank
Holiday) at the Greenway on London Road (A20),
West Malling, about two miles west of Maidstone.
Ceramics and glass only, all before 1920. About
50 dealers from all over Britain sell at this fair,
which is one of the largest for ceramics and glass.
An expert identification service is available. Ad-
mission to the public is £1. Organized by
Wakefield Antiques Fairs, 1 Fountain Road, Rede
Court, Rochester, Kent, telephone (0634) 723461.

Wallington, Surrey

(Please also see Croydon and London.)

Two Missionary Auctions
Auctions are held the last two Thursday and
Friday of many months at 7:30 p.m. at Crusader
Hall, Stanley Park Road. Though these sales are
somewhat smaller than many others, they are of
interest because held in the evening. They offer
jewelry, silver, clocks, and other antiques and collectables. Viewing is held the Wednesday evening
prior to the sale, and all day Thursday.
Catalogues are available several days before the
sale, and cost 25p. For further information, contact Two Missionary Auctions, telephone 01-647
8437.

Waltham Abbey, Essex

(Please also see Epping, Harlow, Hatfield, Hertford, London, and Loughton.)

Antiques and collectors fair five Sundays of the year (usually second Sunday of April, June, August, October, and November, but check with the organizer) from 10:30 a.m. to 5 p.m. at Waltham Abbey Town Hall, on Highbridge Street. This fair is a local fair, with about fifty vendors of all types of small antiques and collectables, but little furniture. Admission is 40p, children 20p, but the fair is free to members of the antiques trade. The fair is signposted from Junction 25 of the M5 Orbital Motorway. Parking is available, not all free. Access is more difficult by public transport: train to Cheshunt, then a long walk to Waltham Abbey. For further information, contact Bartholomew Fayres, Executive House, The Maltings, Station Road, Sawbridgeworth, Hertfordshire CM21 9JX, telephone (0279) 725809.

Ware, Hertfordshire

(Please also see Epping, Hatfield, Hertford, Waltham Abbey, and Ware.

"Fanhams Halls & Gardens Fair" first Friday, Saturday, and Sunday of May (Bank Holiday) from 11 a.m. to 5 p.m.; the trade is admitted from 10 a.m. (card or other proof required). Held at Fanhams Hall in the town. Antiques and collectors items, none from after 1930. Access by A10 north from London, and follow yellow AA signs in the area, or by rail to Ware. Organized by Chilterns Fairs, Chorleywood, telephone (0928) 2144.

Wareham, Dorset

Antique fair four times a year on Sunday from 10 a.m. to 5 p.m. at Springfield Country Hotel on Grange Road (hotel telephone (09295) 2177). This is a small local antique indoor fair. Admission is

20p. Free parking is available at the hotel. For exact fair dates and further information contact Mrs. S.J. Lunn, Flat 2, Stanton Court, 11 Greenhill, Weymouth, Dorset DT4 7SW, telephone (0205) 789193.

S.W. Cottee & Son, Auctioneers

Auction every other Tuesday at the Wareham Markets Sale Rooms on East Street in the town center. This country auction offers various used goods and antiques, but auctions are not further specialized. No catalogues are issued; inspection is the day before the sale from 1 to 5 and 6 to 8 p.m. and immediately before the sale. You can mail leave bids, but cannot bid by telephone. There is no buyer's premium. Access by car or train to Wareham. Organized by S.W. Cottee & Son, Wareham Markets Sale Rooms, East Street, Wareham, Dorset BH20 4AF, telephone (09295) 2826.

Wells, Somerset

(Please also see Shepton Mallet.)

Antique and collectors fair held the last Saturday of every other month from 9 a.m. to 5 p.m. at the Wells Town Hall. These are small, local fairs, offering collectables and antiques. Admission is free. Organized by Tony Weekes, Pickwick Fairs, Shepton Mallet, telephone (0749) 3595 (evenings only).

Weston-super-Mare, Avon

(Please also see Bristol and Portishead.)

Lalonde Fine Art Auctioneers

Auctions are held every other Tuesday at 11 a.m. at the auctioneer's officers on Station Road. All types of antiques, collectables, and used goods are offered, including furniture, miscellaneous items, and some silver. A free calendar of auctions is available upon request. Catalogues are issued (price usually £1) about two weeks before the sale. Bids may be left, mailed, or made by telephone. The buyer's premium is 10%. Sales are held at and further information is available from Lalonde Fine Art Auctioneers, Station Road, Weston-super-Mare, Avon BS23 1XU, telephone (0934) 331 74.

Weymouth, Dorset

(Please also see Abbotsbury.)

"Antique Fair at Moonfleet" every two months on a Sunday at the Moonfleet Manor Hotel near Weymouth. This is a small regional fair of antiques and collectables. Admission is 20p. Free parking is available at the hotel. For exact fair dates and further information, contact Mrs. S.J. Lunn, Flat 2, Stanton Court, 11 Greenhill, Weymouth, Dorset DT4 7SW, telephone (0205) 789193.

Whitton, Middlesex

Antique and collectors fair first Wednesday of every month year round from 10 a.m. to 4 p.m. and third Sunday of every month from 11 a.m. to 5 pm. at the Winning Post on Great Chertsey Road (A 316). Approximately 40 to 50 stalls of odds and ends and some local dealers. Admission is 15p. Information from Magna Carta Country Fayres, Slough, telephone (0753) 685098.

Winchester, Hampshire

(Please also see Southampton and Stockbridge.)

"Collectors Spring Fair" second Sunday of May and "Collectors Autumn Festival" from 11 a.m. to 5 p.m. at Winchester Guildhall near the Cathedral on The Broadway. Antiques and collector's items, such as porcelain, gold, silver, brass, coins, stamps, linen and lace are offered, with the exception of large furniture. This large regional show includes three halls. No modern items or reproductions may be shown or sold. Admission is 40p. This organizer occasionally uses this hall for other, irregularly held antiques fairs. Parking is available next to the Guildhall. For further information, contact Ron Emmott Productions, 2 Fourways, Church Hill, West End, Southampton, Hampshire SO3 3AU, telephone (0703) 474862.

Windsor, Berkshire

(Please also see Ascot.)

Antiques and collectables fair every Saturday from March through October from 8 a.m. to mid afternoon on Thames Avenue at River Street. This fair takes place inside and outside, and offers about 40 vendors of all types of antiques and collectables, but there are few if any large items. An overflow market sometimes takes place along the river, but there is little of interest in this part. Street parking is difficult in the immediate area, but a car park is across the street and a block away at Riverside Station. Access by train to Windsor Central Station, and walk toward the river.

Wisbech, Cambridgeshire

"Annual Fenland Antiques Fair" last Thursday through Saturday of May, usually from 11 a.m. to 8 p.m. at Isle College (telephone (0945) 582561. This is a relatively new fair. All vendors are antiques dealers, who offer a money-back guarantee on all purchases. Organized by Antiques in Britain Fairs, Hopton Castle, Craven Arms, Shropshire SY7 0QJ, telephone (05474) 356.

Woking, Surrey

(Please also see Godalming and Guildford.)

Barbers Fine Art Auctioneers Ltd.
Auctions are held approximately every five weeks on Monday at 11 a.m. at the auctioneer's offices at The Mayford Centre. Auctions include all types of antiques, including silver, carpets, furniture, por-

celain, glass, and other items. Viewing is held the Saturday and Sunday before the sale from 10 a.m. to 5 p.m. The buyer's premium is 10%. Bids may be left, mailed, or made by telephone. Access by public transit is by train to Woking, then by taxi. Access by car is on A320 to Smarts Heath Road, then left into Mayford Centre. Free parking is available on the site. Sales are held at and further information is available from Barbers Fine Art Auctioneers Ltd., The Mayford Centre, Smarts Heath Road, Mayford Green, Woking, Surrey GU22 0PP, telephone (04862) 28939.

Wolverhampton, West Midlands

(Please also see Birmingham and Wombourne.)

"Wolverhampton Antiques, Crafts, and Collectors' Market" held every Tuesday, Wednesday, Friday, and Saturday at the Market Halls in the city center. Approximately 20 to 50 dealers and collectors of all types of items are present. Parking is available in the Council Car Park for 40p per day. Access by rail to Wolverhampton High Level Station and walk. Organized by the Wolverhampton Markets Department, 1st Floor, Heantun House, Salop Street, Wolverhampton, West Midlands WV3 0SH, telephone (0902) 21571 and 2675.

Wombourne, West Midlands

(Please also see Wolverhampton.)

Antique fair every second Sunday of many (but not all) month from 10 a.m. to 5 p.m. at the Wombourne Community Centre, in the town center. Parking is available on surrounding streets. This is a small, local fair, with not more than 40 vendors. Organized by Waverly Fairs, Boreley Cottage, Boreley Nr. Ombersley, Worcestershire, telephone (0205) 620697.

Woodbridge, Suffolk

(Please also see Ipswich.)

Neal Sons & Fletcher
Auctions are held from time to time on Wednesday at 11 a.m. at the Theatre Street Saleroom. Catalogues are issued for all antiques sales, and usually cost £2. Viewing is held the Tuesday before the sale from 11:15 a.m to 4:30 p.m. and 6:30 to 8 p.m. For further information, contact Neal Sons & Fletcher, 26 Church Street, Woodbridge, Suffolk, telephone (03943) 2263.

Woodford Green, Essex

(Please also see Epping, London, Loughton, and Waltham Abbey.)

Antique and collectors fair held the second Saturday of April and December from 11 a.m. to 5 p.m. at the Sir James Hawkey Hall, Broadmead Road. This is a local fair of about 80 dealers of small antiques, bric-a-brac, and collectables. A small admission fee is charged, but entry is free to members of the antiques trade. Access by car from London to Woodford on A121 (High Road) to Broadmead Road. Access by bus on line 275 and by British Rail from Liverpool Street Station to Woodford Station. For further information, contact Bartholomew Fayres, Executive House, The Maltings, Station Road, Sawbridgeworth, Hertfordshire CM21 9JX, telephone (0279) 725809.

Worcester, Hereford & Worcester

Andrew Grant, Fine Art Auctioneers
Auctions are held six times per year at 11:30 a.m. at the Grandstand, Worcester Racecourse, north of the city on A449. Auctions include all types of antiques and collectables, including sterling, jewelry, books, glass, paintings and drawings, glass, porcelain, pottery, and furniture. Catalogues are issued two weeks before the sale;

usual price is £2. Viewing is the day before the sale from 3 to 7 p.m. and two hours before the sale begins. There is no buyer's premium. Bids can be left, mailed, or telephoned, but a 25% deposit may be required. All items must be paid for and removed on the day of the sale. Payment can be made while the auction is still in progress.

Access by car to the racecourse on A38, then toward the river on Castle Street. Park on the site. Access by train to Foregate Station, Worcester, then walk to the racecourse on Foregate and Castle Street. For further information, contact the auctioneer at the office: Andrew Grant, Fine Art Auctioneers, 59/60 Forgate Street, Worcester, Hereford & Worcester, telephone (0205) 52310. On sale dates, call (0905) 25970.

Worthing, West Sussex

(Please also see Brighton.)

Worthing Antiques Fair, first Wednesday of every other month from June to December from 8 a.m. to 2:30 p.m. at the Worthing Pier Pavilion on the shore. This local fair usually has about 60 vendors. Free to members of the antiques trade, 30p to others. Parking available on the street, about a half mile south of the Central Rail Station. Organized by Mostyn Fairs, 64 Brighton Road, Lancing, Sussex, telephone (0903) 752961.

F. H. Ellis & Sons, Auctioneers
Auctions are held three Mondays per month (usually first, third, and fourth, though this can vary) at the auctioneer's office. Each sale consists of a miscellaneous collection of about 400 lots of all types. Previews are held the Saturday before the sale. Sales site and further information are available from F. H. Ellis & Sons, 44-46 High Street, Worthing, West Sussex, telephone (0903) 38999.

Fox & Sons Worthing Auction Galleries
Auctions are held some Tuesdays (check for schedule) at the galleries. Sales consist of about 400 lots of various modern and antique furniture,

and whatever else is brought in. Previews take place Saturday morning and Monday before the sale. Sales site and further information are available from Fox & Sons, 31 Chatsworth Road, Worthing, West Sussex, telephone (0903) 205565.

Yatton, Avon

Antique and bric-a-brac fair the last Saturday of every month from 10 a.m. to 4 p.m. at the Yatton Village Hall. This is a small local fair. For further information, contact the organizer at Yatton (0934) 833629.

York, North Yorkshire

Flea market and collector's fair several times a year (often last Saturday of the month) from 9:30 a.m. to 5 p.m. at the Racecourse Grandstand about one mile south of the railway station between Bishopsgate Road and Tadcaster Road (A1036). This is a regional fair with up to several hundred vendors of all types of items. Admission is 50p. Exact dates and further information is available from Panda Promotions, 24 Westgate, Honley, Huddersfield, West Yorkshire HD7 2AA, telephone (0484) 666144.

"Annual York Antiques Fair" held the last Thursday through Saturday of October from 11 a.m. to 8 p.m. and "York Summer Antiques Fair" last Thursday through Saturday of June from 11 a.m. to 8 p.m. at the Assembly Rooms in Blake Street (hall telephone (0904) 24604). These are long- established, high-quality regional fairs. Only dealers may sell, and all items sold carry a money-back guarantee of authenticity. Admission is charged. Parking is very difficult, since this is inside the old walled city. For further information, contact Antiques in Britain Fairs, Hopton Castle, Craven Arms, Shropshire SY7 0QJ, telephone (05474) 356.

"York Antiques Centre" is a building full of antiques dealers open Monday through Saturday at 2 Lendal in York.

Markets, Fairs, and Auctions in Scotland

Aberdeen, Aberdeen

"Annual Aberdeen Antiques Fair" is a long- established regional fair, held in mid May at the Amatola Hotel on Great Western Road (check organizer for exact date). Items offered, all older than 1890, are mostly small items, with little furniture. All items purchased at this fair have a money-back guarantee if not as described. Organized by Antiques in Britain Fairs, Hopton Castle, Craven Arms, Shropshire SY7 0QJ, telephone (05474) 356.

Edinburgh, Lothian

(Please also see Queensferry.)

"Ingliston Saturday Market" held every Saturday from dawn or 6 a.m. (whichever is earlier) at Ingliston Field, about five miles east of Edinburgh on A8. This large open-air market is held adjacent to the airport. A large (approximately 40-foot) painted gorilla is found on the grounds, and is visible from the road. This market has large quantities of new items. In many ways Ingliston resembles a street market, with clothes and new items, but there is also lots of junk and collectables. Parking is available on the grounds, for which a fixed fee is charged. Access by bus to Ingliston.

"Edinburgh Antiques Fair" several times a year, usually the last Thursday through Saturday week of April, July, and November from 11 a.m. to 8 p.m. at the Roxburghe Hotel, 38 Charlotte Square (telephone (031) 225 3921). Be sure to confirm dates and times! Only dealers may sell, and offer various items from before 1890. All purchases are guaranteed to be as described. Organized by Antiques in Britain Fairs, Hopton Castle, Craven Arms, Shropshire SY7 0QJ, telephone (05474) 356.

Phillips Scotland, Fine Art Auctioneers
Auctions of household and used goods are held
every Thursday and many Fridays at 11 a.m. at
the offices and sale rooms. No catalogues are issued for these sales. Other auctions are specialized sales, such as "Silver & Plate," "Coins," "Furniture," "Oil Paintings," etc. Catalogues are issued for all except weekly household goods sales
at least one week before the sale, price usually £1,
but for special sales can cost as much as £3. Viewing is held the day before and morning of the sale.
Bids may be left, mailed, or telephoned. The
buyer's premium is 10%. Street parking
(metered) is difficult but available, and a parking
structure is found at St. James Centre a few
blocks away. Access by train to Waverley Station
and walk up to the north one block past Princes
Street, then left on George Street. Sales are held
at and further information is available from Phillips Scotland, Fine Art Auctioneers, 65 George
Street, Edinburgh, Lothian EH2 2JL, telephone
(031) 225 2266.

Glasgow, Strathclyde

(Please also see Edinburgh and Hamilton.)

"The Barrows," also called "The Barras," every
weekend from just after dawn in summer (or 6
a.m. in winter) until mid afternoon in the market
area between London Road and Gallowgate. This
is a large outdoor and indoor general market,
with a large number of vendors of collectables,
junk, and antiques. The antiques and collectables
tend to be on the eastern part of the fair. Several
blocks are closed off for the day. Some old
warehouse buildings have been converted into
halls of antique dealers. This market has one of
the best potentials for making finds in all of
Britain. Parking is difficult on market days but
can be found on the streets to the west and east.
A few vacant lots are turned into car parks for the
weekend; a fee is charged.

Christie's and Edmiston's Ltd.

The Scottish branch of Christie's holds frequent sales of all types of antiques and collectables. A schedule of sales is available on request. Catalogues are published for important sales and cost from £1 to £3. Sales are held at and further information is available from Christie's and Edmiston's Ltd., 164-166 Bath Street, Glasgow, telephone (041) 332 8134.

Phillips Scotland, Fine Art Auctioneers

Auctions are held every Tuesday at 10 a.m. and include antiques, silver, porcelain, painting, furniture (both antique and contemporary), carpets, and sculpture at the sale rooms in central Glasgow. In addition, several times a month, specialized sales are held of items including paintings, silver, jewelry, dolls, etc. A schedule of sales is free upon request. Catalogues are issued at least one week before each sale, price usually £1. Viewing is the day before the Tuesday sales from 9 a.m. to 5 p.m. and the morning of the sale, and two days before every special sale from 9 a.m. to 5 p.m. Buyer's premium is 10%. Payment must be made and all items removed by the end of the second working day after the sale. Bids may be left, mailed, or telephoned. Parking is available at 50p. Access by public transit is by bus or train to Queen Street Station or Central Station and walk. Sales are held at and further information is available from Phillips Fine Art Auctioneers, 207 Bath Street, Glasgow G2 4HD, telephone (041) 221 8377.

Sotheby's Scotland

Auctions are held frequently at the offices and salerooms. Sales are specialized into categories. Catalogues are issued about two weeks before each sale and usually cost £1. Viewing is held the day before the sale and the morning of the sale. A free schedule of sales is available upon request. Bids may be left, mailed or telephoned. The buyer's premium is 10%. Sales are held at and further information is available from Sotheby's Auctioneers, 146 West Regent Street, Glasgow G2, telephone (041) 221 4817.

Hamilton, Strathclyde

L.S. Smellie & Son, Auctioneers
Every Monday at 10 a.m. all types of items are
auctioned in no particular order. This is very
much a country sale, with all types of used goods
and items, and antiques scattered in. Items such
as used toasters and children's toys are sold as
well as Victorian cases, silver and silver plate,
and all other types of items. Easily portable items
are sold before the furniture. Several dealers find
much of their stock at this auction. No catalogues
are issued. Viewing takes place the morning of
the sale. Payment must be made the day of the
sale and all items must be removed within two
days. Sales are held at the salerooms, about half
a mile west of the city center at Cattlemarket,
Aucthingramont Road, Hamilton, Strathclyde,
telephone (0698) 282007.

Inverness, Highland

"Highlands Antiques Fair" the first week of
August (usually midweek but can vary) from 11
a.m. to 8 p.m. at the Caledonian Hotel. This is a
small regional fair, but quality is good. Only
dealers can show, and the dateline is 1890. Organized by Antiques in Britain Fairs, Hopton
Castle, Craven Arms, Shropshire SY7 0QJ,
telephone (05474) 356.

Kelso, Borders

Antiques fair twice a year (May Bank Holiday
Sunday and Monday and third weekend of Oc-
tober) at the Ednam House Hotel on Bridge
Street (hotel telephone (0573) 24168). This is a
small, local fair in an out-of-the-way corner of
Scotland. Free parking is available. Organized by
Borough Fairs, 83 Hunstanton Road, Old
Hunstanton, Norfolk, telephone (04853) 33732.

"The Scottish Antiques and Interior Design Fair"
the second weekend of October (Friday 11 a.m. to
8 p.m., Saturday and Sunday 11 a.m. to 6 p.m.) at
Hopetoun House, an excellent early 18th-century
stately home, which Robert Adam remodelled.

This is one of the best Scottish regional antiques fairs. All items are vetted. The dateline is 1880, though a very few more recent pieces are accepted. Access by car on M9 to Junction 2, then east on A904 and local roads to Hopetoun House. Free parking is available on the grounds. Nearest rail station is three miles east in Queensferry. For further information and exact sale dates, contact Robert Soper, Castle Fairs, Bowcliffe Road, Bramham, Wetherby, North Yorkshire LS23 9JS, telephone (0937) 845829.

Perth, Tayside

"Perthshire Antiques Fair" the first weekend of October from 11 a.m. to 8 p.m. at the Station Hotel, Leonard Street across the street from the rail station. Organized by Antiques in Britain Fairs, Hopton Castle, Craven Arms, Shropshire SY7 0QJ, telephone (05474) 356.

Markets, Fairs, and Auctions in Northern Ireland

Belfast, County Antrim

"St. George's Variety Market" every Tuesday and Friday from 7 a.m. to 3 p.m. (more vendors on Friday) is held on May Street (Postal District BT1). All types of bric-a-brac, junk, and new and used items are sold in a flea market atmosphere.

"Belfast Antiques Market" open most Saturdays from 10 a.m. to 5 p.m. an indoor private market offering furniture, small items, and bric-a-brac. The market is located at 126 Donegal Pass, Belfast, County Antrim BT7 1BZ, telephone (0232) 247372.

Antiques and collectables fair held the first Saturday of every month from 10:30 a.m. to 4 p.m. at the organizer's hall. For a schedule and further information, contact Antiques & Collectables Fairs, Hinghan Hall, 13 Botanic Avenue, Belfast, County Antrim BT7 1JG, telephone (0238) 528428.

"May Day Antiques Fair" the first of May at the Conway Hotel, 6 miles south on A1 (hotel telephone 0232) 612101. This is a local antiques fair with all types of small items. Admission is charged. Free parking is available at the hotel. Organized by Mrs. Winifred Bell, Johnston House, 14 Derriaghy Road, Lisburn, telephone (0846) 624412.

"Great Victoria Carousel" is a regular indoor building full of little antiques stands open Tuesday through Saturday from 11 a.m. to 5:30 p.m. Items offered include some furniture, bric-a-brac, books, paintings, and other odds and ends. The "Great Victoria Carousel" is located at 69a Great Victoria Street, Belfast, County Antrim BT2 7AF, telephone (0232) 230215.

Anderson's Auction Rooms
Auctions are held most Wednesdays at 11 a.m. at
the offices and salerooms. Items sold include furniture, jewelry, and other miscellaneous items.
Many items are Victorian or more recent. Viewing is held Tuesday from 9 a.m. to 8 p.m., and
Wednesday before the sale. Sales are held at and
more information is available from Anderson's
Auction Rooms, 28 Linenhall Street, Belfast,
County Antrim BT2 8BG, telephone (0232)
221401.

Kennedy Wolfenden, Fine Art Auctioneers
Auctions are held approximately every two
months at the auctioneer's salerooms and offices.
Items sold include furniture, silver, porcelain,
and jewelry. For auction schedule and catalogues,
contact Kennedy Wolfenden, Fine Art Auctioneers, 218 Lisburn Road, Belfast, County
Antrim BT9 6GD, telephone (0232) 681775.

Osborne King and Megran Auctions
Auctions are held quarterly, usually on the last
Wednesday of a month at the Gallery, Gilford
Castle, Gilford postal district BT63. Items include
fine arts, furniture, and various types of antiques
including silver. Catalogues are issued before the
sale; minimum price is £1. For exact sale dates
and further information, contact Osborne King
and Megran, 17 Castle Arcade, Gilford, BT63,
telephone (0232) 240332.

Boardmills, County Down

Temple Auctions
Auctions are held every other Saturday beginning at 11 a.m. at firm's salerooms and offices.
Items sold include all types of fine arts and antiques. Viewing is on Friday from 9 a.m. to 9 p.m.
and Saturday before the sale begins. For further
information and exact sale dates contact Temple
Auctions, 133 Carryduff Road, Boardmills,
Liburn, County Down BT27 6YL, telephone
(084663) 777.

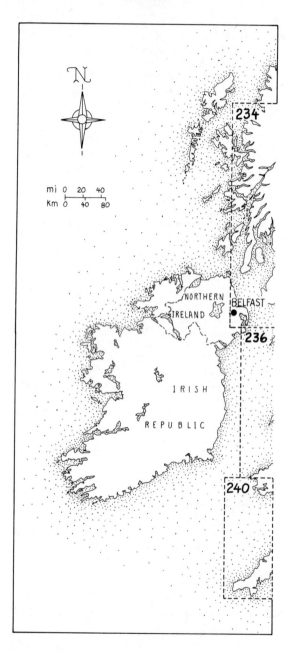

N

mi 0 20 40
Km 0 40 80

234

NORTHERN
IRELAND

BELFAST

236

IRISH

REPUBLIC

240

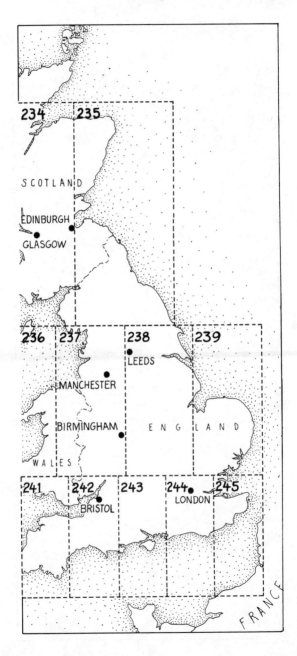

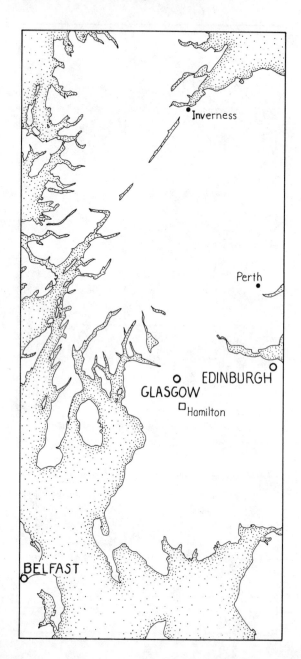

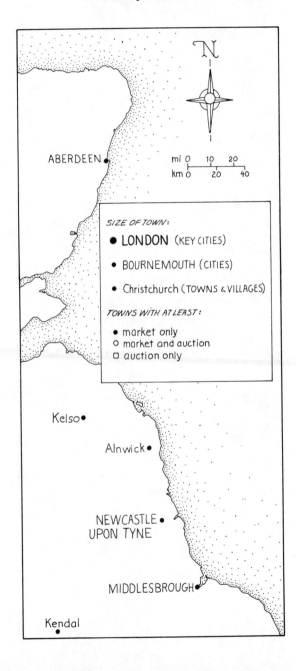

SIZE OF TOWN:

● **LONDON** (KEY CITIES)

● BOURNEMOUTH (CITIES)

● Christchurch (TOWNS & VILLAGES)

TOWNS WITH AT LEAST:

● market only
○ market and auction
□ auction only

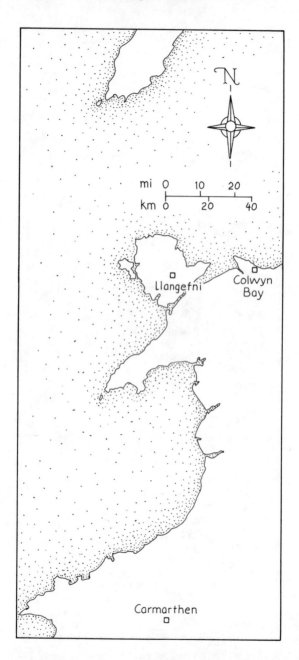

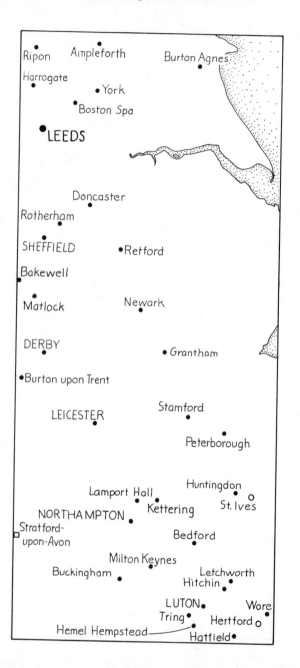

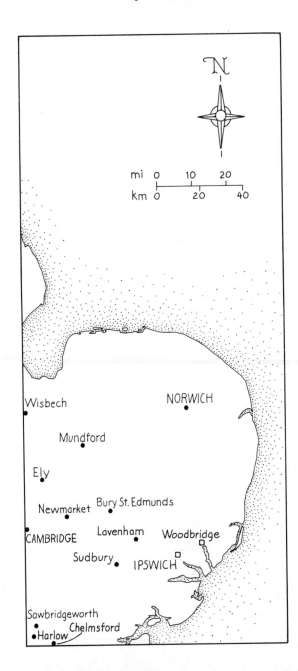

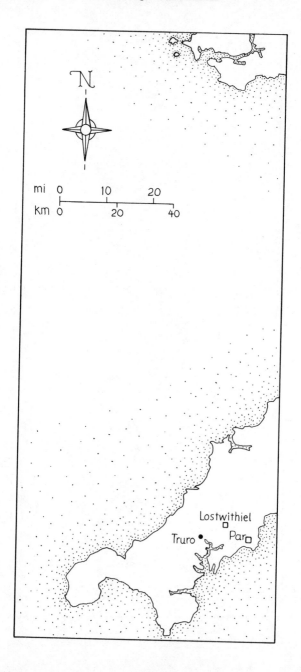

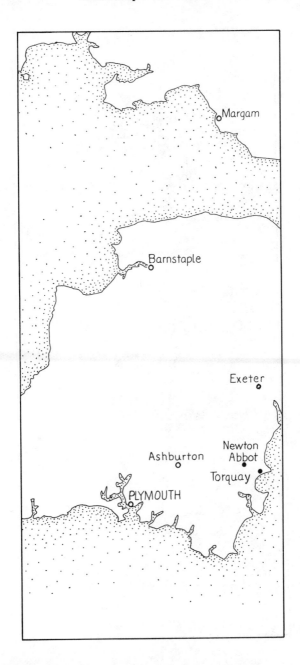

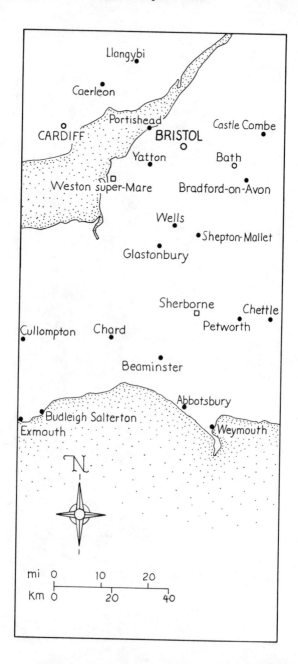

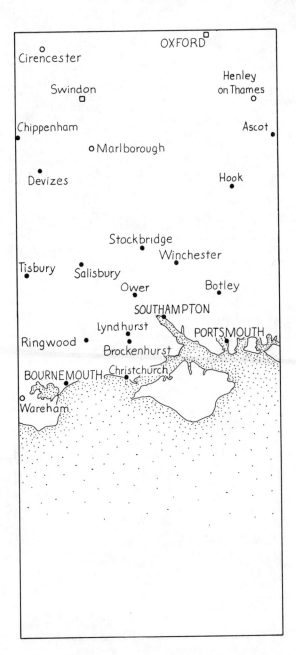

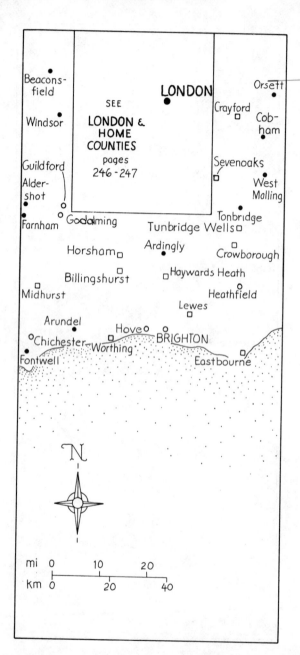

Beacons-field
Windsor

SEE
LONDON & **HOME COUNTIES**
pages
246-247

LONDON
Crayford
Orsett
Cob-ham

Guildford
Alder-shot
Farnham
Godalming
Sevenoaks
West Malling

Horsham
Tunbridge Wells
Ardingly
Tonbridge
Crowborough

Midhurst
Billingshurst
Haywards Heath
Heathfield

Arundel
Chichester
Worthing
Hove
BRIGHTON
Lewes
Fontwell
Eastbourne

N

mi 0   10   20
km 0   20   40

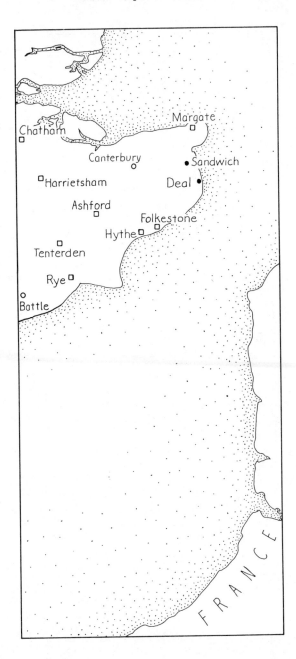

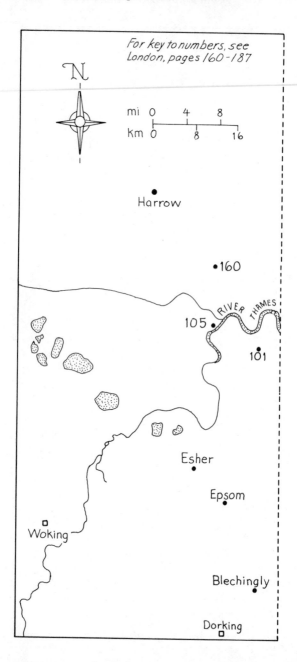

For key to numbers, see
London, pages 160-187

N

mi 0   4   8
km 0   8   16

Harrow

•160

105 • RIVER THAMES

101

Esher

Epsom

Woking

Blechingly

Dorking

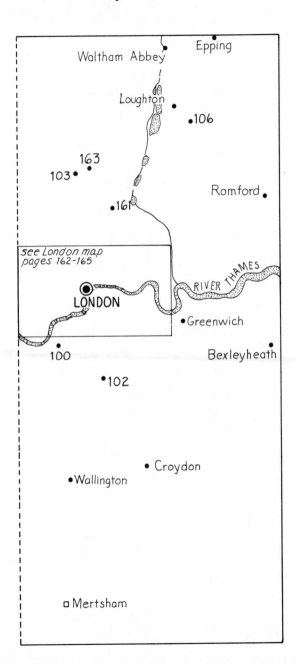

Epping

Waltham Abbey

Loughton •

•106

163
103 •

•161

see London map
pages 162-165

RIVER THAMES

LONDON

•Greenwich

Romford •

100 •

Bexleyheath •

•102

• Croydon

•Wallington

▢ Mertsham

Organizers of Fairs and Markets

Organizers Without Mailing Addresses

Bagatelle Fairs, London, telephone 01-391-2339

Anne Campbell-Macinnes, Bath, telephone (0225) 63727

M & S Fairs, London, telephone 01-440 2330

Bray Enterprises, telephone (0883) 42561

Centre Crafts, telephone (0923) 46559

Stephen Charles, Basildon, telephone (0268) 774977

Chilterns Fairs, telephone (0928) 2144

Dualco Promotions, (Manchester area) telephone (061) 766 2012

Gamlins Exhibition Services, telephone (045) 285 2557

Granny's Attic Antique Fairs, Marlow, telephone (06284) 3658

Christina Page Fairs, telephone (0223) 211736

Hallmark Antique Fairs, Keynsham, telephone (02756) 3795

Mr. Holley, Stalbridge, telephone (0963) 62478

Jubilee Antiques Fairs, London, telephone 01-989 8693

Libra Hall Fairs, telephone (0633) 422489

Magna Carta Country Fayres, Slough, telephone (0753) 685098

Marlborough Oxfam Committee, Marlborough, telephone (0672) 20871

Midas Fairs, Beaconsfield, telephone (04946) 4170

M & S Fairs, London, telephone 01-440 2330

Prestige Promotions, telephone (0533) 56045

Tony Weekes, Pickwick Fairs, Shepton Mallet, telephone (0749) 3595

Ray Ratcliff, London, telephone 01-764 3602

Somerset & Avon Antique Fairs, telephone (0278) 784912

Stagecoach Antique Fairs, telephone (0628) 23790

Fair Organizer, London, telephone 01-657 7414

Fair Organizer, telephone (0423) 770385

Fair Organizer, Yatton, telephone (0934) 833629

Organizers With Mailing Addresses

ABC, 15 Flood St., Chelsea, London SW3, England, telephone 01-351 5353

A.K. Fairs, 693 Stratford Road, Shirley, Solihull, West Midlands, England, telephone (021) 744 4385

Anglian Arts & Antiques, Linthorpe House, Station Road, Halesworth, Suffolk, England, telephone (09867) 2368

Antiques & Collectables Fairs, Hinghan Hall, 13 Botanic Avenue, Belfast, County Antrim BT7 1JG, Northern Ireland, telephone (0238) 528428

Tony Keniston, Antiques in Britain Fairs, Hopton Castle, Craven Arms, Shropshire Y7 0QJ, England, telephone (05474) 356

Antiques and Collectors Club, P.O. Box 14, Horley, Surrey, England, telephone (0293) 772206

Antiques Forum Antiques Fairs, Flat 2—197 Maida Vale, London W9, England, telephone 01-624 3214

A.J. Barrett Fairs, Glenroy, Paynes Lane, Nazeing, Essex, England, telephone (0992) 460929

Antiques & Collectors Fairs, 17 Elm Close, Yatton Nr. Bristol, Avon, England, telephone (0934) 838187

Robert Bailey Antiques Fairs, 1 Roll Gardens, Gants Hill, Ilford, Essex IG2 6TN, England, telephone 01-550 5435

Jenny Scott, Bartholomew Fayres, The Maltings, Station Road, Sawbridgeworth, Hertfordshire CM21 9JX, England, telephone (0279) 725809

Mrs. Winifred Bell, Antique and Collectors Fairs, Johnston House, 14 Derriaghy Road, Lisburn, Northern Ireland, telephone (0846) 624412

Mrs. Irene Poulter, Borough Fairs, 83 Old Hunstanton Road, Old Hunstanton, Norfolk, England, telephone (04853) 2122

Miss Helen Bowman, Bowman Antique Fairs, P.O. Box 37, Otley, West Yorkshire LS21 1RA, England, telephone (0532) 843333 or (0943) 465782

British International Antiques Fair, Exhibitions & Events Division, National Exhibition Centre, Birmingham B40 1NT, England, telephone (021) 780 4171

Canterbury City Council Amenities Department, Council Offices, Military Road, Canterbury, Kent, England, telephone (0277) 51755 extension 389

Robert Soper, Castle Fairs, Bowcliff Road, Bramham Near Weatherby, North Yorkshire LS23 9JS, England, telephone (0937) 845829

Century Antiques Fair Ltd., 58 Mill Lane, London NW6 1N3, England, telephone 01-794 3551

Crown Antiques Fairs, 55 Barton Road, Cambridge, Cambridgeshire CB3 9LG, England, telephone (0223) 353016

Roger Heath-Bullock, Cultural Exhibitions Ltd., 8 Meadrow, Godalming, Surrey GU7 3HN, England, telephone (04868) 22562

Mr. R.F.J. Peck, Darent Antiques & Collectors Fairs, Whitestacks, Crockenhill Lane, Eynsford, Kent, England, telephone (0322) 863383

East Kent Fairs, 201 London Road, Dover, Kent CT17 0TF, England, telephone (0304) 201644

Ron Emmott, Ron Emmott Promotions, 2 Fourways, Church Hill, West End Southampton, Hampshire SO3 3AU, England, telephone (0703) 474862

E & M Enterprises, 28 Nutbush Drive, Northfield, Birmingham B31 5SJ, England, telephone (021) 477 3143

Mrs. K. Crisp, Evergreen Promotions, 118 Main Road, Cleeve, Bristol, Avon BS19 4PN, England, telephone (0934) 833629

Falcon Fairs, Capp House, 96a Southend, Croyden, Surrey CR9 3SD, England

Linda Forster, Forest Fairs, 28 Glenwood Road, West Moors, Dorset, England, telephone (0202) 875167

Ken Graves Fairs, 75 Princes Avenue, Hedon, Hull, Humberside, England, telephone (0482) 896854

Bob Harris & Sons, 2071 Coventry Road, Sheldon, Birmingham, England, telephone (021) 743-2259

Herridges Fairs, Tickencote Mill, Tickencote Nr Stamford, Lincolnshire PE9 4AE, England, telephone (0780) 57163

Heritage Antiques Fairs Harvey (Management Services) Ltd., P.O Box 149, London W9 1QN, England, telephone 01-624 1787

Hitchin Market Office, 22 Churchgate, Hitchin Hertfordshire, England, telephone (0462) 56202

Brian Haughton—Organizer, International Ceramics Fair, 38 Burlington Gardens, Old Bond Street, London W1X 1LE, England, telephone 01-734 5491

IPM Promotions, 2 Frederick Gardens, Brighton BN1 4TB, England

Doug Burnell-Higgs, Isca Fairs, 10 Norman Street, Caerleon, Gwent, Wales, telephone (0633) 421527

K.M. Fairs, 58 Mill Lane, London NW6 1NJ, England, telephone 01-794 3551.

James Quigley, Kingston Promotions, 157 Plymouth Drive, Hill Head, Fareham, Hampshire PO14 3SN, England, telephone (0329) 661780

Mrs. S.J. Lunn, Lunn Antiques Fairs, Flat 2, Stanton Court, 11 Greenhill, Weymouth, Dorset DT4 7SW, England, telephone (0305) 789193

Mrs. L. Smith, Marlborough Oxfam Committee, 27 Oxford Street, Ramsbury, Marlborough, Wiltshire, England, telephone (0672) 20871

Maridale Antique & Collectors Fairs, 9 Mill Ridge, Edgware, Middlesex, England, telephone 01-958 8354

Bob Hopwood, Miniatura, 41 Eastbourne Avenue, Hodge Hill, Birmingham B34 6AR, England, telephone (021) 783 2070

Merlin Fairs, Will o'the Wisp, Moorland Nr. Bridgwater, Somerset, England, telephone (027869) 616

London House, King Street, Hammersmith, London W6 9LZ, England, telephone 01-741 8011

Shirley Mostyn, Mostyn Fairs, 64 Brighton Road, Lancing, Surrey, England, telephone (0903) 752961

The National Crafts Fair, 69 Church Road, Richmond, Surrey, England, telephone 01-940 4608

Panda Promotions, 24 Westgate, Honley, Huddersfield, West Yorkshire HD7 2AA, telephone (0484) 666144

Nepicar Farm Boot Fairs, Wrotham Heath, Sevenoaks, Kent TN15 7SR, England, telephone (0732) 883040

The Park Lane Hotel Antiques Fair, London House, 271-273 King Street, London W6 9LZ, telephone 01-741 8011

Ralph Paulett, Peak Fairs, Hill Cross, Ashford, Bakewell, Derbyshire DE4 1QL, England, telephone (062981) 2008

Mrs. Caroline Penman—Director, Penman Fairs, Cockhaise Mill— Lindfield, Haywards Heath, West Sussex, (Mail to P.O. Box 114, Haywards Heath, West Sussex RH16 2YU, England), telephone (04447) 2514

Philbeach Events Ltd., Earls Court Exhibitions Centre, Warwick Road, London SW5, England, telephone 01-385 1200

Ms. Linda Berkman, Pig & Whistle Promotions, 53 Muswell Ave., London N10, 2EH England, telephone 01-883 7061 and 01-249 4050

Antony Porters Fleamarkets, Whitegates, Netherton, Huddersfield, Yorkshire, England, telephone (0484) 662429

Ms. Lorna Quick, Quick Fairs, 6 Post Office Lane, Glemsford, Sudbury, Suffolk, England, telephone (0787) 281855

Sherman & Waterman Association Ltd., 12/13 Henrietta Street, Covent Gardens, London WC2 8LH, England, telephone 01-240 7405/6

Silhouette Fairs, 25 Donnington Square, Newbury, Berkshire, England, telephone (0635) 44338

The Somerset & Avon Antiques Fairs Ltd., P.O. Box 15, Burnham-on-Sea, Somerset, England, telephone (0278) 784912

Step in Exhibitions, 105 Warwick Road, London SW5, England, telephone 01-370 1267

Ms. A. Stroud, Will o' the Wisp, Moorland Near Bridgwater, Somerset, England, telephone (0278) 69616

Taunton Antique Center, 27-29 Silver Street, Taunton, Somerset, England, telephone (0823) 89377

Top Hat Exhibitions Ltd., 66 Derby Road, Notting ham, Nottinghamshire, England

Treasure House Antiques Market, Crown Lane, Arundel, West Sussex, England, telephone (0903) 883101

Patrick Smith, Upper Gardner Street Traders Association, 47 Hove Park Way, Hove BN3, telephone (0273) 505560

Unicorn Fairs, P.O. Box 30, Hereford & Worcester HE2 8SW, England, telephone (098) 987339

Wakefield Antiques Fairs, 1 Fountain Road, Rede Court, Rochester, Kent, England, telephone (0634) 723461

Waverly Fairs, Boreley Cottage, Boreley Nr. Ombersley, Worcester, England, telephone (0205) 620697

West Country Antiques & Crafts Fairs, The Dartmoor Antiques Centre, Off West Street, Ashburton, Devon, England, telephone (0364) 52182

Westfairs, P.O. Box 43, Weston-super-Mare, Avon BS23 2DS, England, telephone (0934) 33596

Geoffrey Whitaker, Antique Fairs, 25B Portland Street, P.O. Box 100, Newark, Nottinghamshire NG24 1LP, England, telephone (0636) 702326

Keith Atkins, General Manager, Wolverhampton Markets Department, Salop Street, Wolverhampton WV3 0SH, England, (0902) 21571 or 26528

Alan Kipping, Wonder Whistle Enterprises, 1 Ritson Road, London E8, England, telephone 01-249 4050

Auctioneers

All of these auction houses have sales of antiques and collectables. Auction schedules and sales are usually available upon request.

Abridge Auction Rooms, Market Place, Abridge, Essex, England, telephone 01-849 2107

Alberts Auction, Farm Buildings, Maiden Lane, Crayford, Kent DA12 4LX, England, telephone (0322) 528868

Aldrige's, 130 Walcot Street, Bath   Avon BA1 5BS, England, telephone (0225) 52839

George Allen, Tudor Salesrooms, 28 High Street, Carcroft, Doncaster, South Yorkshire, England, telephone (0302) 725029

Allen & Harris, The Planks, Old Town Swindon, Wiltshire SN3 1QP, England, telephone (0793) 615915

Allman Auctions, 10 Middle Row, Chipping Norton, Oxfordshire OX7 5NH, England, telephone (0608) 3087

Ambrose Auctions, 149 High Road, Loughton, Essex ILG10 4LZ, England

Anderson's Auction Rooms, 28 Linenhall Street, Belfast, County Antrim BT2 8BG, Northern Ireland, telephone (0232) 221401

The Auction Rooms & Furniture Warehouse, 101 Hoe Street, Walthamstow, London E17, England, telephone 01-520 3215

Edward Bailey & Son, 17 Northgate, Newark, Nottinghamshire NG24 1EX, England

Bainbridges Auctioneers and Valuers, St. Johns Yard, St. Johns Parade, Mattock Lane, Ealing, London W13, telephone 01-579 2966

Ball & Boyd, 17 Madoc Street, Llandudno, Gwynedd, Wales, telephone (0492) 77239

Barbers Fine Arts Auctioneers Ltd., The Mayford Centre, Smarts Heath Road, Mayford Green, Woking, Surrey GU22 0PP, England, telephone (04862) 28939

Bearnes Auctioneers & Valuers, Rainbow, Avenue Road, Torquay, Devon TQ2 5TG, England, telephone (0803) 26277

Bell Court Auction Rooms, 67 High Street, Bidford-on-Avon, Warwickshire, England, telephone (0789) 772611

Berkeleys of Brentwood, 45 North Road, Brentwood, Essex, England, telephone (0277) 224599

Biddle & Webb, Ladywood, Middleway, Birmingham B16 0PP, England, telephone (021) 455 8042

Bloomsbury Book Auctions, 3/4 Hardwick Street, London EC1R 4RY, England 01-833 2636

Bonhams, Montpelier Galleries, Montpelier Street, London SW7 1HH, England, telephone 01-584 9161

Bonhams Chelsea, 65-69 Lots Road, London SW10 0RN, England, telephone 01-351 0466

Bonsor Penningtons, 82 Eden Street, Kingston-upon-Thames, Surrey KT1 1DY, England

Boulton & Cooper Ltd., St Michaels House, Malton, North Yorkshire YO17 OLR, England

Michael J. Bowman, Redstone Lodge, 3 Shiplay Lane, Torquay, Devon, England

Brown & Merry, 41 High Street, Tring, Hertfordshire HP23 5AB, England, telephone (044282) 6446

William H. Brown Auctions, Westgate Hall, Westgate, Grantham, Lincolnshire, England, telephone (0476) 68861

Burling Wilson, St. Mary's Auction Rooms, Buxton Old Road, Disley, Stockport SK12 2BB, England, telephone (0663) 64854

Burstow & Hewett, Abbey Auction Galleries, Lower Lake, Battle, East Sussex TN33 0A7, England, telephone (04246) 2374 or 2302

Butler & Hatch Waterman, 102 High Street, Tenterden, Kent, England, telephone (05806) 3233

Capes Dunn Auction Galleries, 38 Charles Street, Manchester M1 7DB, England, telephone (061) 273 1911

Christie's & Edmistons, 164-166 Bath Street, Glasgow G2 4TG, Scotland, telephone (041) 332 8134

Christie's, 8 King Street, St. James, London SW1Y 6QT, England, telephone 01-839 9060

Christie's South Kensington, 85 Old Brompton Road, London SW7 3LD, England, telephone 01-581 3933

Clarke & Le Quesne, 3 Victoria Road, Coventry, West Midlands, England, telephone (0203) 23377

Cobbs Burrows & Day, 39/41 Bank Street, Ashford, Kent, England, telephone (0233) 24321

Colliers Bigwood & Bewlay Auctioneers & Valuers Ltd., The Old School, Tiddington, Stratford-upon-Avon Warwickshire CV37 7AW, England, telephone (0789) 69415

Comins, 3 Chequer Lane, Ely, Cambridgeshire CB7 4LW, England, telephone (0353) 58141

Cooper Hirst, Goldlay House, Parkway, Chelmsford, Essex CM2 7PR, England, telephone (0245) 58141

S.W. Cottee & Son, Wareham Markets Sale Rooms, East Street, Wareham, Dorset BH20 4AF, England, telephone (09295) 2826

Dacre Son & Hartley, 1-5 The Grove, Ilkley, West Yorkshire LS29 9HS, England, telephone (0943) 600655

Dee & Atkinson, The Exchange, Driffield YO25 7LD, England, telephone (0377) 43151

A. E. Dowse & Son, Scotland Street, Sheffield S3 7DE, England, telephone (0742) 25858

Dowell Lloyd & Co., 118 Putney Bridge Road, London SW15, England, telephone 01-788 7777

Eddisons Auctions, 4/6 High Street, Huddersfield, West Yorkshire, England

H. Evans & Sons, 1 Parliament Street, Hull, Humberside, England

Henry Duke & Son, 40 South Street, Dorchester, Dorset, England, telephone (0305) 65080

Elliott & Green, The Auction Sale Room, Emsworth Road, Lymington, Hampshire, England, telephone (0590) 52310

Fellows & Sons, Bedford House, 88 Hagley Road, Edgbaston, Birmingham B16, England

John Francis Auctions, King Street, Carmarthen Dyffed, Wales, telephone (0267) 233456

Andrew Grant, 59/60 Foregate Street, Worcester, Hereford & Worcester, England, telephone (0205) 52310

Geering & Colyer, 22-24 High Street, Tunbridge Wells, Kent, England, telephone (0892) 25136

Glendining & Company, 7 Blenheim Street, New Bond Street, London W1Y 9LD, telephone 01-493 2445

Gorridges Auction Galleries, 15 North Street, East Sussex, telephone (0273) 472503

Grays Auction Rooms, Alfred Street, Grays, Essex, England, telephone (0375) 31181

Graves Son & Pilcher Fine Arts, 71 Church Road, Hove, East Sussex BN3 2GL, England, telephone (0273) 735266

Hanbury Williams Auctions, 34 Church Street, Cromer, NR27 9ES, England

Hatton Garden Auctions Ltd, 36 Hatton Garden, London EC1 HP, England, telephone 01-405 0511

Heathcote Ball & Co., Castle Auction Rooms, 78 St. Nicholas Circle, Leicester LE1 5NW, England

Hobbs & Chambers, At the Sign of the Bell—Market Place, Cirencester, Gloustershire, England, telephone (0285) 4736

Holloway's, 49 Parsons Street, Banbury, Oxfordshire OX16 8PF, England, telephone (0295) 53197

Hothersall Forrest McKenna & Son, Bank Salerooms, Clitheroe, Lancashire, England

James of Norwich, 33 Timberhill, Norwich NR1 3LA, England, telephone (0603) 24817

Kennedy Wolfenden, 218 Lisburne Road, Belfast, County Antrim BT9 6GD, telephone (0232) 681775

Kent Sales, Kent House, 4 New Road, South Darenth Kent, England

Lacy Scott Fine Art Auctioneers, Risbygate Street, Bury St. Edmunds, Suffolk, England

Lalonde Fine Arts Auctions, Bristol Auction Rooms, Oakfield Road, Bristol, Avon BS8 2BE, England, telephone (0272) 734052

Lawrence of Crewkerne, South Street, Crewkerne, Somerset TA18 8AB, England, telephone (0460) 73041

Lefevre & Partners, 80 Grosvenor Street, London W1X 9DE, England, telephone 01-408 0578

Leigh Auction Rooms, 88-90 Pall Mall, Leigh-on-Sea, Essex SS0 1RG, England

Lewes Auction Rooms, 66 High Street, Lewes, East Sussex, England, telephone (0273) 478221

Locke & England, Walton House, The Parade, Leamington Spa, Warwickshire, England, telephone (0926) 27988

London Bridge Auctions, 6 Park Street, London SE1, England, telephone 01-407 9577

Lots Road Chelsea Auction Galleries, 71 Lots Road Chelsea, London SW10 0RN, England, telephone 01-531 7771 or 01- 351 5784

Loves of Perth, South St. Johns Place, Perth, Tayside PH1 5TB, Scotland

Lowery's, 24 Bridge Street, Northampton, Northamptonshire NN1 1NT, England

Frank R. Marshall & Co., Church Hill, Knutsford, Cheshire, England, telephone (0565) 41872

Michael Matthews Auctions, Dowell Street, Honiton, Devon, England, telephone (0404) 41872

Messenger May Baverstock, 93 High Street, Godalming, Surrey GU7 1AL, England, telephone (04868) 23567

Morgan Evans & Co. Ltd., 30 Church Street, Llangefni, Gwynedd, Wales, telephone (0248) 723303

Moore's Auction Rooms, 217/219 Greenwich High Road, London SE10, England, telephone 01-858 7848

Morphets of Harrogate, 4/6 Albert Street, Harrogate, North Yorkshire HG1 1JL, England, telephone (0423) 502282

Neales of Nottingham, 192 Mansfield Road, Nottingham, Nottinghamshire, England, telephone (0602) 624141

Neale Sons & Flecher, 26 Church Street, Woodbridge, Suffolk 1P12 1DP, England, telephone (03943) 2263

D. M. Nesbitt, 7 Clarendon Road, Southsea, Portsmouth PO5 2ED, England, telephone (0705) 864321

Newington Green Auctions, 55 Green Lanes, London N16 4TD, England, telephone 01-246 4222

Michael Newman Auctions, Kinterbury House, St. Andrews Cross, Plymouth Devon PL1 2DQ, England, telephone (0752) 669298

B. J. Norris, The Quest, West Street, Harrietsham Nr. Maidstone, Kent, England, telephone (0622) 859515

Norris & Duvall, 106 Fore Street, Hertford SG14 1AH, England, telephone (0992) 582249

Northampton Auction Galleries, The Old Albion Brewery, Commercial Street, Northampton, England, telephone (0604) 37263

Nuttal Richards & Co., The Town Hall, Axbridge, Somerset, England, telephone (0934) 732969

Old Amersham Auctions, British Legion Hall, Whielden Street, Old Amersham, Buckinghamshire, England, telephone (02403) 22758

Onslow Auctioneers, 123 Hursley, Winchester, Hampshire, England, telephone (0962) 75411

Osborne King and Megran Auctions, 17 Castle Arcade, Gilford, BT63, telephone (0232) 240332

Outhwaite & Litherland, Kingsway Galleries, Fontenoy Street, Liverpool, Merseyside, England, telephone (051) 236 6561

Parkins, 18 Malden Road, Cheam, Surrey, England, telephone 01-644 6127

Pearsons Ormistons, 54 Southampton Road, Ringwood, Hampshire, England, telephone (04254) 3333

Phillips, 7 Blenheim Street, London W1Y OAS, England, telephone 01-629 6602

Phillips (Bath), 1 Old King Street, Bath, Avon BA1 1DD, England, telephone (0225) 310609

Phillips (Cambridge), 42 Newnham Road, Cambridge, Cambridgeshire CB3 9EY, England, telephone (0223) 66523

Phillips (Cardiff), 9-10 Westgate St., Cardiff, Wales CF1 1DA, telephone (0222) 396453

Phillips (Chester), New House, 150 Christleton Road, Chester CH3 5TD, England, telephone (0244) 313936

Phillips (Colwyn Bay), 9 Conwy Road, Colwyn Bay, Clwyd LL29 7AF, Wales, telephone (0492) 33406

Phillips (Cornwall), Cornubia Hall, Par, Cornwall PL24 2AQ, England, telephone (072681) 4047

Phillips (Edinburgh), 65 George Street, Edinburgh EH2 2JL, Scotland, telephone (031) 225 2266

Phillips (Exeter), Alphinbrook Road, Exeter EX2 8TH, England, telephone (0392) 39025

Phillips (Folkestone), Bayle Place, 11 Bayle Parade, Folkestone, Kent CT20 1SQ, England, telephone (0303) 45555

Phillips (Glasgow), 98 Sauchiehall Street, Glasgow G2 3DQ, Scotland, telephone (041) 221 8377

Phillips (Ipswich), Dover House, Wolsley St., Ipswich, Suffolk 1P1 1UD, England, telephone (0473) 55137

Phillips Marylebone, Hayes Place Lisson Grove, London NW1 6UA, England, telephone 01-723 2647

Phillips (N. Ireland), O'Harabrook, Ballymoney, Northern Ireland

Phillips (Norwich), 3 Opie Street, Norwich, Norfolk NR1 3DP, England, telephone (0603) 616426

Phillips Sanders & Stubbs, 32 The Avenue, Minehead, Somerset, England

Phillips (Sherborne), Long Street, Sherborne, Dorset DT9 3BS, England, telephone (0935) 815271

Phillips (Leeds), 20 Fountain Street, Morley Leeds, West Yorkshire LS21 9EN7, England, telephone (0532) 448011

Phillips (Oxford), 39 Park End Street, Oxford, Oxfordshire OX1 1JD, England, telephone (0865) 723524

Dennis Pocock & Drewett, Salerooms, High Street, Marlborough, Wiltshire SN8 1AA, England, telephone (0672) 53471

Prudential Property Services (Fine Art/Chattels Division), The Salerooms, The Market, St. Ives, Cambridgeshire PE17 4JA, England, telephone (0480) 68144

Reeds Rains, Trinity House, 114 Northenden Road, Sale, Manchester M33 3HD, England, telehone (061) 962 9237

Riddetts Auctions, Richmond Hill, Bournemouth, Dorset, England, telehone (0202) 25686

Rowse, Jeffery & Watkins, 5 Fore Street, Lostwithiel, Cornwall PL22 0BP, England, telephone (0208) 872245

Russell, Baldwin & Bright, 38 South Street, Leominster, Hereford, England, telephone (0586) 4123

Sandgate Auctions, 42 Fort St, Ayr, Ayrshire, Scotland

Simmons & Lawrence, 32 Bell Street, Henley-on-Thames, Oxfordshire RG9 2BHH, England, telephone (0491) 571111

L.S. Smellie & Sons, Auctioneers, Cattlemarket, Auchingramont Road, Hamiton, telephone (0698) 282007

Sotheby's, 34/35 New Bond Street, London W1A 2AA, England, telephone 01-493 8080

Sotheby's Chester, Booth Mansion 28-30 Watergate Street, Chester, Cheshire CH1 2NA, England, telephone (0244) 315531

Sotheby's Sussex, Sommers Place, Billingshurst, West Sussex RH14 9AD, England, telephone (040381) 3933

Southgate Antique Auctions, Southgate Town Hall, Green Lanes, London N13, England, telephone 01-886 7888

Henry Spencer & Sons, 20 The Square, Retford, Nottinghamshire DN22 6KJ, England

J. Straker Chadwick & Sons, Market Street, Chambers, Abergavenny, Gwent NP7 55D, Wales, telephone (0873) 2624

Stride & Son, Southdown House, St. John's Street, Chichester, West Sussex PO19 1XQ, England, telephone (0243) 782626

Summerley Auction Rooms, Limmer Lane, Felpham, Bognor Regis, West Sussex PO22 7LF, England

Taylor Lane & Creber, 38 North Hill, Plymouth, Devon, England, telephone (0752) 670700

Tennant's of Yorkshire, 26-27 Market Place, Leyburn, North Yorkshire, England

James Thompston, 64 Main Street, Kirkby Lonsdale, Cumbria, LA6 2AJ, telephone (0468) 71555

Temple Auctions, 133 Carryduff Road, Boardmills, Liburn, County Down BT27 6YL, telephone (084663) 777

Tiffin, King, & Nicholson, 14 Lowther Street, Lewes, East Sussex, telephone (07916) 3137

Vidler & Co. Rye Auction Galleries, Cinque Ports Street, Rye, Sussex, England, telephone (0797) 222124

Duncan Vincent, 105 London Street, Reading, Berkshire, England

Two Wallington Missionary Auctions, Crusader Hall, Stanley Park Road, Wallington, Surrey, England, telephone 01-647 8437

Wallis & Wallis, West Street Auction Galleries, Lewes, East Sussex BN7 2NJ, England, telephone (0273) 47137

Waltham Forest Auctions, 101 Hoe Street, Walthamstow, London E17, telephone (01) 520 2998

Warren & Wignall, The Mill Earnshaw Bridge, Leyland Lane, Leyland, Lancashire, England, telephone (0772) 453252

Weller & Dufty Ltd., 141 Bromsgrove Street, Birmingham B5 6RO, England, telephone (021) 692 1414

Wellington Salerooms, Clifton House, Mantle Street, Wellington, Somerset, England

Noel Wheatcroft & Son, Old English Road, Matlock, Derbyshire, England, telephone (0629) 4591

Woolley & Wallis Salesrooms, The Castle Auction Rooms, Castle Street, Salisbury, Wiltshire, England

Wright-Manley Auctions, Beeston Sale Center, Beeston Nr. Tarporley, Cheshire CW6 0DR, England, telephone (08293) 2151

Index

Will You Help?

Time passes, events change. Almost as soon as this book went to the printer, things changed: some shows moved location, others were cancelled, others increased in size or scope, others gained a focus on a particular type of item. Some flea markets may move because of urban renewal or other reasons.

Won't you please let us know? If you do, we'll be able to improve future editions of this book. Then, future readers can benefit from your findings.

Either tear out this page, or feel free to use other sheets of paper.

Sincerely, *Travel Keys.*

What did you find different?

What problems did you find?

Are there any tricks you know to avoid this problem?

What markets or fairs moved time or place?

What was your greatest success and most wonderful find?

Thank you very much!

Please send your comments to:

Travel Keys
P.O. Box 160691
Sacramento, Calif. 95816 U.S.A.

Will You Help?

Time passes, events change. Almost as soon as this book went to the printer, things changed: some shows moved location, others were cancelled, others increased in size or scope, others gained a focus on a particular type of item. Some flea markets may move because of urban renewal or other reasons.

Won't you please let us know? If you do, we'll be able to improve future editions of this book. Then, future readers can benefit from your findings.

Either tear out this page, or feel free to use other sheets of paper.

Sincerely, *Travel Keys*.

What did you find different?

What problems did you find?

Are there any tricks you know to avoid this problem?

What markets or fairs moved time or place?

What was your greatest success and most wonderful find?

Thank you very much!

Please send your comments to:

Travel Keys
P.O. Box 160691
Sacramento, Calif. 95816 U.S.A.

Order Form

We'll ship your order postpaid as soon as we receive it and a check, money order, or credit card information.

Title   *Total*

Manston's Travel Key Guides

Manston's Travel Key Britain (1988) $9.95 _____

Manston's Flea Markets of France $9.95 _____

Manston's Flea Markets of Germany $9.95 _____

Manston's Travel Key Europe $9.95 _____

Collins Phrase Books

French Phrase Book $4.95 _____

German Phrase Book $4.95 _____

Greek Phrase Book $4.95 _____

Italian Phrase Book $4.95 _____

Spanish Phrase Book $4.95 _____

Californians add sales tax:
Postage & handling included
Overseas Airmail: Add $8.20 per
book

0 . 00

_____

Total: **$**   _____

Payment by check:
Please make checks and money orders payable to Travel Keys.

If your check is not drawn on a U.S. bank, please send in your currency and add equivalent of $4.00 to cover costs of exchange.

Please do not send checks drawn on a foreign bank in U.S. dollars.

(Over, please for credit cards orders and mailing address for orders)

Credit card orders:

We accept VISA and MasterCard, as well as Access and Carte Bleu. Credit card orders may be placed by telephone as well as by mail.

You may call (916) 452-5200 24 hours a day for credit card orders.

For all credit card orders, we need:

Credit Card number:

Expiration Date:

4-Digit Bank # (M/C only):

Signature:

Date:

Mail to:

Travel Keys
P.O. Box 160691
Sacramento, California 95816 U.S.A.

We will send the order to:

Name:

Address:

City, State or Province:

Zip or postal code:

Your daytime telephone number:

About the Author:

Peter B. Manston, travel and food writer, has been roaming through Europe for years, searching for antique fairs and street markets, collectors' meets and auctions for almost as long. He's collected centuries-old silver, glass, crystal, and wood carvings.

His fascination with antiques and collectables and the hunt for them are clearly evident in the details of the markets, fairs, and auctions described: not only how large each one is, but what types of items predominate, how to find them, and more.

He has organized the material to make it easy to use this book, and hopes you'll find as many delightful and valuable items as he has.

Good Luck and Happy Hunting!